MULTINATIONAL ENTERPRISE AND WORLD COMPETITION

UNIVERSITY OF READING EUROPEAN AND INTERNATIONAL STUDIES

This new series will include books which discuss some of the major contemporary European and international issues from a comparative perspective. National experiences with a relevance for broader European and international issues will also be covered by this series.

The collection is interdisciplinary in nature with the aim of bringing together studies that emphasise the role of political, economic, historical and cultural factors in shaping the course of international co-operation and international conflicts, particularly from the point of view of Europe and its relations with the rest of the world.

The influence of the processes of European integration (economic, political, cultural) on both the European polity-economy and the rest of the world, as well as the impact on Europe of global integration processes and non-European integration schemes, will be some of the themes that will run through the volumes planned for inclusion in the series.

Already published

Jeremy Clegg
MULTINATIONAL ENTERPRISE AND WORLD
COMPETITION
A Comparative Study of the USA, Japan, the UK, Sweden and West Germany

George N. Yannopoulos (*editor*)
GREECE AND THE EEC: Integration and Convergence

Series Standing Order

If you would like to receive future titles in this series as they are published, you can make use of our standing order facility. To place a standing order please contact your bookseller or, in case of difficulty, write to us at the address below with your name and address and the name of the series. Please state with which title you wish to begin your standing order. (If you live outside the UK we may not have the rights for your area, in which case we will forward your order to the publisher concerned.)

Standing Order Service, Macmillan Distribution Ltd, Houndmills, Basingstoke, Hampshire, RG21 2XS, England.

MULTINATIONAL ENTERPRISE AND WORLD COMPETITION

*A Comparative Study of the USA, Japan, the UK,
Sweden and West Germany*

Jeremy Clegg

Lecturer in Management, University of Bath

Foreword by
John H. Dunning

M
MACMILLAN
PRESS

in association with
THE GRADUATE SCHOOL
OF EUROPEAN AND
INTERNATIONAL STUDIES
UNIVERSITY OF READING

First published 1987

Published by
THE MACMILLAN PRESS LTD
Houndmills, Basingstoke, Hampshire RG21 2XS
and London
companies and representatives
throughout the world

Typeset by Latimer Trend & Company Ltd, Plymouth

Printed in Great Britain by
Camelot Press Ltd, Southampton

British Library Cataloguing in Publication Data
Clegg, Jeremy,
Multinational enterprise and world competition: a
comparative study of the USA, Japan, the UK, Sweden
and West Germany.—(University of Reading European
and international studies)
1. International business enterprises
I. Title   II. University of Reading, Graduate
School of European and International Studies
III. Series
388.8'881713   HD2755.5
ISBN 0–333–43227–4

To my parents

Contents

List of Tables

Foreword

This book represents a revised version of the author's PhD thesis. When Dr Clegg began his graduate studies at the University of Reading in 1976, most of the empirical research on the determinants of international production, i.e. production financed by foreign direct investment and undertaken by multinational enterprises (MNEs), was of three main kinds. The first consisted of cross-sectional or time-series studies which focused largely on the geographical distribution, i.e. the *where* of foreign direct investment; the second were bi-national inter-sectoral studies which sought to identify *why* the share of the domestic output of one country, accounted for by foreign affiliates of another country's MNEs, was greater in some sectors than others; while the third centred on trying to explain the form of involvement by MNEs in foreign countries, e.g. whether by equity investment or contractual arrangement.

The particular merit of Dr Clegg's approach is that it is multi-faceted. Indeed, it is ambitiously so, since the author not only attempts to explain the industrial distribution of the different forms of foreign involvement in, or by, five countries; it also does so for three years over a ten-year period for both inward and outward investment. The data, carefully assembled, rigorously analysed and sensibly interpreted, enable the author to make one of the first cross-country, cross-industry, cross-form of involvement and cross-time studies ever undertaken.

It is a thorough and original piece of work and deserves the widespread and careful attention of scholars. It provides many insights into the importance of country and industry characteristics in explaining the extent and pattern of foreign direct investment, exports and non-equity resource transfers; the institutional modes by which goods and services are transacted across national boundaries, and how these have changed over time. The comparisons between the inward and outward capital stake patterns of the USA and Germany, and those of the UK and Japan, are particularly instructive; while the changes which have taken place in the character and form of Japanese outward economic involvement between 1965 and 1975 suggest that the belief by some Japanese scholars that a different theory is necessary to explain the activities of Japanese, compared with US MNEs, may be misguided.

One major conclusion of this book, which includes a comprehensive review of the major theoretical and empirical research on MNEs, is that any worthwhile theory of international production must be part and parcel of a more general paradigm which also explains the possible alternatives to such production. This involves answering questions relating to both the location and ownership of economic activities, and hence drawing upon different strands of economic theory, notably the theory of international trade and the theory of the firm. Dr Clegg also reveals that students of international production must cross traditional disciplinary boundaries, and that, depending on the precise question to be answered, the researcher on MNEs is required to embrace an amalgam of concepts, methodologies and analytical tools.

In the 1980s, many of the issues dealt with by Dr Clegg in this book are the subject of detailed research. But this does not detract from the pioneering contribution of the author in taking a holistic view of the activities of MNEs. The thesis well deserved the joint first prize for the best doctoral dissertation in international business awarded by the Academy of International Business in 1985.

University of Reading   JOHN H. DUNNING

Preface and Acknowledgements

The modern theory of the multinational enterprise is far more than a review of the mysteries of large international firms. While it begins with the most fundamental question of all – 'why do they exist?' – it considers in great detail the interrelationships between the ways in which firms compete in the international economy.

The multinational enterprise is at the centre of international competition, and indeed international economics. As the statistics in this book show, the pervasiveness of multinational firms' operations is continually increasing, to the extent that direct foreign investment has grown faster than any other form of competition. What is more, multinationals are involved not only in direct foreign investment, but in trade and many other international transactions – it is easy to underestimate their importance.

The approach taken here is to assess the lessons that a comparative study of five major international economies, the USA, Japan, UK, Sweden and the Federal Republic of Germany, can teach us about the causes and methods of international competition.

This study arises from my PhD at Reading University, in the course of which research I have become greatly indebted to many individuals and institutions. I should like to thank the many economists and government statisticians with whom I have corresponded, unfortunately too numerous to mention by name. In particular I should like to thank the officers and heads of sections of the following institutions: the US Department of Commerce, Bureau of Economic Analysis, the Swedish Statistiska Centralbyran and the Deutsche Bundesbank, all of whom readily provided invaluable material and guidance on statistics.

I should also like to thank Joji Kobayashi of the Japan Securities Research Institute, Professor Mark Casson for most helpful advice and comments, and Panos Michael of the University of Liverpool for his most invaluable counselling on my empirical work.

I am particularly grateful to Mrs Jill Turner, Mrs Meg Wells and Mrs Pat Elgar for the preparation of the typescript, despite the unreasonable demands put upon them by the time available.

I should like to express my deepest gratitude to Professor John H. Dunning, my PhD supervisor at Reading, for his continued academic encouragement, indispensable advice and unswerving support for my endeavours in this most challenging area of research.

JEREMY CLEGG

1 Introduction and Summary

1.1 WHY THIS BOOK IS NEEDED

There is now a coherent body of theoretical work on the economics of the multinational enterprise (MNE). Empirical work, however, has been severely hampered by the lack of information, particularly of a statistical kind, on the nature and extent of multinational operations. As theory has progressed this deficiency has only become more apparent.

Modern theory emphasises that the economic activities of MNEs must be appraised within the context of the full range of international economic competitive routes, by which firms may contend for international markets. As a direct result the data requirements for the critical investigation of theory have become increasingly demanding.

Furthermore, a number of predictions have been made on the nature of anticipated significant differences between countries in respect of their roles both as sources of, and hosts to, MNEs. This logically implies that a comparative study be made between countries. To date there has been none.

That these projections should be subjected to formal testing cannot be stressed too much, when it is appreciated that this area of research constitutes the economic basis of important policy issues. There exists, therefore, a pressing need for empirical analysis consistent with the modern theoretical perspective. It is the aim of this book to make a contribution towards the satisfaction of this need.

1.2 THE SCOPE OF THE STUDY

Theoretical Approach

While it may be true that there is no single universally agreed theory of international competition, there is a focal point in the literature

1

which provides a clear analytical framework for the elements that a general theory should contain. The approach used in this study uses the analysis of the eclectic theory (Dunning, 1977) and the internalisation approach (Buckley and Casson, 1976). A further advantage of the line of reasoning of this approach is that, in principle, all earlier theoretical approaches relevant to any one or other of the methods by which firms compete internationally, can be better expressed within this framework.

This need for an integrated approach is now generally recognised. In a large number of previous empirical works, typically before the late 1970s, the generality of the conclusions that could be drawn was severely limited. For example, an enquiry based on the industrial organisation approach, e.g. for the USA, could produce results at the forefront of the literature in the early 1970s, but would nevertheless beg the question of whether a truly generally applicable model had been found. Worse than this, the implications of the then-popular industrial organisation approach were that any model obtained should be the same for all countries. The most marked reaction to this doctrine came from Japan (Kojima, 1973), vehemently refuting both the theory and the welfare implications in the case of Japanese investment. Unfortunately, none of these exchanges brought economists any nearer to a general understanding of the factors which explain all forms of international involvement.

It is now possible to look again at these heterogeneous contributions and draw out some which can be fitted into an integrated theory. More recent empirical works have done this for various source countries and hosts, and particularly notable here has been research by economists associated with what can be usefully called the Reading School, and in addition, notably, Swedenborg (1979) and Lall (1980). The distinguishing feature of these studies is that they analyse both trade and production generated by direct foreign investment (DFI), and explicitly recognise the country-specific aspects of their results.

Empirical Approach

The present study takes the need for an integrated framework as its starting point, and extends the analysis for the first time to international licensing, in a manner analogous to the treatment of trade. Also, as modern theory requires, explicit tests are made for international differences in the models obtained for a selection of five major developed countries, using comparable data. Furthermore, the analysis is applied to data on both outward and inward involvement. The principal method of investigation used is regression analysis.

The five developed countries selected for this enquiry are the United States, Japan, the UK, Sweden and the Federal Republic of Germany. In 1975 these together accounted for 73.9 per cent of the estimated world stock of direct foreign investment (Dunning, 1979a). The period covered by the present study is 1965–75. There are several advantages to the choice of a standard time period, and to this one in particular. Comparative statistical investigation requires a close correspondence between the data to be analysed in terms of quality and measurement. The time dimension is one important aspect of measurement. Given this, more trustworthy inferences about the real nature of differences between countries can be made which might not be possible if they were being studied at different times in their development.

The period chosen is particularly appropriate, both because many modern patterns of competition are well developed and because the quality of comparative data is particularly high. This is true to the extent that a similar comparison for a later set of years could not be attempted for as compelling a selection of countries. As it is the analysis is restricted to manufacturing industry. However, this does occupy a central place of interest in the study of the MNE. The information used in this enquiry has been gathered from many national and international sources.

1.3 THE CONCEPT OF INTERNATIONAL PRODUCTION

Here the term 'international production' is used in a wider sense than in some other works, for example Dunning (1981a). The reason for this is simply to standardise on the concept of production for international markets, and to clarify the distinctions among its constituent parts. To this extent the present usage resembles that of Parry (1975), though with the addition of licensing.

Defining international production as production for international markets, therefore, includes the operations of both MNEs and of non-MNEs, where the latter group may only be involved in trade or licensing. The definition of the MNE adopted here is in many ways the simplest, being the threshold definition which states that the MNE is a firm which owns and controls income-generating assets in more than one country (Dunning, 1973).

International production is, therefore, a very broad concept and includes all the business linkages which can occur in the international economy. This will cover all international transactions in goods, services and assets. The business relationship within which these transactions take place is of central interest here. Aside from direct exporting, there is considerable interest in novel forms of international industrial co-operation, which contrast with the full ownership and control of foreign subsidiaries. Such new forms include joint ventures, contractual arrangements for transfers of technology and skills, and services via management contracts (Buckley and Casson, 1985).

In practice, there are three forms of international production with which economists and economic theory are most concerned, although these do represent stylisations of actual behaviour. However, they are the three dominant forms of international competition by value, and this study will make the assumption that they are exhaustive of the value of international production.

The routes which are considered here are trade, direct foreign production (DFP) and licensed foreign production (LFP). DFP is the value of output generated by direct foreign investment (DFI), and LFP is analogous, being the output generated by licensing. Throughout this study the terms 'DFI' and 'DFP' are used interchangeably, except where the distinction is crucial; their relationship to one another is discussed in Chapter 3. The concept of DFI as a measure of foreign involvement is inferior to that of DFP, therefore; despite this DFI is only referred to here because of its currency in the literature. The definition and measurement of DFI is both more complicated and less instructive than that of DFP, and this is also discussed in Chapter 3.

The relationships of the three routes of international production can be readily appreciated when represented in Figure 1.1.

Unless otherwise stated, the licensing referred to in this study is non-affiliate licensing as opposed to affiliate licensing. Non-affiliate licensing is defined as that between otherwise independent transactors, not related by ownership.

Valuation of Transactions

There will be few other avenues for non-affiliate licensing transactions, other than those recorded in the non-affiliate licensing statistics, so these may be taken as the total, although undervaluation of the

TOTAL DIRECT SALES*   FOREIGN PRODUCTION

DIRECT
TRADE

DIRECT
FOREIGN
PRODUCTION

LICENSED
FOREIGN
PRODUCTION

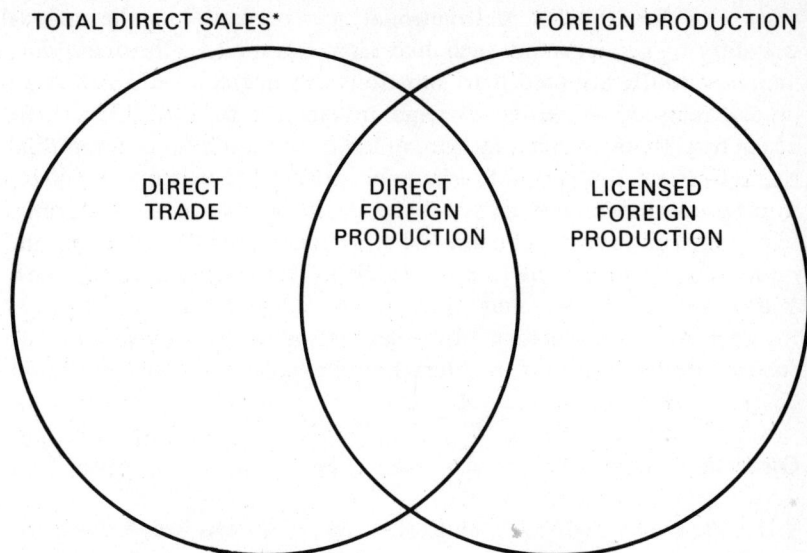

*production owned by the source country firm.

FIGURE 1.1 *International production*

data itself can be a problem. The published trade statistics do not differentiate between non-affiliate and affiliate trade, and the only justification for using their sum as representative of total non-affiliate trade is that internalised trade is believed to have been less important over the period studied. This is not an indefensible assumption unless the level of disaggregation used is particularly high, when affiliate trade may well reach significant proportions of total direct trade.

While international markets external to firms may not exist for various types of transactions in goods, assets and particularly services, this is not necessarily true of markets internal to firms. Here, transactions may not be classified accurately according to the actual subject matter concerned. However, some limited data do exist on affiliate transactions. In such transactions, as with all transactions internal to the firm, statistics or nominal values may not be an accurate measure of the value of, for example, services or technology transferred internationally within the firm. No reasonably objective value is available as it is for non-affiliate licensing; indeed, many internal transactions remain unpriced.

It is therefore impossible, in practice, to build up a composite picture of the extent of multinational involvement from the various transfers of services and such like from parent to subsidiary. The method usually adopted is to substitute the degree of direct foreign involvement by the direct foreign investment position. Thus, the direct foreign investment data are not used to signify failure in capital markets alone, nor would this be appropriate. The existence of direct foreign investment is almost invariably indicative of the failure of some external international market to match or improve on the returns available via the internal market. This occurs when external markets are imperfect, and where buyer and seller are not brought together at a satisfactory arm's length price. Such instances are covered in the review of the literature in Chapter 2.

Ownership Control

The reason why ownership control is then chosen is because it is the route which maximises the net return to the owner of any (broadly defined) technology advantage. In principle the internal market achieves this by avoiding the transactions costs involved in accurately identifying and apportioning the value added by the input of technology or service to the owner. Instead, this value is assigned automatically to the owner of capital by right. Thus, ownership – the control of capital is itself a service – is often chosen where markets other than capital are imperfect, and this is notably so in international operations. In a few and rare instances, minority control of a foreign operation can effect the maximum net return to the owner of an advantage, if there is control of a crucial stage elsewhere in the total production process.

External market co-ordination is then properly viewed as the other end of a spectrum of co-ordinating relationships, and there is every reason to believe that this is a continuous spectrum. The use of direct foreign investment as the world's dominant mode of foreign production is ultimately explicable by the rights which are upheld by law. For this reason some economists have argued that only changes in law can make any impression on the preference for foreign ownership.

Direct foreign investment is generally recognised to be capital-intensive activity. It is true that adequate capital needs to be raised for foreign operations. However, this is no less true of new domestic activity. Capital is but one, albeit major, input. Rather more significantly, as argued above, it is a factor for which property rights are customarily well observed. The inference from this argument is that the existence of DFI need represent not so much the advantage a firm has in access to capital, as in access to other essential factors of production (for which property rights may not be so robust), such as technology and other assets and services for which external factor markets are notably imperfect. Thus, the extension of the firm, including multinationality, is symptomatic of access to internal assets.

The basis of this logic is discussed further in Chapter 2, where the other elements of modern theory are discussed, including the role of country and location on the pattern of international competition.

Limitations of this Study

There are, inevitably, limitations to the present study in respect of the empirical analysis which can be attempted. The theoretical framework itself suggests that direct foreign investment can be of different types. From the point of view of the firm, DFI could substitute for imports to the foreign market. Alternatively, DFI could be raw materials-based, or be export-platform oriented (to exploit low-cost foreign labour), or form part of a conglomerate diversification policy.

This study deals with DFI of the import-substituting type essentially because of the data available. The classification of the data into industries in manufacturing excludes the possibility of investigating how firms may invest abroad in activities other than the main industry to which they are classified. The data are not available on a company basis for the purposes of this study and this would be essential to investigate strategies other than import substitution.

However, to the extent that this study focuses on five developed countries, both as source nations of DFI and as hosts, import substitution is all the more tenable, whereas it might be expected, as a general rule, to be inappropriate to a less developed host nation. As most DFI is between developed countries, this suggests that much outward DFI will be of this type. Where this assumption is particularly questionable is in the case of Japanese outward DFI, but even here, despite the way the investigation is set up, there is no reason to believe that any contrast with other countries will be suppressed and, indeed, all the tests made fully investigate the possibility of such contrasts.

Another important avenue for research, but not one that can be directly investigated here, is the existence of intermediate product trade. In the present context this would relate to trade between the member affiliates in a multinational group, which constitute the MNE. This trade will be international in nature when the affiliates are located in different countries. Such trade increases as the MNE becomes more vertically integrated, and is particularly incident for firms in industries where production in manufacturing has been geographically rationalised to take advantage of economies in the various stages of the production process.

While this behaviour is a significant feature of the pattern of DFI adopted, it is not directly tested for here. Nevertheless, its effect in terms of trade complementing DFI (to the extent that trade is with the same partner country as DFI) are not excluded.

1.4   PRINCIPAL FINDINGS

This section briefly reviews the principal findings of this study in Chapters 4 and 5. As noted in the previous section, the empirical work is conducted in such a way as to both establish models for each of the five countries, with respect to trade, direct foreign investment and licensing, including their relationship with each other, and to make direct comparisons between the models of each country. Furthermore, changes in the explanation of each country's pattern of competition over time are investigated, to capture the dynamic aspect of competition.

Outward Competition

At an early stage it was recognised that no single model was appropriate to the five countries. In terms of our theoretical approach, this supports the hypothesis that country-specific factors dominate in the determination of international production. This is an important finding because it formally demonstrates that the theory of international competition is required to be very much more complicated than, for example, the industrial organisation approach or the product cycle theory. The discovery of quantifiable country-specific differences verifies both that a unified theoretical approach is required and that this should be flexible enough to provide for the many different contingencies influencing international competition.

A corollary of this is that international involvement, and particularly the form with which this study has been primarily concerned – direct foreign production – can be explained and sustained by a wide range of source-country advantages. Indeed, the one equation for which no common model was found between any two countries was that of outward direct foreign production.

It was found that in many cases the orthodox expectations of the effects of variables did not apply. However, for certain equations and variables a greater concordance was obtained across countries.

The one universal result of these equations is that exports are promoted by innovation, as proxied by research intensity. This could be expected to apply to manufacturing trade as a whole, and this result is reassuring. The other findings, however, strongly support the contention that country-specific influences dominate. Innovation and DFI have a significant relationship for countries other than the UK and Japan. For the UK, the prominence of DFI in mature industries is held to be responsible. For Japan the Kojima (1973) prediction is obtained, although the reasoning behind this prediction is held to be faulty, and other findings of this study suggest the Japanese pattern is changing.

For the USA and the UK, DFI is characterised by capital intensity, and it is argued here that this, being a country-specific phenomenon, reflects the advantages of large existing MNEs from these countries in access (including internal access) to capital.

Inward Competition

As with the findings for outward competition, the important results are almost entirely country-specific. The interpretation of the relationship between, say, inward DFI and an explanatory variable, where both data are for the host country, is that the nature of the coefficient obtained indicates whether foreign firms' advantages lie in the same activities or not as the host country.

Thus, in the case of the USA, where it is found that inward DFI is unrelated to US technology intensity, it is inferred that foreign firms do not enter the US market on the basis of their technological superiority. The causes of US technological superiority have been well investigated in the literature. However, a simple stylised explanation is afforded by the product cycle model. It is found that capital intensity does characterise DFI into the USA, and this indicates that capital-advantaged MNEs are best placed to enter the US market by this route.

Both inward DFI and licensing are high-technology in nature in Japan, and this is more pronounced than for any other host country. The conclusion from this is that Japanese government policy of limiting inward DFI and the licensing of technology to key sectors has had a profound and quantifiable effect on the pattern of inward competition in Japan. This does not mean that inward DFI is extensive – it is not by comparison with other host countries. However, it does highlight the premium put on the technological component of any production transferred to the Japanese market.

As a matter of record, the value of estimated sales from licensing in the Japanese market exceeds that of inward DFI in each year studied. This is a very different picture from the other hosts and reflects the preference in Japan for technology transfer without ownership, a preference traditionally associated with government and industry alike.

A number of other results for each of the countries, and other explanatory hypotheses, are reported. All support the original contention of this study that the country pattern of international competition differs widely, and that these differences are amenable both to quantitative analysis and interpretation by modern theory.

1.5   ORGANISATION OF THE BOOK

The main focus of this book is the comparative empirical work conducted for the five countries. However, it is essential to appraise the various theoretical and previous empirical contributions to this subject area. This is the role of Chapter 2, the emphasis of which, from the theoretical viewpoint, is on theories of the MNE and, in particular, the most recent work on DFI and internalisation theory. Studies relevant to the statistical work in Chapters 4 and 5, in terms of their similarity of approach, are also reviewed in Chapter 2.

Chapter 3 surveys the information which is available on international competition for the five countries, and also looks at the problems encountered in measuring the true extent of international competition.

Chapter 4 details the statistical framework of the study. The results of separate regression equations for each of the five countries are presented and discussed, and the interrelationship between trade, licensing and DFI is investigated.

Chapter 5 presents the results of detailed comparisons between the countries in which contrasts and similarities are clearly revealed by statistical tests. The causes of international differences are discussed, and an overview of the findings is made in the light of previous studies.

Chapter 6 reviews the implications of the approach, together with the inferences from the results, for policy formulation at the national and international level. Chapter 7 draws conclusions from the study as a whole and assesses the implications for future research.

2 Theory and Evidence on International Production: A Critique and Development of Recent Work

2.1 INTRODUCTION

In 1960 S. H. Hymer noted that 'There are as many kinds of advantage as there are functions in making and selling a product' (1960, 1976 edition, p. 41). Much of the theoretical literature on foreign investment through the 1960s and 1970s has been occupied with identifying the principal candidates among such advantages, in the process of moving towards an improved explanation of direct foreign investment. At the same time empirical research has been directed to the few areas where appropriate quantitative assessment is possible.

While not all work on direct foreign investment has rested on Hymer's original arguments, many of his contentions and observations have survived to be viewed as special cases not inconsistent with the most recent and promising research on the multinational enterprise. This review is not intended to be exhaustive of all the theories which have at one time or another been associated with the explanation of direct foreign investment or direct capital flows. In preference it focuses on the mainstream of thinking which emphasises the multinational enterprise as the agent of international competition.[1]

It now seems to be well recognised that any attempt to explain the existence and operation of multinational firms in the long-run must draw on contributions made in the fields of industrial organisation, location theory and the failure of markets (Dunning, 1977; Calvet, 1981) – an assimilation process which has been under way since the early 1970s.

2.2 HYMER: AN APPRAISAL

The fundamental contribution made by Hymer (1960) was in distinguishing between direct and portfolio foreign investment, and noting that they were in no way substitutes for each other. He stressed that the possession of financial capital, or favoured access to it, was not sufficient for direct foreign investment, indeed were capital itself the sole advantage then portfolio capital alone would flow from low to high interest rate countries. In this case there would be foreign ownership of financial assets, but not control. It is the control component that explains the empirical observation that direct capital can flow between countries simultaneously, although such flows would be inter- rather than intra-industry in nature.

It may be helpful to restate the original contentions made by Hymer on the determinants of the form, industrial pattern and extent of international operations of firms, not least because this will aid further discrimination of where the most important advances have subsequently been made. Hymer identified the following as sufficient conditions for direct foreign investment by a profit maximising firm:

1. the existence of a firm-specific advantage, such as production technology, for which the international licensing market is imperfect.
2. a negative covariance between the incomes of firms in different countries (belonging to the same industry), that is, international interaction, for which it happens that there is no market solution. It is not clear whether Hymer considered geographical diversification (based on imperfectly correlated incomes between plants in different locations) to be a significant and sufficient motive for direct foreign investment; in any case he did not investigate its explanatory power (Rugman, 1978).

According to the first approach a characteristic of direct foreign investment was the transfer of technical knowledge and the 'flow of business technique and skilled personnel' (Hymer, 1960, p. 69). As Hymer put it, the firm 'internalises or supersedes the market' (*ibid.*, p. 48), transferring the advantage abroad within the firm at 'a marginal cost close to zero' (*ibid.*, p. 219), owing to the cost of using the market mechanism (elaborated by Kindleberger, 1969). The market costs were identified to be the result of buyer uncertainty about the true value of the advantage to be traded (Hymer, 1960, p. 50). Direct foreign investment, however, ensures full control over the use of the advantage and permits full 'appropriation' of the returns on skills and abilities, which the market could not affect at anything less than prohibitive cost. As to the origin of these advantages Hymer noted that 'historical accident' in the distribution of skills and chance resource endowments between countries has a role, particularly where a firm's present ability is a function of its past experience (*ibid.*, pp. 72–6); it was only held to be the recent integration of world economies and the reduction in isolation between firms in different locations that led to the simultaneous realisation of national firms in the same industries in different countries (*ibid.*, pp. 53, 94). This said, Hymer predicted that direct foreign investment would be profitable only so long as the firm can surmount the fixed cost of 'foreignness' involved in operating abroad.

The second of Hymer's explanations, often viewed as more controversial, is the hypothesis that international conflict between firms, in either the intermediate or final product markets, precipitates direct foreign investments aimed at removing oligopolistic competition (horizontal interaction) or bilateral monopoly (vertical interaction). The motive is to achieve joint profit maximisation in the absence of collusion or an efficient long-term contract being feasible. The environmental prerequisite of this hypothesis is that there should be few firms involved, e.g. a horizontally concentrated market structure. It should be noted that technical knowledge need not accompany such direct foreign investment (*ibid.*, pp. 217–18).

Although there is a distinction between the first and second hypotheses, for Hymer they were very much related. The strong conclusions that Hymer reached about the infeasibility of licensing are largely the result of the assumption running through his treatise of concentrated market structure being an industry-specific characteristic. Thus a potential licensor perforce faces an imperfect market for technology licensing (Calvet, 1981). This is not surprising considering the dual role of monopolistic advantages in Hymer's thesis; firstly they act as barriers to entry, and secondly as income-generating ownership-specific assets.

Although host-country factors are not explored by Hymer, he did recognise that the incidence of licensing as an alternative to direct foreign investment could vary geographically where external factors that raise the cost of direct control are faced (Hymer, 1960, pp. 92–3).

The principal implication of the Hymer approach is that direct foreign investment is industry-specific in nature, and stretching the point, that internalisation is indicated wherever industry-specific production processes require large firms relative to the size of the market. Accordingly Hymer predicted, although cautiously, that direct foreign investment will be uncharacteristic of industries where there are many small firms (*ibid.*, p. 95).

Subsequent Contributions and Hymer's Theory

The most noteworthy contributions have been made to those areas of Hymer's thesis where gaps occur or the argument has been the weakest. The limitations of Hymer's work might be classified as follows:

1. Hymer never did distinguish conditions sufficient for trade from those sufficient for direct foreign investment (see also Calvet, 1981). The possession of an ownership-specific advantage is a necessary condition for direct foreign investment, but merely a sufficient condition for trade (Dunning, 1977). Hymer's emphasis was on concentrated industries where the pattern of direct foreign investment may indeed follow that of trade (Hymer, 1960, p. 92) in response to the erection of tariffs or changes in cost conditions. This presumption that all trade can be explained by ownership-specific advantages was even in 1960 at variance with received trade theory, although it has more recently been argued that some advantages are more likely to promote trade than direct foreign investment through their inherent physical immobility (Lall, 1980).

   Thus systematic theoretical work on how locational factors explain trade and direct foreign investment, notably by Dunning (1977) and Parry (1975) has paid dividends.

2. Hymer's approach, while it did not entirely beg the question of how some countries might industrialise before others, did not develop an explicit theory of how ownership advantages are generated. It was left to Buckley and Casson (1976) to advance the concept of the firm as a generator of knowledge.

3. The excess costs of using the external market to transfer an asset advantage were assumed to derive solely from concentrated market structure, whereas there are many other sources of costs unrelated to structure which underlie the neoclassical theory of the firm elaborated by Coase (1937), Williamson (1979) and

applied to multinational firms by Buckley and Casson (1976).

4. In common with many industrial organisation economists Hymer's approach did not explore the internal costs of the expansion of the firm internationally, and the costs of internalisation and internal organisation in general. However, he did recognise the role of more traditional costs such as capital costs and financial constraints which might attenuate expansion in addition to the novel concept of the cost of foreignness to international expansion.

5. Largely because of the presumption of imperfect markets for all types of ownership advantages, Hymer's approach did not discriminate which sorts of advantage were more costly to transfer between firms. With the benefit of hindsight it is clear that external markets are not equally impedient to every type of advantage.

6. Neither did the industrial organisation approach entertain or deal with vertical direct foreign investment within manufacturing industries, although at the time of Hymer's writing the phenomenon had not assumed its present empirical significance. From a normative viewpoint this would have been of interest to Hymer as he had noted that centralised control extended vertically is less likely to lead to divergence of price and marginal cost than control extended horizontally (1960, p. 200). This is an omission partly addressed by new contributions concerning the choice of business form in international economic linkages, themselves relevant to point 4, e.g. Dunning and Norman (1983).

7. Not least because barriers to long-run entry were assumed, the analysis was in the main static, and did not investigate how structural and internalisation conditions might change over time (Dunning, 1982). Nevertheless, Hymer did recognise that the firm needed to regenerate advantages susceptible to diffusion.

8. The last point to emerge is that because Hymer's empirical study concerned a single source country, the United States, this limited the generality of some of the conclusions he was able to make, particularly those on the industry-specific nature of direct foreign investment. Additionally, the variation in strategy according to the nature of the host country was not investigated.

Although the full importance of country-specific effects was generally understated by Hymer, he did note that government discrimination, consumer and supplier preferences and exchange risk augmented the cost of foreignness, and that somehow the extent of direct foreign investment was influenced by past and present home and host stages of development. This line of argument had been investigated in more recent literature, notably by Dunning (1981a).

Theoretical work continued to clarify the distinction between the original industrial organisation approach and the theory of internalisation, in effect to develop the criticism in point 3 above. Dunning and Rugman (1985) have delineated the most clearly between the structural market imperfections identified and emphasised by Hymer, and the cognitive imperfections facing the firm which arise as the natural cost of doing business. The behaviour of firms under these two types are very different: the imperfections in structure may be created strategically (endogenously) by firms in order to exploit the rents on monopolised assets; with the second type, firms act in response to existing (i.e. exogenous) market imperfections (missing or inefficient markets), circumventing these by creating internal markets. It is this second type which underpins the more general theory of internalisation, although the role of business strategy does need to be assimilated far more than it has been into the economics of the MNE.

Much work has since been done elaborating the themes appearing in Hymer's study. What is clear from Hymer's thesis is that whilst initiating a theory of direct foreign investment and international production known as the 'industrial organisation approach', Hymer presciently touched on other factors which were not related to market structure. To this extent it was evident that from an inspection of Hymer's thesis alone, the definitive theory was yet to be developed. Rugman (1980) has argued that all contributions to the theory of the multinational enterprise can be subsumed within the internalisation approach associated with Buckley and Casson (1976). Often viewed, mistakenly, as merely a generalisation of industrial organisation, it has proved to be a remarkably robust structure through which to look at international involvement.

The internalisation theory sees the multinational firm as a special case of a national firm (Calvet, 1981; Teece, 1981). Indeed in principle the theory is the same, the only difference being that 'There are presumably more imperfections and greater transactions costs in international than in domestic markets' (Rugman, 1980, p. 369), which is consistent with Hymer's view that the higher the perception of risk in international transactions, the more likely direct control will be.

2.3   INTERNALISATION THEORY

The theoretical rationale underlying the internalisation approach derives from the contributions of Coase (1937), Williamson (1971; 1975; 1979; 1981) and Arrow (1969; 1974). The theory of internal versus external organisation rests on the concept of transactions costs, and on which form of organisation minimises them. If transactional cost functions are identified for both organisation within the firm (internalisation) and through the external market, then internalisation theory has something to say about the conditions which determine the choice of either route. It becomes apparent from this scheme that the industrial organisation approach neglected the internal cost function aspect (point 4 above).

It is necessary to consider the nature of the item being traded (be it commodity, asset or service), and the importance of this is looked at in Section 2.4. The general principles are, however, that while the volume of transactions clearly has a large role in determining the average cost of transacting, via either route, the precise parameters of each cost function nevertheless depend on the scale of the impediments inherent in each route. Transactions costs are incurred to overcome these impediments, such as risk and efficiency loss. The source of these impediments are, according to Coase, uncertainty (principally in external markets) and the loss of managerial control (within the firm).

Williamson (1971) adds that opportunistic behaviour by transactors is necessary to realise the potential risks from uncertainty in the external market, and notes that innovation in firm organisational structure can significantly reduce the loss of control within the firm (Williamson, 1975; 1981). This latter point helps explain the growth of large, particularly multinational, firms.

Lastly, there are two observations that we will find useful for the next section. Williamson points out that there exist both natural and socially provided (for example, legal) constraints on opportunism. The inference is that where there are such provisions, the cost of using the external market will be lowered. The same applies to trust (often based on experience and goodwill) which can be transactor-specific (Arrow, 1969). Williamson also notes that uncertainty, and therefore the inability to draft complete contracts, only arises in a dynamic world. In particular technical change is the most problematic constraint. One can conclude that the effect of this uncertainty will be to raise the costs of the external market relative to the firm (Williamson, 1979).

In the real world there is, of course, a spectrum of business relationships, from the external spot market to the wholly-owned and controlled activities within firms. To explain all of them would not elucidate the principles any further, as many are hybrids in terms of the above analysis. Caves (1982, pp. 1–24) provides the most accessible explanation of pure internalisation theory, but our main interest now is to apply these principles to the MNE. The relevance of this approach is readily apparent if the choice is being considered between an owned and controlled form of international competition, especially DFI, and a form such as licensing.

Internalisation and the Multinational Enterprise

Buckley and Casson (1976) were the first to apply the theory of internalisation as an explanation of the form of international competition adopted by firms. They observed that the MNE is characteristically vertically integrated, being engaged on a multitude of activities in addition to the regular production of its final output.

The question then arises of why these activities, or stages in production process, are controlled by the firm. The answer is that the trade flows in knowledge or goods that they represent face imperfect external markets. Accordingly Buckley and Casson identify the principal causes of these relatively high transactions costs as impediments to free trade, which arise by industry, country (region and nation) and firm.

At the industry level the following factors cause it to be particularly expensive to bind the parties to a contract, which is viewed as the alternative to organisation within a firm:

1. where research and development is involved, this requires the co-ordination of resources over time.
2. the need for discriminatory pricing to maximise profit on quasi-monopolistic information.
3. the existence of bilateral monopoly.
4. buyer uncertainty over the value of knowledge to be traded.
5. perishability of products and uncertainty over security of supply.
6. investment in durable transaction-specific goods requiring planning.

7. *ex ante* monopoly of a unique resource requiring discriminatory pricing.

The emphasis of this argument is that uncertainty and market failure are most likely to occur due to novelty and technological change and/or where co-ordination over time is required.

The country-specific reasons for internalisation affect any internationally-oriented firm, because such a firm faces market conditions which are not solely industry-specific, but depend also on the relationship with the foreign country. The first set of influences arise naturally, and are called 'region-specific'. The higher the general level of development and the cultural similarity between two countries the lower the cost of contracting internationally compared to DFI.

The second set of country influences are those artificially imposed, and Buckley and Casson term these 'nation-specific'. This includes political, legal and fiscal attempts by governments to influence economic activity, and their general effect will be to raise the costs of using external markets relative to multinational control. An example would be tariffs causing local production to rise relative to imports. However, government policy could equally be fashioned to increase the level of external market transfers, an example is Japanese policy on inward licensing.

The third category of influences on the degree of internalisation is at the level of the individual firm. Each firm will have some expertise both in transacting with outside agents and in administering resources within the firm. The firm's experience in organising internally is particularly important, and this will be embodied often in transaction-specific investments, whose value to the firm will exceed the price obtainable in the external market (otherwise for example, consultancy arrangements, etc., may be feasible). Therefore, particular firms, more than others, will be capable of internalising activities.

Within this framework, the internalisation of transactions in knowledge leads to the common ownership of similar production stages, that is, horizontal integration, and the internalisation of transactions in intermediate products between adjacent production stages constitutes vertical integration. In both cases 'internalisation of markets across national boundaries generates multinational enterprises' (Buckley and Casson, 1976, p. 33).

The internalisation approach can be distinguished from the industrial organisation approach in at least two important ways. Unlike industrial organisation, there is a theory of the creation of new knowledge, where firms invest in research in much the same way as for any investment project. Because research is particularly risky, this explains why internalisation is likely to be extensive in research-intensive industries, not simply because final product markets are concentrated.

Internalisation depends not on market structure alone, but on transactions-cost augmenting factors which imply that internalisation can be country-specific. The internalisation approach does not elaborate greatly on the internal organisation of the firm, but remains consistent with the Coasian theory which emphasises that the efficiency of internal organisation is an element in competition, along with the quality of entrepreneurship.

The framework of Buckley and Casson (1976) injects some much needed determinism into both internalisation theory and the study of the MNE. Testable predictions can be generated using such an approach. The only major omissions are details on the dynamics of the development of firms over time (Buckley, 1983a).

Also associated with internalisation theory are contributions by other authors, who in effect emphasise particular aspects of the motives for internalisation noted above. At the industry level the appropriability theory of Magee (1977a and 1977b) in essence revises the appropriability of knowledge issue introduced by Hymer (1960; 1976), who suggested that the returns on knowledge were more fully secured through DFI than licensing. This approach emphasises failure in the international market for technology, and argues that DFI will always earn higher rents on knowledge as a consequence.

Another approach in harmony with internalisation theory is that of Swedenborg (1979), termed 'endogenous technical progress'. This approach stresses the transactions-specific nature of investments, particularly in knowledge and skills, which accrue to a firm over time as it gains expertise in a particular industry.

This 'learning by doing' would seem to apply particularly to skills and productional know-how. Although phrased at the level of the firm, its implications for the country would be dynamic scale economies in particular industries in which the country has long productional experience. It is probably no coincidence that this theory seems to apply particularly well to Sweden, the country investigated by Swedenborg (1979). This supply-sided type of dynamic approach has much in common with Dunning's hypotheses on the origin of country-specific advantages, noted below and in Section 2.8.

A number of other hypotheses at one time or another have been proposed as key elements in the explanation of DFI. Most receive some support, either for a particular industry, country or time period. Some more enduring hypotheses, and especially those with which this study is concerned, are reviewed in Sections 2.7 and 2.8.

The Eclectic Theory

The eclectic theory is associated especially with the writings of Dunning, but also with earlier contributions by Hirsch (1976) and Lundgren (1975). As the name suggests, this approach draws on various schools of thought within international economics, industrial organisation theory, location theory and the theory of the firm. By doing so it contains the ingredients to create a unified approach to international trade, direct foreign investment and international contractual arrangements.

As with internalisation theory, the central theme is the cost of transactions in external markets, to which is added an analysis of location costs. The income generating advantages of firms are termed 'ownership-specific' or 'ownership' advantages because they are the property of the firm. Such advantages represent the capitalised value of knowledge or property rights, which appeared in the earlier synopsis of the internalisation approach of Buckley and Casson (1976).

The ownership advantage is a useful concept because it helps predict who internalises transactions. The internalisation theory elaborates on the causes of impediments to trade and transactions costs, but provides no shorthand for the direction internalisation takes.

The eclectic theory, following Dunning (1979) predicts that a country's international competitive position will be the result of:

1. the net ownership advantages of home firms over foreign firms, i.e. determining the extent of foreign involvement.
2. the relative efficiency to the firm of internal versus external market exploitation of its ownership advantages, i.e. determining the choice between directly-owned production (exports plus direct foreign production) versus licensing.
3. the relative location costs of home versus host-country production, i.e. motivating the choice between exports and direct plus licensed foreign production.

The eclectic theory makes the internalisation theory operational by adding locational factors, and so assisting the assimilation of the theory of the MNE into international economics. Predictions can be made about international trade flows and the location of production as well as the ownership of production.

This constitutes a significant improvement on both the Hymer approach and orthodox trade theory when taken on their own. For direct and licensed foreign production, it is a necessary condition that firms have net ownership advantages over foreign firms, and that comparative production costs are lower in the foreign location. For direct foreign production to be efficient, it is necessary that the transactions costs of transferring the relevant ownership advantages are higher in the external than internal market of the firm.

Ownership advantages, or the advantages which one firm might have over another, have been extensively classified by Dunning (1979). Essentially they can be viewed in two groups:

1. exclusive access to markets, inputs or intangible assets.
2. economies of scale or size, including those of international or multinational operation.

These distinctions are to prove very important in the decision to use firm or external market allocation.

In parallel fashion to this, Dunning (1982) distinguishes ownership advantages which:

1. could feasibly be marketed, through external markets, such as those embodied in patents, franchises, technical service, management or turnkey agreements.
2. cannot be marketed, for example, those advantages enjoyed by a multinational firm by virtue of its international integration of activities. These would include joint production economies, centralised purchasing, organisational economies and financial economies, which increase with size and geographical spread.

Arguably the second class of advantages are not saleable because of the problems of extreme contractual incompleteness; like Williamson's (1971) flow process economies they can only be legally transferred through the sale of the entire firm. Dunning points out that the non-saleable type of advantages have greater permanence than those whose rights can be transferred through regular external markets. Additionally, the two classes have very different implications for the growth of MNEs. The first may promote any form of international competition, whereas the second can only be exploited via DFI, being entirely firm-specific in nature.

One last element of the eclectic theory concerns the explanation of why ownership advantages should vary between countries. Dunning observes that 'many of today's ownership advantages of firms are a reflection of yesterday's location advantages of countries' (Dunning, 1980, p. 10). Thus specialisation initiated by supply conditions can generate competitive expertise. This agrees with Swedenborg's own endogenous technical progress theory.

The value of the eclectic theory is its systematic bringing together of theoretical knowledge, and the rigour this imposes on the analysis of the MNE. In contrast to the industrial organisation approach, modern theory suggests there is every reason to expect the pattern of DFI to vary between countries.

2.4   THE PRODUCT CYCLE AND THE LOCATION OF PRODUCTION

The purpose of this section is to evaluate certain lessons from the product cycle theory. This is an essentially descriptive account of US DFI and trade in the 1950s and 1960s. In much empirical work on the US, it still neatly summarises the position up until the 1970s, and can provide a useful stereotype against which comparisons with other countries can be made.

In addition, the product cycle approach addresses the issue of the location of production, and is a useful simple framework within which the effect of locational factors on import-substituting DFI can be appraised.

This theory originated in the work of Vernon (1966) and has received much attention in the literature. It is not, in itself, a complete theory of DFI as it does not explain the ownership of production (Stobaugh, 1968); to do so it is necessary to refer to internalisation theory.

According to the product cycle (PC) the USA, having the highest per capita income in the world, and the highest cost of labour time, leads all developed countries in terms of tastes for labour-saving and high-income goods. Because US incomes are rising, research is continually required to manufacture superior products, thus US industry is characterised as research-intensive. It is also likely to be capital and human capital-intensive, because high incomes also connote high average saving propensities. As incomes and tastes lag behind the USA in other developed countries, the USA eventually becomes an exporter of these technology-intensive goods.

As new product technology itself eventually becomes standardised, it becomes less costly to transfer to foreign locations. An incentive to transfer the technology exists because when existing products are superseded by even newer models in the USA, and the main markets for the previous generation exist mainly in other developed countries, which also have lower wage costs, production will be more profitable outside the USA. It is even tenable that what residual demand there is in the USA for older generations of products will be catered for by imports.

The original PC did not address directly the precise means by which production transfers from the USA. It could, from a modern perspective, be effected via DFI, licensing, or even diffusion or foreign imitation. However, taking DFI and licensing as the key routes, it is possible to incorporate a microeconomic rationale for the PC stylisation.

A straightforward approach is provided by Buckley and Casson (1981). This dynamic model argues that where an expanding market is being serviced (e.g. Europe), DFI will never precede licensing, licensing will never precede exporting, and consequently DFI will never precede exporting, assuming the firm always adopts the most efficient means of market servicing. It is argued that exporting, licensing and DFI are in ascending order of fixed costs, and descending order of variable costs, especially for a firm servicing a foreign market for the first time.

The choice of method of market servicing, in the absence of differential familiarisation effects between methods, depends on the size of the foreign market. This would typically result in the movement through the exporting phase, possibly through licensing if it were efficient, to DFI. The initial immobility of the technology, explaining why exporting is the first strategy, is the result of the deferral of foreign production while the technology becomes more standardised, so reducing the capital outlay eventually required for DFI or licensing.

Knowledge is often viewed as a public good within the MNE, but this stylisation (e.g. Johnson, 1968, Swedenborg, 1979) was mainly in order to emphasise the relative triviality of marginal intra-firm transactions costs compared to those of the external market. The importance of appreciating the temporary location-specificity of new technology has been recognised by Lall (1980), and the above argument can help explain the portrayal of US international competition.

Most observation is a cross-sectional snapshot of the dynamic process of trade. In empirical work it is found that innovation intensity favours exports over DFI. This result is obtained because the bulk of exports in the highest technology products (industries) have not been switched to DFI. DFI will have mainly occurred in the more mature industries, for which foreign markets will have already expanded. For this to be a continuing pattern, it is necessary that the US has a comparative advantage in novel technology products, that is, precisely as contended in the product cycle.

The role of licensing can also be clarified in the PC. From the analysis of Buckley and Casson (1981) it is established that the larger is the foreign market, the lower is the average total cost of DFI compared to that of licensing. As DFI is anticipated to have lower variable costs (and higher fixed costs), it is, therefore, most suited to high volume markets. As most US trade takes place with developed economies, it follows that US DFI will also prevail in these countries rather than in LDCs.

The costs of transacting have been referred to frequently in the context of licensing, and in the present analysis these are equal to the fixed and variable costs of a licensing arrangement. It is, therefore, perfectly tenable that licensing may never be efficient if these transactions costs are high. However, as empirical work shows (Section 2.8), such costs are likely to be lowest between developed countries.

The product cycle is not purveyed as a general theory of international involvement, and indeed its relevance to the US is thought to have waned. A product cycle may apply to a few products from non-US countries engaging in investment in lower income countries, but in statistical analysis this would produce unclear results unless there was an absence of third-country competition in particular hosts. A more telling caveat is that, while labour costs perform the function of a locational factor in the PC, there are other important factors which affect access to markets, such as tariffs, so high domestic labour costs are not a *sine qua non* for DFI.

The PC relates to a unique period during which the US enjoyed primacy in terms of income per capita. Furthermore, the PC is primarily a theory of new DFI, and it has little to say on the extension of existing investments by a mature foreign-investing nation. To explain such DFI recourse must be made to ownership advantages other than scientific technology alone. Thus, a shortening of the PC is argued; even for the US, as it has the most extensive DFI of all countries (Vernon, 1979). For any firm with existing DFI, the capital costs of transferring technology are significantly reduced by the possibility of using existing foreign capacity more intensively. It is, therefore, even feasible that the exporting and licensing phases may be absent altogether.

Although the PC does not constitute a general theory of international involvement, it does encapsulate the popular conception of the 'American model' which we will find useful as a comparison in the statistical testing in Chapters 4 and 5. The PC is for most purposes too restrictive, and we are better off with the more general eclectic theory, the value of which is enhanced when the PC is found, quite simply, not to explain much observation.

2.5 KOJIMA AND JAPANESE-STYLE DIRECT FOREIGN INVESTMENT

The previous section considered the 'American model' of international involvement. In many ways the Japanese account of Japanese DFI is a reaction to the restricted explanatory power of the PC, but it goes further than that to emphasise the merits of Japanese DFI and the demerits of US DFI.

Kojima's macroeconomic or general equilibrium approach to direct foreign investment has been elaborated in a sequence of works (Kojima, 1973; 1977; 1978 and 1982) and contains descriptive, theoretical and welfare elements (Buckley, 1981a). The key contention is descriptive. This is that US DFI in technology advanced industries is premature, in complete contrast to Japanese investments which are optimally timed and are in standardised labour-intensive activities.

Support is derived for this view especially from Vernon's oligopolistic explanation of direct investment in the product cycle (1971), a process encapsulated by Knickerbocker's (1973) study of oligopolistic entry by US multinationals into Europe. Accordingly Kojima asserts that, far from the PC generating technology gap trade with a gradual staged migration of production abroad, in fact this trade is curtailed by DFI, leaving the USA with chronic balance of payments difficulties. Such direct foreign investment has been labelled, at its most fulsome, as 'anti-trade reorganisation oriented' (Kojima, 1977), i.e. it is destructive of trade based on the comparative costs doctrine.

In pronounced contrast, Japanese direct foreign investment is held to obey the law of comparative advantage, and is portrayed as taking place at the bottom of what is the counterpart of the product cycle. In this case investment is 'pro-trade reorganisation oriented', not least because trade would be extinguished from Japan anyway by foreign competition. Kojima (1982), however, stresses that the international transfer of production from Japan takes place only in industries in which Japanese firms have a comparative trade disadvantage, not simply when the absolute cost of foreign production appears relatively lower to the firm; this represents an attempt to distinguish the macroeconomic theory from the product cycle, an issue which is returned to below.

To sustain this argument Kojima presents US industry as being dualistic, consisting of an oligopolised high-technology industrialised sector, and a competitive less technology-intensive sector. It is, therefore, the behavioural consequences of oligopolistic interaction that drive US direct foreign investment. By implication Japanese industry must be devoid of such imperfections, implying an accordance between private and social aims. Empirically it has been recognised that in the 1960s and 1970s Japanese DFI took place on primarily location cost grounds, first in domestically unavailable natural resources, and then secondly in labour-intensive, low-technology manufacturing industries when domestic wage rates rose with the upgrading of the Japanese domestic industrial structure. Japanese manufacturing investment abroad, therefore, occurred in the less technology-intensive activities, i.e. those in the lower half of Japan's own dual economy (Cohen, 1975), in marked contrast to the US pattern.

Roemer (1975; 1976) has argued persuasively that this transfer of production resulted mainly from certain special circumstances:

1. the proximity and availability of cheap labour in South-East Asian countries.
2. financial and managerial assistance to small firms to invest abroad (see Chapter 3).
3. the sheer rapidity of Japanese domestic industrial restructuring.

All this suggests that such Japanese DFI was a once-and-for-all phenomenon. The technology transferred to Asia was not firm but industry-specific know-how, and more correctly described as public-good in nature (Buckley, 1983b). As argued below, this is not to say that market imperfections hypotheses cannot explain early Japanese DFI, but these would then relate to the availability of finance and marketing expertise.

More recent Japanese direct foreign investment is not so amenable to this account, resembling more closely the US type, both in industry composition and firm behaviour (Roemer, 1975; 1976; Sekiguchi and Krause, 1980). There seems to be little evidence that domestic Japanese markets in technology-based industries are structurally very different from those in the USA (although the government has pursued a very interventionist role), nor that Japanese firms react any differently to barriers to trade in their principal overseas markets (the US and Europe).

Overviewing Kojima's approach, there are several aspects that are unsatisfactory. It is, as noted before, based on normative premises, arguing that direct foreign investment should take place on social cost and benefit criteria. It, therefore, addresses a different question to the positive theories of multinational enterprise. If we accept that not all US direct foreign investment has been oligopolistic (which would imply that private and social values diverge), then Kojima's account has remarkably little to say, and we must accept that some alternative theory is more appropriate. Additionally, it is by no means clear that the use of internal markets *per se* generates external social costs. The internalisation literature is not synonymous with oligopoly, and social cost-reducing behaviour is perfectly possible within its framework, especially where new knowledge is created and exploited — an issue Kojima avoids (Buckley, 1983b).

Moreover, it is not evident that even earlier Japanese foreign investment accords with Kojima's account. Sekiguchi and Krause (1980) have pointed out that the reason Japanese firms were advantaged over local Asian firms was primarily due to marketing prowess. The privileged final market was often Japan, which posed significant barriers for non-Japanese firms. A much-vaunted merit of Japanese direct foreign investment is its low degree of foreign (Japanese) ownership, but this would then become immaterial if most of the returns were earned through lower prices to Japanese parents and in the marketing process generally. Thus, there is support for the contention that Kojima's account of Japanese direct foreign investment is actually best explained by market imperfections, particularly in the marketing process. Furthermore, these market imperfections also conform to our expectations as to country-specificity, because all independent non-Japanese firms face these additional costs of marketing in Japan. The result is that internalisation of earlier Japanese foreign production occurred in precisely the standardised production industries Japan was losing competitiveness in, but for which products a market still existed. Because of market imperfections only Japanese-related affiliates were able successfully to continue to sell to the Japanese market.

To a certain extent Kojima's account can also be accused of picking the facts to suit the theory. There is a large amount of global direct foreign investment by countries such as the UK and the Federal Republic of Germany which his approach remains silent on. Explanations are required for non-Japanese direct foreign investment which has not been anti-trade oriented, as well as new Japanese DFI.

Kojima's account is in fact not a theory of choice in international operations, for it seems that there is a presumption, based on early Japanese direct foreign investment, that firms which venture abroad are idealised as single product firms. This portrayal may well have had some relevance to Japanese experience at a time when even the leading Japanese firms had neither the foreign market experience nor the proprietary rights to the technology they were using. It cannot then be considered a good predictor of the sort of direct foreign investment that leading and innovationary Japanese firms are likely to engage in in the future.

2.6   THE STRATEGIC OPTIONS IN INTERNATIONAL COMPETITION

As outlined in Chapter 1, this study is concerned with the three main theoretical and empirical methods of competition in international markets. This section translates the theoretical concepts of direct foreign investment, licensing and comparable measures used in the statistical analysis in Chapters 4 and 5. In addition, these variables resemble very closely the expression of those used in the empirical studies whose results are reviewed in Sections 2.7 and 2.8.

It has been established that the various means of market servicing are part alternatives, and that we should expect common factors to have explanatory power. As this is the case, in order to make comparisons between the strength of each explanation for each competitive route, the measures of competition themselves must be rendered into comparable measures. Here it is chosen to express them as output values. Trade statistics are already recorded in this way, however this is not the case for DFI and licensing. Where necessary, output values have been estimated from the DFI position.[2] These data then accord with the concept of foreign production owned by the MNEs or direct foreign production (DFP).

The data on licensed foreign production (LFP) have been estimated from statistics on licensing. As these transactions are primarily on a royalty rate basis, the method used follows Buckley and Davies (1981) in multiplying the transactions values by a factor of twenty, assuming an average royalty rate of 5 per cent. Thus data on international receipts and payments in licensing agreements are converted to outward licensed foreign production and inward licensed foreign production respectively, both being estimates of the sales value of output generated using the technology transfer.

The Endogenous Variables Defined

In common with most empirical work this study is not concerned with explaining the absolute level of international production and its components, as these are affected by the size of the industry. In order to obtain variables measuring the degree of involvement, the data are standardised through dividing by the value of domestic gross output, in both the cases of outward and inward variables. Additionally, as this procedure has been followed in several other studies, the results should be amenable to comparison. The dependent variables used in the statistical enquiry are expressed as follows:

INTPRODOUT   the sum of exports plus direct foreign production abroad plus licensed foreign production abroad, divided by domestic industrial production (in the source country).

EXP   exports divided by domestic industrial production.

DFPOUT   direct foreign production abroad divided by domestic industrial production.

LFPOUT   licensed foreign production abroad divided by domestic industrial production.

INTPRODIN   the sum of imports plus inward direct foreign production plus inward licensed foreign production divided by domestic industrial production (in the recipient country).

IMP	imports divided by domestic industrial production.
DFPIN	inward direct foreign production divided by domestic industrial production.
LFPIN	inward licensing foreign production divided by domestic industrial production.

Section 4.2 in Chapter 4 notes usage of these data in the statistical tests. However, it is worth remarking that there is a fair amount of changeability in correlation coefficients calculated between the above variables (for each country) over the three years for which data are used. This is preferable because it signifies some variation in the data. Therefore when used in the statistical analysis, with the data pooled across years, it is not the case that, in effect, the same data are being used three times over.

2.7   INDUSTRY- AND FIRM-SPECIFIC DETERMINANTS OF COMPETITION

This section and Section 2.8 attempt to apply the theoretical framework outlined in Sections 2.3 and 2.4 to leading empirical work on DFI and the multinational enterprise. Emphasis is necessarily given to those studies that go some way to uniting the various routes of international competition in their theoretical approach, and whose results are of relevance to this study.

Industrial and Firm-Level Studies

Horst (1972a) in his empirical work first drew the theoretical distinction between what are now conventionally known as ownership and locational advantages. His study of US multinationals' sales in the Canadian market found that research intensity explained the total involvement of US MNEs better than direct foreign production and exports taken separately. He concluded that these two routes were substituting for each other because each was an alternative means of exploiting US MNEs' technological superiority. Further regressions using effective and nominal Canadian tariff rates as locational variables explained the ratio of US exports to total sales in Canada, with the correct negative sign.

Research intensity is a commonly used industrial characteristic, and there are good theoretical reasons why we would expect innovations to be internalised, as noted in Section 2.3. If other ownership advantages are internalised, then we should expect a positive relationship between them and the size of the firm. Indeed it is possible to regard firm size as a composite proxy for ownership advantages (Dunning, 1980).

However firm size also holds an important place in industrial organisation theory, as a structural determinant of oligopolistic behaviour and therefore as a cause of DFI. Horst (1972b) used firm size to explain US DFI in Canadian manufacturing industry. From his results he concluded that 'Once inter-industry differences are washed out, the only influence of any separate significance is firm size ... all this suggests that with respect to intra-industry factors a theory of foreign investment behaviour may be structurally identical to an industrial organisation theory of domestic market shares' (Horst, 1972b, p. 261). Despite the terminology of the conclusion, the essential notion is that irrespective of the possibility of oligopolistic behaviour, the same factors which explain the size of the firm in domestic markets also help explain the multinational extension of the firm into foreign markets. This is, of course, entirely in the spirit of the internalisation theory of the MNE.

Corroboration of this interpretation of Horst's original work comes from a later study by Owen (1982) again of the Canadian market, which uses internalisation theory explicitly. Owen's significant results, explaining the share of US subsidiaries in the total sales of the Canadian market, are almost exclusively for ownership variables, such as research intensity and advertising intensity, which explain the US share successfully. Owen finds no significant effect for US domestic market concentration, as Horst's own industrial organisation thesis would have suggested. However, this does provide more general support for the internalisation approach.

One last point of interest in Owen's study is that if Canadian measures of the ownership variables (that is, Canadian data) replace the US measures, then very similar results are obtained, only the level of significance falls. Thus one might expect lower levels of significance were host explanatory data to be used. This is of relevance to the work of Lall and Siddarthan (1982) and my own statistical work on inward competition in Chapter 4 of this book. The above studies consider the relationship between ownership advantages and foreign involvement, and this is most relevant to our perspective. However, work has been done on the ancillary question of the domestic opportunity cost of ownership advantages, namely the issue of domestic conglomerate diversification, this is also held to be an alternative to DFI.

A study by Wolf (1977) expressly considers this within the context of DFI and exports for a large sample of US manufacturing industries. His results indicate that ownership advantages as measured by technical manpower intensity and the catch-all size of firm promote both DFI and exports, which become net substitutes for each other, but that domestic industrial diversification is not to this extent an alternative in the use of technical expertise. The reason, most probably, is the specific nature of certain ownership advantages to a particular industry. Wolf's results suggest that domestic diversification is less related to international competition than each of the results of international competition are to each other. This provides some justification for leaving domestic diversification aside as a separate issue for the purposes of an international study.

Perhaps the most comprehensive study in this area is that of Swedenborg (1979), which uses a methodological basis structured around the equivalent of the internalisation approach (noted in Section 2.3). In this wide-ranging investigation of the determinants of Swedish DFI and exports, ownership variables such as research intensity and labour skills intensity are confirmed as key factors, while firm size *per se* is found to have no more than a proportionate relationship with DFP and exports. The issue of how far these results resemble those of the more plentiful US studies is looked at in Section 2.8.

Two further studies with particular relevance to and similarity with the empirical work in Chapter 4 are Lall (1980) and Lall and Siddarthan (1982). The first study uses a sample of US foreign investing industries, in order to test whether orthodox ownership variables tend to favour DFI or exports. In the context of the US, the basic hypothesis is that the product cycle description should apply to the profile of US international competition.

The gradual standardisation of new technology and its eventual transfer to production abroad plus the locational-specific skills, on the one hand, and on the other the more freely mobile ownership advantages such as product differentiation and firm managerial services, provide the basic model: new technology and immobile skills should favour exports, while other knowledge and services should favour DFI. Lall, however, emphasises that this model can only be expected to apply to the USA, because the USA is the leader in terms of tastes and (at least in 1970, being the vintage of the data) had a virtual across-the-board absolute advantage in technology.

In this way, new product technology and the high skill levels of US firms (measured by average US wage), are quasi-locational advantages, as well as being ownership advantages of firms. In his statistical tests Lall found, as anticipated, that the coefficients of research intensity and skills were higher and more significant for exports for direct foreign production (see Table 2.1 on p. 39).

The ownership advantages hypothesised to be more mobile within the firm internationally also found some support, but with less significance. Advertising intensity, as a measure of product differentiation, favoured DFI and the proportion of salaried employees, as a measure of mobile organisational services or entrepreurial spare capacity gained some weak support. Variables such as capital intensity were insignificant.

In a second set of regressions to explain the export versus total sales to foreign markets propensity of US MNEs, Lall finds that skills of US production workers (measured by their average wage) as hypothesised favours exports over DFP, on the grounds that such skills are almost wholly immobile internationally.

Lall's study has much relevance and similarity with that part of the empirical work in Chapter 4 concerning the USA. The second study by Lall, in co-authorship with N. S. Siddarthan (Lall and Siddarthan, 1982) has equal relevance to our own study of inward DFI in the US. This study sought to explain the share of foreign-owned production in the USA (using data for 1974). The explanatory variables were derived from host-country data, and because of the presumed superiority of US industry it was hypothesised that these variables should be either unrelated or negatively related to foreign shares.

Lall and Siddarthan's findings are therefore largely negative, in the sense that the hypotheses which do not explain inward DFI are supported, and because the data are all derived from the host, no measures of foreign ownership advantages that do promote DFI are available. They find that research intensity, advertising intensity, average US wage and the proportion of non-production workers (salaried employees), measuring the same ownership advantages as Lall (1980), prove to be insignificant. These are variables which closely resemble those used in this study, however other than these the authors find a measure of multiplant operations (firm size economies) and effective tariff protection (US locational advantages) to be the most significant variables.

The implications of the Lall and Siddarthan study are that we should not be surprised that entry into the USA is based on a different structure of advantages than that of US industry. This conclusion applies with most force to the US firms because, if again it is presumed US firms are absolutely advantaged in technology-, advertising-, etc., intensive industries, then intra-industry foreign penetration will be low. Consequently what inter-industry inward DFI there is will then be in industries not intensive in the characteristics cited above, but rather in characteristics not directly measured by the host data. The variables the authors do find significant, however, confirm that entrants must have advantages of size and perhaps capital (they are by definition MNEs) and that tariff protection has the postulated effect. Thus a large amount of inward DFI must be import-substituting.

It can be seen from this overview of a few selected studies how the emphasis in empirical work has shifted since the early 1970s away from the testing of hypotheses with strong affinities to industrial organisation theory, towards more general investigations (though using similar variables) less wedded to the notion that the US model must apply to all countries. Ultimately the investigations implied by received theory (Sections 2.3 and 2.4) need to address differences between countries in the patterns of international competition and to discover if, for example, DFI from non-US countries requires different hypotheses. Studies, or aspects of studies, going some way towards this objective are reviewed in Section 2.8.

There are a number of empirical works which are related but are not directly relevant to this present study. This may be because the hypotheses being tested use rather different variables, or because different aspects of international competition are being investigated. Broadly there are two groups of such closely related studies, whose conclusions nevertheless are instructive.

Firstly, there are several valuable works which investigate the determinants of intra-firm trade in visible goods. Such trade may be in intermediate or final goods for sale, but the distinguishing feature of each is that they flow between the parent and subsidiary or between the subsidiaries of an MNE. Rather than trying to explain the value of production in a host market, or direct foreign production, these studies are looking at the particular characteristics of product markets that cause internalisation in the first place. Thus the failure in an intermediate market internationally leads to vertical integration, which implies DFI. Here vertical integration is used very broadly and simply implies specialisation to some degree between the units of an MNE, such specialisation is, of course, extremely common in manufacturing.

Studies investigating this aspect of MNEs include Helleiner (1978), Helleiner and Lavergne (1979), Dunning and Pearce (1981), Buckley and Pearce (1981), Panic and Joyce (1980) and also Swedenborg (1979). The general conclusions are consistent with internalisation theory, but we are reminded that orthodox locational factors such as resource availability or low-wage labour can generate flows of raw materials or intermediate products internationally. However, this of itself does not explain why such trade is internalised, for which the causes are generally found to be the imperfections in international commodity markets. Within manufacturing industry internal trade is found to be positively related to research intensity, and certain skills, which are well-known industrial characteristics measuring novelty and ownership advantages associated with internalisation.

The second group of related studies is concerned with the choice of firms in using external markets versus internal allocation to transfer invisibles. Such invisibles include services and technology. These works are relevant to our inclusion of licensing in the statistical work in Chapters 4 and 5. However the approaches are a little different, mainly because in this study licensing is treated in an analogous statistical form to direct foreign production.

By focusing on licensing versus DFI, the *raison d'être* of DFI is presumed to be to some extent failure in international technology markets. Licensing is a substitute mechanism in this scheme for horizontal DFI, that is, DFI in similar production processes to the 'licensor' or originator of the technology. Many studies confirm that licensing is evaluated by firms as an alternative to DFI. However this is most often as a precursor, and the indications are that the degree of licensing by a firm depends not only on the extent of its proprietary licensable technology, but also on its capacity – or lack of capacity – to exploit its technology via DFI. Thus a small firm may lack the access to managerial resources or capital to engage in DFI, or the value of the technology itself may not warrant such commitment.

Added to these considerations, the normal internalisation criteria apply, for example the degree of uncertainty over the value of technology and the behaviour of the parties (including the technology gap) for which costs of transacting exist to secure the arrangement. Also host or recipient country factors, such as market size, can be influential.

The importance of the nature of the technology and the theoretical internalisation criteria, which can change over time, are emphasised in a number of studies, for example, Telesio (1979), Buckley and

Davies (1981), Davidson and McFetridge (1984 and 1985) and Conractor (1980a and 1980b). Each investigate aspects of firm-, industry- and country-specific determinants of licensing and actual licensing behaviour. All of these studies confirm the general applicability of the internalisation approach to licensing.

2.8   VARIATIONS IN COMPETITION BY SOURCE AND HOST COUNTRY

The previous section looked at the evidence for the internalisation theory at the product (or industry) and firm level. In addition internalisation theory argues that the form of international business will depend on international differences in the costs of transacting through external markets, which are associated both with the country of origin and the partner country.

The eclectic theory furthermore suggests that, quite apart from differences in the chosen form of international business, the types of ownership advantages generated will tend to differ systematically between source countries; also that differences in the locational advantages of countries will determine the location of production, the direction of trade and the choice between trade and local production.

Therefore there are compelling reasons to anticipate differences in the pattern, form and extent of international business by country. However, such differences began to transpire in advance of the theory, especially in empirical studies of a comparative nature. Caves (1974) found his model of host-country market shares accounted for by US MNEs differed between the UK and Canada. From the perspective of the host country Orr (1973) found in his study of foreign market shares in Canada, that US penetration was distinguished by its research intensity alone as compared to non-US source countries.

Later host-country studies confirmed the distinctive nature of US DFI as opposed to DFI by other foreign investing countries. Samuelsson's (1977) investigation of foreign-owned production in Swedish industry identified US DFI as intensive in technical skills and capital (implying a bias to producer industries) and European DFI as associated more with advertising intensity (implying a bias to consumer industries).

It is possible to argue that any particular contrast between the DFI of two such source countries, or groups of countries, may apply in one host country, but vanish or be replaced by a different contrast in another host. There is likely to be some truth in this, particularly where certain source countries have 'zones of influence' or special relationships with particular hosts, for example, the British Commonwealth. However, gradually a general picture builds up of systematic source-country differences, and this is best illustrated by comparing total outward competition by two (or more) source countries across all hosts.

Swedenborg (1979) contended that Sweden had a 'comparative advantage' in skill-intensive industries. The basic methodology of her study resembled that of US studies, while her results, it would seem, do not. Table 2.1 summarises the results of her study together with those of Lall (1980) in respect of two variables that appear in both studies. The variable SAL appears only in Lall's work and is defined as the proportion of salaried employees. As noted in Section 2.7 it is a measure of capacity in organisational services.

Lall's results are from three separate regressions, and should be taken as representative. Although research intensity favours exports over DFP in both countries, there is some support for Swedenborg's contention of a relative emphasis on skills in Swedish DFI, as skills appear not to influence Swedish exports. For both countries the finding on the influence of research intensity suggests a product cycle, which is tenable as Sweden is a very high-income country (see Table 3.1), but on skills there is at least *prima facie* evidence of international differences between the two source countries.

TABLE 2.1   *A comparison of US and Swedish empirical work*

	USA			Sweden	
	DFPOUT	*EXP*		*DFPOUT*	*EXP*
R and D	0.489 (4.20)[a]	0.618 (4.89)[a]	R and D	3.35 (1.05)	9.00 (2.38)[a]
Skills	2.263 (2.19)[b]	2.988 (2.56)[a]	Skills	1.04 (2.26)[b]	0.69 (1.20)
SAL	0.344 (0.918)	−0.603 (−1.52)[c]			

Figures in parentheses are *t* statistics.
Significance levels are denoted by: a(1%), b(5%) and c(10%).
SOURCES: Lall (1980, table 2) and Swedenborg (1979, table 5.7).

All the studies cited above are based on universe industrial data for foreign involvement by one source or in one host country. Thus the scope for international comparison is limited. They do suggest, however, that firstly the sort of international involvement is different by source and by host country (e.g. research-intensive, advertising-intensive, etc.) and secondly that there is a predisposition, again depending on country, to associate with one form of international business competition (e.g. DFI versus exports). The existence of DFI *per se* testifies to the capacity of firms from a country to internalise international transactions, and it may also say something about the characteristics of host countries (e.g. the size of market, level of development or international political relations).

A separate group of studies can be identified which at the outset aim to be able to test (source) country-specific differences. These are those drawing on the extensive and homogeneous data sets compiled by Dunning and Pearce (1975; 1981) on the world's largest companies. Using these data on leading firms such studies also test certain ownership hypotheses to explain industrial differences, with similar conclusions to those noted in Section 2.7. Because the set of firms covers those from a number of source countries, data are available to isolate source-country differences, usually using dummy variables to identify countries.

Studies such as Buckley and Casson (1976), Buckley and Pearce (1977), Buckley, Dunning and Pearce (1978), Dunning and Pearce, (1981) and Buckley and Pearce (1981), find that the multinationality of firms can vary widely between source countries. Firms from the UK, Benelux, Switzerland, Sweden, Canada are implicated as being more multinational than US firms, while Japanese and Spanish firms are found to be significantly less so. It is not possible to ascribe these country-specific differences to the concentration of source-country firms in particular industries as the regressions are completely unrestricted and industry effects are also accounted for by dummy variables. The conclusion is that, irrespective of industry, firms from certain countries tend to be more multinational.

It is true, however, that these empirical results mix country-specific effects and locational effects. So, for example, it would be impossible to say whether UK firms were more multinational because they were very competitive and capable of investing abroad, or because they had to produce abroad to avoid the disadvantages of manufacturing in the UK.[3]

Source-country-specific effects do suggest that internalisation is, at least in part, a country-specific phenomenon, but the influence of locational variables needs to be estimated separately from ownership variables to establish this. This is the framework used to test the eclectic theory (Dunning, 1977).

Dunning's own tests of the eclectic theory attempt to isolate theoretical influences. For example, Dunning (1980) uses source-country data for just the USA, but is able to specify seven hosts. Ownership hypotheses explain the total extent of US outward involvement while locational variables explain the form, in this case the ratio of US exports to affiliate sales.

It is also found that the model seems to differ as between developed and developing hosts. Firstly, certain ownership hypotheses do not explain involvement in less-developed hosts (human capital intensity) and secondly the locational equation shows some instability. This probably arises from differences in the appropriateness of certain advantages to production in LDCs and the fact that DFI in LDCs is more likely to be of an export-platform nature, i.e. represents production for third-country markets rather than the host.

An issue which cannot be tackled in a single source-country study is why ownership advantages and DFI patterns should vary so widely between source countries. This question was raised by Dunning (1979b) and investigated again by Dunning (1981b). From a statistical analysis of the net (outward minus inward) DFI position of sixty-seven countries it is found that the model explaining this measure is very different between the stages of development of countries. An example which might be suggested is that a country at an early stage of industrial development, with some locational attributes (resources, or a market for a particular product) may receive inward DFI. The income-generation of this DFI and eventual industrial spill-overs cause the creation of host ownership advantages. In turn these advantages may form the basis of the host country's own outward DFI.

Thus at a low level of development locational advantages explain inward DFI, but at higher levels they help explain the origin of a country's ownership advantages. Much depends on the character of the original investment, and historical accident, but the role of this supply-sided explanation of differences in firms' ownership advantages between source countries seems a significant one.

In reviewing variations in competition by country we have so far concentrated on DFI and trade. Again this ignores a number of licensing studies which suggest, more directly than studies of DFI alone, that the incidence of internalisation varies markedly by both source and host country.

The results of a number of studies (for example, Contractor, 1981b; Dunning and Cantwell, 1982; Davidson and McFetridge, 1984 and 1985) using a variety of methodologies, all seem to point to some general conclusions. These concern the factors influencing the transactions costs involved in licensing. The more sophisticated, and therefore less standardised, the technology the higher the transactions costs of licensing are likely to be, and therefore the more likely is DFI. Developed countries produce the most sophisticated technologies, and this explains their high level of DFI.

However, a second influence is the extent of the technology gap between the licensor and licensee. If it is extensive, then studies suggest the transactions costs of successful licensing will also be high, and DFI is likely to be preferred. It is generally found that this technology gap is inversely correlated with host industrial development.

Thus the observed international pattern of licensing is that, while the absolute volume of DFI is highest between developed countries (which have larger markets favouring inward DFI) the relative incidence of licensing is also nevertheless highest among developed countries, as these have the licensee firms that are most competent to assimilate new technology. Therefore the broad pattern of international licensing is amenable to explanation using the internalisation theory.

2.9 CONCLUSION

Hymer's approach identified the industry-specific motives for internalisation, but made the presumption that licensing markets almost invariably would be so imperfect as to prohibit their use. The dynamic nature of markets rather than the static treatment under the industrial organisation approach was emphasised by Coase and Williamson. This type of analysis paved the way for the application of internalisation theory to the MNE by Buckley and Casson.

In a dynamic world uncertainty and risk characterise economic activity. As uncertainty and risk are not solely industry-specific, the costs of overcoming them similarly do not vary with industry alone. This explains observation that a firm can license in one market and yet produce via direct foreign investment in another market. Such transactions cost-augmenting factors vary with partner country.

The eclectic theory adds the concept of the accrued value of rights to technology and assets, described as 'ownership advantages', to the theory of internalisation to determine under whose ownership the integration of activities occurs. With the addition of location advantages, representing relative location costs of production, the theory is able to explain the location of production and trade flows. The eclectic theory represents an extension of internalisation theory into international economics. In the spirit of international economic theory, it also suggests that the origins and nature of ownership advantages will be distributed differently between countries, in an analogous fashion to the origins of comparative trade advantage.

Other theories of the MNE and DFI can, for the most part, be explained as special cases within the more general approach above.

Empirical work initially concentrated on the USA, to which early theory was most appropriate. However, the investigation of non-US countries, both as sources and as hosts, confirmed that a more general explanation of differences in the patterns of DFI and ownership advantages was required.

US DFI appeared to be characterised as research-intensive in nature, while empirical work on Swedish DFI suggested that other factors were relatively more important, such as skills. This constituted *prima facie* evidence that the origins of competitive ability were not identical as between direct investing countries, as theory had suggested.

Empirical work has always found it more arduous to capture successfully the influence of location variables, but where their effect is significant it accords with theory. In addition, studies on DFI and licensing, and DFI and trade have traditionally been separate, because of difficulties in combining empirical analysis. However, taken together, the evidence supports the theoretical approach outlined in this chapter.

One last point concerns the distinction between those ownership advantages which can be sold in external markets, and those which arise primarily as firm-level economies, for which external markets do not in general exist. It is suggested that the more significant are firm-specific economies, then the larger is likely to be the size of MNEs, and consequently the greater the proportion of DFI will be in world competition. It can be noted that these economies have less to do with national origins than, say, technology advantages, because they are related to the extension of the firm itself.

3 International Production by the Five Countries

3.1 DEFINITIONS, MEASUREMENT PROBLEMS AND SOURCES OF DATA

It is the purpose of this chapter to provide some dimensions to the theme pursued by this study. Both theory and statistical analysis by their nature obscure the magnitudes of international production and its components. Data for the three routes of international production – trade, direct foreign production and licensed foreign production – are assembled here on a comparative basis, although more emphasis is given to direct and licensed foreign production.

Some of the statistics presented in this chapter also constitute the basic data used in the statistical analysis in Chapters 4 and 5. These are the data distributed by industrial groups within manufacturing industry. The information used in the later statistical analysis are all in terms of output values, on the premise that international involvement is best measured in this way, rather than as inputs or partial inputs (Dunning, 1973). However, other data on direct foreign investment positions, and licensing transactions (as well as trade) are presented here as they are available on a more general basis, particularly by geographical distribution.

The official criteria for a direct investment being deemed to exist vary between countries, and what differences and difficulties there are, are noted in Appendices C and D. In certain cases the output values from direct foreign investment were estimated to provide the direct foreign production data for manufacturing industry, and Appendix F briefly notes where this has been done for particular countries.

Apart from these considerations, the general bases for the statistics vary in nature, quality and trustworthiness between countries. For example, data on Japanese outward direct foreign investment derives from the approval values for specific projects authorised by the Japanese Ministry of Finance under the Foreign Exchange and Control Act (1949). Since these projects need not be effected immediately, nor in some cases up to the full value of the authorisation, there is at least a lag before a capital outflow is recorded. In general the authorised amounts of direct foreign investment exceed the actual balance of payments outflows, on a cumulative basis. The balance of payments statistics are compiled by the Bank of Japan, and these are the ones submitted to the IMF.

The data presented here for direct foreign investment abroad by Japan, although based on the geographical and sectoral distributions available from approval data, have been reduced to accord with the balance of payments outflows actually recorded. This may do nothing to reduce any inherent distortions within the data, but it does ensure that the absolute level of outward Japanese direct foreign investment is not seriously overstated. By 1975 the cumulative value of actual balance of payments direct investment outflows stood at approximately 52 per cent of the official approved direct investment outflows. This adjustment allows more accurate international comparisons to be made.

In the Federal Republic of Germany, both outward and inward direct foreign investment figures have been provided on a cumulated balance of payments flow basis since 1952 and 1961 respectively. These data are specified by country and industry and are presented at the actual transactions values recorded by the Deutsche Bundesbank. Since the late 1960s the Deutsche Bundesbank has made efforts to trace the recipients of these direct investment flows to revalue the data to the actual value of direct investments held, culminating in a full survey for the year 1976. Thus, later in this chapter, two sets of data are presented, one on the balance of payments basis and the other from the surveys which have the merit of providing some geographical breakdown for manufacturing industry alone. We can note now, however, that as would be expected, the balance of payments data tend to be underestimates.

Other than these considerations noted for Japan and the Federal Republic of Germany, the data for other countries are based on survey values which provide a higher degree of homogeneity, and their origin is noted in Appendix D. In all the tables presented here, an attempt has been made to report data for years 1965, 1970 and 1975, as used in the later statistical analysis itself, in order to improve comparability. If this has not been possible, the actual year the data relates to is indicated. In all tables, the figures refer as closely as possible to end-year values.[1]

This study has adhered to the convention of reporting direct foreign investment according to the activity, or principal activity, of the foreign affiliate in which the investment is held. As a matter of interest, what comparison is available between the activity of the parent and foreign affiliate suggests that, at least in manufacturing, horizontal investment, within the confines of the industrial groupings used here, is highly dominant. The average industrial correspondence by value between the investing firm and affiliate for UK DFI in 1974 was 90.64 per cent (see Clegg, 1985, Appendix J).

In all data on international economic involvement, the general problem is one of undervaluation: while trade statistics are relatively accurate, figures on direct foreign investment are well-known to suffer from this problem, but it also extends to licensing data. However, with these reservations, the rest of this chapter uses what statistics there are to convey a picture of outward and inward production for these five countries.

The Measurement of a Direct Foreign Investment

The most common measure of the commitment to production with a foreign market is that of a direct foreign investment. We have already noted that it would be preferable to use a measure of output but this is not the basis on which most statistics are collected. The prevalence of the usage of direct foreign investment as an indicator, particularly in official sources, owes much to the fact that these figures were initially compiled at a time when economists' interest (and that of governments) lay more in the creditor status of a nation, than in the extent to which its firms added value in foreign locations as a means of competition. The perspective on inward direct foreign investment was analogous. The concept of direct foreign investment is the most complicated of the statistics used here, more so than in the case of less common data such as licensing transactions, where at least some market values are available.

For all the data on international involvement, therefore, but especially for FDI, the theory of what we should measure as a means of international competition by firms, and the statistics which are in practice available, stand in sharp contrast to each other. In general terms, a direct investment comprises the book value of the net assets of a foreign (domestic) affiliated enterprise that is attributable to a resident parent enterprise (non-resident), together with all advances and loans that this shareholder has granted the affiliated enterprise. The precise definition generally adhered to is the IMF definition, and this is noted in Appendix C, along with the practical problems encountered in valuation.

The modern usage of the term 'direct foreign investment' rests on the assumption that if a direct foreign investment can be suitably defined, the international flow of control services can be inferred. This transfer is the hallmark of internalisation, but it is virtually never directly measured; indeed, it may not be given monetary values even by the firms concerned. The actual practice reduces to the choice of a minimum shareholding threshold, above which *de jure* control is deemed to exist, thus its correspondence to *de facto* control need not be a close one.

It would be reassuring to know that, by value, most direct foreign investment which is owned is also fully controlled. What information there is does support this contention. Taking the measure of fully controlled DFI as that which is more than 50 per cent owned, then for countries other than Japan, about 85 per cent by value was fully controlled during the 1970s. For manufacturing industry alone, the appropriate proportion in general is a little higher (though possibly not for the UK), arguably because the importance of scientific technology in most manufacturing tends to increase the use of whole ownership, as suggested by the internalisation theory outlined in Chapter 2.

Average ownership proportions of Japanese DFI are considerably lower, at around 61 per cent, and even lower at 45 per cent for manufacturing alone. This marked international difference is likely to be the result of substantial Japanese DFI in Asia, where control is exercised more easily at low shareholdings, and the consequence of the standardised nature of production, particularly in textiles. However, there are indications that as the industry composition of new Japanese DFI changes (especially that in Western economies) the preference for whole ownership is increasing (Ozawa, 1981). Ownership patterns of DFI in Japan are also distinctive, being very much lower than in the other developed countries, although it appears that as regulation of foreign ownership has been relaxed, the foreign proportions have risen.

3.2   THE NATIONAL ECONOMIES IN PERSPECTIVE

While each of the five countries in this study are highly developed, there are some noteworthy contrasts. Table 3.1 presents some basic data covering the period analysed in the later statistical investigation. In terms of absolute size the US clearly ranks first, and Sweden last. However, this divergence disappears in respect of income per capita. By 1975 Sweden has a GNP per capita higher than the USA.

By 1975 the UK occupies the fifth place in terms of GNP per capita, while the country with the slowest growth rate is the USA, though this is of course from a high base. Unquestionably Japan has experienced the fastest growth, with its absolute market size rising from fourth to second place. A lower, but considerable rate of growth is achieved by Germany, and slightly lower still, by Sweden. These figures confirm

TABLE 3.1   *International perspectives on the five countries*

(a) Estimates of population, 1975 (mid year), millions and rank

USA	213.56	(1)
Japan	111.57	(2)
UK	55.89	(4)
Sweden	8.19	(5)
FGR	61.83	(3)

(b) Gross domestic product US$bn. Rank and percentage increase, 1963–75

	1963	1970	1975	1963–75%
USA	594 (1)	981 (1)	1526 (1)	256.8 (5)
Japan	68 (4)	205 (2)	502 (2)	756.2 (1)
UK	85 (3)	121 (4)	2304 (4)	271.3 (4)
Sweden	18 (5)	33 (5)	69 (5)	388.6 (3)
FGR	96 (2)	185 (3)	420 (3)	439.6 (2)

(c) Gross domestic product per capita, US$. Rank and percentage increase 1963–75

	1963	1970	1975	1963–75%
US	3142 (1)	4789 (1)	7148 (2)	277.5 (5)
Japan	704 (5)	1961 (5)	4498 (4)	638.9 (1)
UK	1586 (4)	2199 (4)	4123 (5)	260.0 (4)
Sweden	2347 (2)	4107 (2)	8466 (1)	360.7 (3)
FGR	1660 (3)	3055 (3)	6798 (3)	410.5 (2)

SOURCE: See Appendix B.

that while the US retains primacy in absolute terms, other countries are making significant gains, and it should be expected that similar developments will also be reflected in international competition.

Estimates of total worldwide competition are presented in Table 3.2. These are obtained by summing the output values of trade, direct foreign production and licensing for each country. These output values are those used in the statistical analysis, and are overviewed in the following sections.

Table 3.2 makes it clear that as a group, and also individually, the five countries are engaged in considerably more competition outside their home markets than within them. For each country outward competition exceeds that of inward, although this is the most marked for the USA. This tendency has decreased only for the UK over the period.

TABLE 3.2   *Total international competition for the five countries 1965–75, US$bn*

	USA	Japan	UK	Sweden	FGR	All
Outward						
1975	275	87	91	23	136	613
1970	115	23	40	9	47	234
1965	67	9	24	5	21	126
Inward						
1975	109	36	68	17	106	336
1970	50	17	28	7	41	143
1965	28	6	16	4	17	70

SOURCE: See Appendix A.

The statistics on total international competition provide an idea of the importance of world markets for each country, but not the importance of any one form, nor the geographical or industrial distribution. The following sections look in more detail at these different patterns, by country.

3.3   TRADE PATTERNS

The emphasis of this study is not on trade *per se*, although trade is an integral part of international competition. This section briefly overviews the salient features of the trade patterns of the five countries. Table 3.3 conveys the broad geographical distribution.

TABLE 3.3   *Trade patterns of the five countries in manufactures, 1975, percentage distribution*

	USA	Japan	UK	Sweden	FGR
Exports					
Developed	62.6	50.6	71.6	84.7	80.5
Developing	37.4	49.4	28.4	15.3	19.5
Imports					
Developed	80.5	78.2	90.3	96.1	91.1
Developing	19.5	21.8	9.7	3.9	8.9

NOTE: The distribution is derived from manufactures' trade, defined here for convenience as Standard Industrial Trade Classification (SITC) sections 1, 4, 5, 6, 7 and 8.
SOURCE: See Appendix A.

It is evident that Sweden and Germany have the highest proportion of their export markets in developed countries. For Sweden there is also an appreciable natural resource content to exports, a feature which also applies to the USA. Japan, on the other hand, exports most intensively to developing countries, and while this carries over to Japanese imports of manufactures, Japan nevertheless maintains a very large balance of payments surplus in manufactures trade.

The industrial distribution of trade flows reveals some insight into the character of certain countries. In 1965 Japan's exports of textiles comprised 20 per cent of total manufactures exports. By 1975 this has fallen to just 7 per cent. This occurred at precisely the time when Japan's locational advantages in such labour-intensive sectors were rapidly deteriorating. Another example of a locational factor underlying trade patterns is Sweden's high proportion of exports in paper and related products. This group formed 23 per cent of Swedish exports in 1965 and was still high at 19 per cent in 1975. The availability of timber resources is a classic locational advantage explaining this distinctive comparative trade advantage.

3.4   DIRECT FOREIGN INVESTMENT

Geographical Patterns of Outward Investment

There is a large body of work on the specialisation patterns of countries in international trade (for example, Balassa, 1977). By comparison there is very little on the structure of direct investments and still less on licensing.

Nevertheless, DFI does follow particular patterns, both by partner country and industry. In the analysis of trade, there is found to be a tendency for the commodity export structures of large high-income nations to become increasingly similar as incomes grow (Hufbauer, 1970). As we saw in Section 3.3, much of this trade is with other developed countries, and it has also been argued that the pattern of DFI may well follow that of trade (Dunning, 1981b).

Table 3.4 presents the distribution of outward DFI for the five countries, for all industrial sectors (manufacturing and non-manufacturing), and for manufacturing alone. Only for Sweden is non-manufacturing data unavailable, and accordingly manufacturing alone is taken as the total. The indications are that Swedish DFI is indeed predominantly in manufacturing (see the discussion of industrial patterns later in this section).

We can identify three areas of concentration in US DFI: Canada, Europe and Latin America. The high degree of manufacturing DFI in Europe conforms to the product life cycle account, and so to the argument that DFI patterns follow trade. However, while total US DFI has become increasingly directed to developed hosts, manufacturing DFI has shown a perceptible redirection towards less developed countries, probably symptomatic of export-platform investment rather than the import-substituting type identified with Europe. A clear shift away from Canada ('North America') is evident over the period, as is the increasing preference for countries in the EEC other than the more traditional host of the UK.

Japanese DFI is principally attracted to the North American market (the USA) amongst the developed countries, and to Asia and Latin America within the developing regions. The geographical concentration of Japanese manufacturing DFI is the reverse of the US pattern, being instead predominantly in less-developed hosts. Economists such as Kojima have addressed themselves to explaining this distinctive Japanese pattern.

Here we can briefly note the special conditions under which early Japanese DFI arose. Firms in Japan producing standardised products, especially textiles and metal products, experienced rising labour costs, losing labour to the technologically advanced industries (Cohen, 1975). Normally such small and medium-sized firms would simply cease trading, having none of the classical proprietary advantages to enable DFI; indeed what technology was used was at the diffusion stage, and the final product markets were price-elastic.

Such small Japanese firms were able to invest abroad only because of the organisational, managerial and financial assistance provided by the Japanese trading companies, and the overseas scanning services of the governmental Overseas Trade Development Association (Ozawa, 1978). The distinctive Japanese financial structure of a high ratio of debt to equity carried over to foreign operations, financed substantially by government and the Japanese conglomerate trading companies. These facilities, coupled with host import-substitution polices, encouraged DFI. Effective control of foreign operations was maintained not through ownership, but through the supply of intermediate products and the marketing of final output.

Japanese economists stress the 'macroeconomic' causes of Japanese DFI, in the sense of the locational factors and general conditions causing the transfer of production abroad. However, the above account of early DFI refers to a unique period, where production in low-technology industries was transferred to developing countries by small firms. New Japanese DFI has been in activities where MNEs have true proprietary ownership advantages, and this has followed a movement towards whole ownership of subsidiaries, as in the established Western pattern (Ozawa, 1981).

The UK stock of outward DFI is the result of more recent trends superimposed on an earlier distribution. Pearce (1977) notes that the age structure of UK DFI is older in developed rather than developing countries, and consequently is less concentrated in manufacturing. Both the historical pattern and more recent trends are evident in Table 3.4. The proportion of DFI in developed hosts has risen appreciably, and within Europe the share of manufacturing is increasing fastest. The developing countries' share of UK DFI is clearly falling.

The inference is that UK MNEs are turning towards developed markets. This predated the UK's accession to the EEC, though tariff discrimination cannot explain subsequent growth. More recent UK DFI in the US has been part of this new pattern (Young and Hood, 1980; Hood and Young, 1981; Buckley, 1981). A preference for acquisition in the US by UK MNEs, has supported the notion that UK firms have capital-raising advantages. The locational attractions of the US include large market size, and this helps explain why the share of UK DFI going to Canada has consistently fallen.

Sweden's DFI is concentrated in three main geographical areas, Europe (especially the EEC), North America and Latin America. Of these Europe and Latin America have increased their shares. The

TABLE 3.4 The geographical distribution of outward direct foreign investment, by major host region, percentage distribution for available years

Host Region	USA			Japan			UK		
	1965	1970	1975	1965ᵇ	1970	1975	1965	1971	1974
North America	30.96	27.84	25.02	25.12	25.50	24.57	21.83	21.98	21.77
	(35.53)	(28.89)	(26.29)	(17.84)	(23.50)	(16.18)	(26.09)	(25.41)	(22.16)
Europe	28.27	33.46	39.75	2.58	17.84	15.79	15.37	21.92	27.47
	(39.33)	(44.51)	(46.55)	(1.88)	(3.88)	(5.00)	(15.27)	(24.77)	(29.06)
EEC (9)	23.56	26.63	31.26	—	—	—	11.93	17.88	21.87
	(36.60)	(39.31)	(40.78)				(12.54)	(21.51)	(25.20)
Other Europe	4.70	6.82	8.49	—	—	—	3.45	4.05	5.60
	(2.72)	(5.19)	(5.76)				(2.73)	(3.27)	(3.86)
Other developed	6.08	7.35	8.34	0.70	7.85	5.84	29.91	29.77	30.07
	(7.56)	(8.96)	(8.45)	(1.88)	(5.58)	(6.30)	(35.72)	(31.70)	(32.00)
Latin America	22.00	17.17	17.87	28.92	15.33	18.08	8.52	7.33	4.57
	(15.22)	(14.62)	(15.32)	(39.90)	(29.61)	(30.52)	(7.85)	(7.02)	(5.98)
Middle East	3.10	2.05	−3.26	20.48	9.34	6.12	0.45	0.49	0.61
	(0.23)	(0.21)	(0.29)	(0.47)	(0.48)	(2.50)	(0.24)	(0.11)	(0.04)
Africa	2.81	3.22	1.95	1.20	2.58	3.13	9.62	8.92	7.00
	(0.28)	(0.45)	(0.41)	(2.35)	(2.67)	(1.15)	(4.43)	(4.06)	(4.72)
Asia	2.76	2.99	4.63	20.83	20.98	26.46	14.02	10.12	8.32
	(1.84)	(2.35)	(2.69)	(36.15)	(34.47)	(38.34)	(10.11)	(6.47)	(5.96)
Unallocated	4.01	5.92	5.70	—	—	—	—	—	—

Table cont. p. 54

TABLE 3.4—continued

Host Region	USA			Japan			UK		
	1965	1970	1975	1965[b]	1970	1975	1965	1971	1974
Developed total	65.32	68.65	73.11	28.57	51.26	46.20	67.11	73.68	79.31
	(82.42)	(82.36)	(81.28)	(21.13)	(32.77)	(27.44)	(77.08)	(81.89)	(83.22)
Developing total	30.67	25.43	21.19	71.43	48.74	53.80	32.60	26.33	20.50
	(17.57)	(17.64)	(18.71)	(78.87)	(67.48)	(72.52)	(22.92)	(18.10)	(16.79)
Total	100.00	100.00	100.00	100.00	100.00	100.00	100.00	100.00	100.00
[Value US $m all industries]	[49474]	[75480]	[124050]	[581]	[1592]	[8238][a]	[11800][a]	[17017][a]	[24508][a]
[Value US $m manufacturing]	[19339]	[31049]	[55886]	[213]	[412]	[2602]	[5895]	[10043]	[14351]

Host Region	Sweden			FGR			
	1965	1970	1974	1965	1970	1975	1976
North America	16.44	11.56	10.47	16.23	16.45	16.96	17.50
	16.44	11.56	10.47				(21.58)
Europe	65.70	69.72	69.48	53.80	56.91	59.07	52.58
	65.70	69.72	69.48				(46.82)
EEC (9)	57.38c	58.26c	59.19c	28.23	34.45	35.35	34.50c
	57.38	58.26	59.19				(28.78)
Other Europe	8.32c	11.46c	10.29c	25.58	22.46	23.72	19.09c
	8.32	11.46	10.29				(18.04)
Other developed	4.58	4.07	4.37	3.37	2.45	2.69	3.85
	4.58	4.07	4.37				(4.94)
Latin America	8.51	12.26	13.25	18.98	17.36	13.06	13.06
	8.51	12.26	13.25				(21.90)
Middle East	–	–	–	0.67	0.66	1.71	3.86
	–	–	–				(2.37)
Africa	1.10	0.46	0.45	4.77	4.75	4.99	1.85
	1.10	0.46	0.45				(0.65)
Asia	3.68	1.92	1.97	2.22	1.42	1.52	1.63
	3.68	1.92	1.97				(1.74)

Table cont. p. 56

TABLE 3.4—continued

Host Region	Sweden			FGR			
	1965	1970	1974	1965	1970	1975	1976
Unallocated	—	—	—	—	—	—	5.69
	—	—	—	—	—	—	
Developed total	86.72	85.36	84.32	73.36	75.80	78.72	73.93
	86.72	85.36	84.32	—	—	—	(73.34)
Developing total	13.28	14.64	15.68	26.64	24.19	21.28	20.37
	13.28	14.64	15.68	—	—	—	(26.66)
Total	100.00	100.00	100.00	100.00	100.00	100.00	100.00
[Value US $m all industries]	[1551]	[3019]	[6665]	[2076]	[5788]	[16013]	[20536]
[Value US $m manufacturing]	[1551]	[3019]	[6665]	—	—	—	[11751]

NOTES:

Figures may not sum precisely to totals due to rounding.
— Signifies that data are not available or are not applicable.
Figures in parentheses ( ) are for manufacturing industry alone.
Swedish data are for total assets, and are available for manufacturing industry only.
Figures for the Federal Republic of Germany refer to 1976 for all industries and 1977 for manufacturing alone. Both years are derived from surveys which are not precisely comparable with the previous years.

[a] Unspecified detail is included in the totals.
[b] The distribution of Japanese data for 1965 is estimated using several sources.
[c] Irish Republic is included in Other Europe.

SOURCE: See Appendices A and B.

tariff discrimination hypothesis may help explain DFI in the EEC (as opposed to EFTA) by Sweden (Swedenborg, 1979). Of the five source countries, Sweden's DFI is most concentrated in developed countries and, therefore, likely to be horizontal in nature. To this extent it resembles the US pattern of DFI in Europe, and so in general appears oriented towards large market size. Even within Latin America, the major host is Brazil, having the largest market.

Two sets of data are available for the Federal Republic of Germany: firstly, the balance of payments data for 1965 to 1975, and secondly, the survey data for 1976. There are some discrepancies indicated between 1975 and 1976, and the survey data does have an unallocated portion. The correspondence between the data is quite a close one, and the distribution does not appear unduly distorted. Assuming the balance of payments data give an accurate impression of the trend, it appears that the geographical distribution of German investment is becoming more concentrated. This appears in Table 3.4 as an increase in the share of Europe, and in particular the EEC. The share of total German investment received by Latin America has declined appreciably over the period. However, Latin America is mainly a recipient of manufacturing investment, while Europe receives relatively more non-manufacturing. The motive often cited for German investment in Latin America concerns the need to relocate labour-intensive industry abroad as domestic German labour costs rise. On the other hand, German investment in the EEC is more likely to be directed to the integration of operations, and this would be expected to increase.

Industrial Patterns of Outward Investment

This study is mainly concerned with manufacturing investment. However, it is significant that the proportion of total DFI devoted to manufacturing varies widely between our five countries. For the USA the proportion is around 40 per cent and rising. Japan's is lower and more volatile because of the low absolute value of its DFI stock, at around 30 per cent. Since 1965 the UK's proportion has steadily risen from 35 per cent to around 50 per cent in the 1970s. Information of sufficient quality for Sweden is only available for 1970, when the proportion was 74 per cent, the highest among the five countries. For Germany in the 1970s the relevant figure is probably between 60 and 70 per cent.

By restricting our analysis to manufacturing, our conclusions may, therefore, vary in their applicability to each country. However, there can be no question of the intrinsic importance of this sector. One means of conveying the significance of manufacturing DFI is to relate it to domestic production in the source country. Table 3.5 does this by expressing the estimates of manufacturing output from DFI as percentages of domestic production. These figures are the weighted averages of the direct foreign production propensities used in the statistical analysis in Chapters 4 and 5.

TABLE 3.5   *Direct foreign production as a percentage of home manufacturing, 1965–75*

	USA	Japan	UK	Sweden	FGR	All
1975	19.1	7.1	24.4	15.4	17.2	16.7
1970	11.8	2.0	19.1	13.2	10.2	10.6
1965	8.5	1.1	12.0	10.1	3.6	7.6

SOURCE: See Appendix A.

The importance of multinational production is striking: for the UK almost one-quarter as much again is produced outside the UK (that is production which is owned by UK companies). For each country the importance of such production has grown over the period, at a rate which exceeds the rate of growth of trade even for Japan.

Aggregate figures, however, obscure the distribution of activity between industries, and it is the specialisation of countries by industry that conveys their country-specific character. Table 3.6 presents the distribution of our estimates of direct foreign production by industrial group.[2]

The stylisation of the USA as a direct foreign investor in technology-intensive industries is borne out by the figures for direct foreign production, even though the share of transportation has visibly declined. By comparison, Japan is the reverse pattern, and the relocation of Japanese production in textiles is very much in evidence, at precisely the same time as Japanese exports in this industry were declining.

The strengths of UK MNEs lie unequivocally in the food, drink and tobacco industries. It is not strictly accurate to characterise this as a standardised product industry, as it is intensive – particularly in

TABLE 3.6 *Outward direct foreign production, percentage distribution by industry group*

	USA	Japan	UK	Sweden	FGR	All countries
1975						
Food, drink and tobacco	8.91	9.63	33.52	0.81	10.92	12.80
Chemicals and allied products	17.40	11.53	16.18	8.48	25.52	17.71
Primary and fabricated metals	4.57	12.51	4.03	12.57	6.73	5.72
Mechanical and instrument engineering	19.21	7.51	7.62	35.21	7.18	14.92
Electrical engineering	10.59	10.20	9.74	16.58	16.48	11.45
Transportation equipment	15.16	7.23	6.31	7.25	21.40	13.86
Textiles, leather, clothing and footwear	3.04	22.31	6.19	1.08	6.95	5.84
Paper, printing and publishing	3.38	10.78	7.26	10.57	0.96	4.44
Other manufacturing	17.75	8.30	9.13	7.45	3.86	13.26
Total manufacturing	100.00	100.00	100.00	100.00	100.00	100.00
Value (US $bn)	(184.24)	(29.17)	(47.43)	(6.85)	(47.61)	(315.30)
1970						
Food, drink and tobacco	10.18	10.62	30.34	1.15	8.92	13.41
Chemicals and allied products	19.16	4.91	15.99	9.67	26.23	18.77
Primary and fabricated metals	8.61	12.81	4.30	12.33	4.44	7.56
Mechanical and instrument engineering	18.90	7.95	7.76	45.44	6.23	15.62
Electrical engineering	10.03	7.63	13.28	13.06	17.81	11.56
Transportation equipment	18.26	8.51	3.67	4.40	25.79	15.94
Textiles, leather, clothing and footwear	2.47	19.01	7.36	0.64	6.28	4.31
Paper, printing and publishing	3.89	22.34	5.62	7.06	0.67	4.48
Other manufacturing	8.50	6.20	11.69	6.26	3.64	8.34
Total manufacturing	100.00	100.00	100.00	100.00	100.00	100.00
Value (US $bn)	(72.03)	(3.71)	(19.89)	(2.61)	(13.74)	(111.98)

Table cont. p. 60

TABLE 3.6—continued

	USA	Japan	UK	Sweden	FGR	All countries
1965						
Food, drink and tobacco	12.94	13.31	44.61	0.34	8.16	18.13
Chemicals and allied products	20.28	2.23	12.02	13.11	17.11	18.13
Primary and fabricated metals	9.62	13.98	8.28	8.99	7.21	9.29
Mechanical and instrument engineering	17.15	7.98	2.64	50.90	8.38	14.73
Electrical engineering	9.24	2.05	9.11	16.21	18.69	9.82
Transportation equipment	21.41	12.96	5.30	2.34	27.99	18.22
Textiles, leather, clothing and footwear	1.84	19.52	6.28	0.39	5.43	3.10
Paper, printing and publishing	4.16	20.40	7.58	3.78	1.71	4.90
Other manufacturing	3.34	7.56	4.16	3.95	5.33	3.69
Total manufacturing	100.00	100.00	100.00	100.00	100.00	100.00
Value (US $bn)	(40.38)	(0.89)	(10.23)	(1.43)	(3.16)	(56.08)

NOTE: Figures may not sum precisely to totals due to rounding.
SOURCE: See Appendix A.

marketing – but it is clearly not research-intensive in the same sense as, say, engineering. This example does show how ownership advantages other than scientific technology are quite capable of supporting direct foreign investment.

Of all the countries, Sweden's DFP structure is the most concentrated, and this will partly result from the dominance of a few large Swedish MNEs. However, the specialisation in these particular industries is explained by the national expertise in engineering, and ultimately by the locational advantages in ferrous metals. As a case study, Sweden, more than any other country, shows how the ownership advantages of firms are influenced by factors which are specific to countries. In Sweden's case the pattern of specialisation has been led by the availability of natural resources.

Although it is not so obvious, this argument also applies to the paper industry. Blessed with extensive timber reserves, Sweden's industrial know-how is such that she is now a substantial direct foreign investor in this industry. Unlike Japan, where the motive is in securing supply, Swedish firms have amassed considerable proprietary skill in this manufacturing industry. Indeed, if we rank the paper industry by research intensity and skills intensity, it is fifth and first in Sweden, but for the five countries as a whole it ranks sixth and fifth. This is perhaps the clearest example of national specialisation.[3]

The specialisation of Germany has been strong in chemicals throughout its industrial past, and it is again such a background that helps explain the high level of DFI in this sector, based on accumulated expertise and proprietary technology. Although no longer representing the largest share of German DFI by 1975, transportation is the second most significant industry of concentration.

Geographical Patterns of Inward Investment

Most inward investments, and certainly those in our five countries, originate from a relatively small number of source countries. The USA is the only country with an appreciable proportion of inward investment from less developed countries.

As Table 3.7 shows, however, the countries of the EEC (9) are the dominant investing group in the USA. In fact, the UK is the largest investor in US manufacturing, although second to the Netherlands in all industries combined. The increase in the absolute level and the share of European investment in the USA has attracted comment.

TABLE 3.7 *The geographical origin of inward direct foreign investment, by major source region, percentage distribution for available years*

Source Region	USA 1970	USA 1974	USA 1980	Japan 1965	Japan 1970	Japan 1975	Japan 1975*	UK 1965	UK 1971	UK 1974
North America	23.49	19.53 (24.78)	13.49 (12.98)	72.71	71.34	71.78	55.62 (67.33)	77.34	71.23 (74.65)	61.97 (72.76)
Europe	72.00	63.55 (62.33)	67.77 (69.60)	20.33	24.02	24.17	32.75 (25.63)	19.86	23.26 (23.34)	28.66 (24.92)
EEC (9)	57.89[a]	53.31 (44.03)	58.31 (54.15)[d]	11.07	13.44	15.18	—	9.38	13.06 (12.79)	16.87 (13.02)
Other Europe	14.11[a]	10.24 (18.28)	9.46 (15.45)[d]	8.97	10.46	8.99	—	10.47	10.30 (10.46)	11.79 (11.88)
Other developed	—	0.57 (3.88)	5.86 (3.54)	—	—	—	—	1.04	4.11	4.62 (1.70)
Latin America	1.87[b]	9.20 (8.94)	11.29 (13.60)	1.53	1.19	0.78	—	—	1.02	1.64
Middle East	0.91	6.67	1.11 (0.25)	—	—	—	—	—	—	—
Africa	—	0.47	0.18 (—[c])	—	—	—	—	—	−0.02	0.2
Asia	—	0.02 (0.07)[c]	0.34 (0.12)[c]	0.19	0.48	1.04	—	—	0.31	3.09

	USA			Japan				UK		
Source Region	*1970*	*1974*	*1980*	*1965*	*1970*	*1975*	*1975**	*1965*	*1971*	*1974*
Unallocated	—	—	-0.04 (-0.09)	5.34	2.97	2.24	11.73 (7.04)	—	—	—
Developed total	97.21[b]	83.64 (90.97)	87.12 (86.11)	92.36	95.36	95.95	—	98.23	98.69 (99.21)	95.25 (99.38)
Developing total	2.79[b]	16.36 (9.04)	12.92 (13.97)	1.72	1.66	1.82	—	1.78	1.31 (0.79)	4.75 (0.62)
Total	100.00	100.00	100.00	100.00	100.00	100.00	100.00	100.00	100.00	100.00
[Value US $m all industries]	[13720]	[265111]	[79950]	[524]	[841]	[1924]	[1023]	[5605]	[9743]	[15423]
[Value US $m manufacturing]	—	[8242]	—	—	—	—	[554]	—	[8118]	[11040]

Table cont. p. 64

TABLE 3.7—continued

Source Region	Sweden†			FGR[1]			FGR[2]		
	1965	1970	1975	1965	1970	1975	1965	1968	1973
North America	47.01 (41.14)	46.69 (46.26)	41.78	48.16	47.69	41.60	39.94 (42.72)	45.61 (42.72)	44.49 (50.24)
Europe	52.90 (58.86)	52.52 (53.74)	58.05	50.23	49.93	53.63	60.06 (57.28)	54.39 (53.69)	53.69 (49.58)
EEC (9)	48.19 (50.29)	46.64 (43.24)	51.55	30.23	32.40	34.89	40.25 (35.09)	35.58 (35.36)	34.23 (30.22)
Other Europe	4.71 (8.57)	5.89 (10.50)	6.50	20.00	17.53	18.74	19.82 (22.19)	18.82 (18.32)	19.47 (19.36)
Other developed	—	—	0.04	0.16	0.44	1.91	—	—	1.82 (0.17)
Latin America	—	—	0.12	1.24	1.72	1.65	—	—	—
Middle East	—	—	0.00	0.16	0.14	1.02	—	—	—
Africa	—	—	0.00	0.00	0.02	0.02	—	—	—
Asia	—	—	—	0.05	0.07	0.15	—	—	—
Unallocated	—	—	—	—	—	—	—	—	—

Source Region	Sweden†			FGR^1			FGR^2		
	1965	1970	1975	1965	1970	1975	1965	1968	1973
Developed total	100.00	100.00	99.87	98.55	98.06	97.15	100.00	100.00	100.00
	100.00	100.00							
Developing total	—	—	0.12	1.45	1.94	2.85	—	—	—
Total	100.00	100.00	100.00	100.00	100.00	100.00	100.00	100.00	100.00
[Value US $m all industries]	[1104]	[1784]	[4122]	[1935]	[5922]	[16192]	[3255]	[4506]	[11681]
[Value US $m manufacturing]	[350]	[562]	—	—	—	—	[1978]	[3317]	[7577]

NOTES:

Figures may not sum precisely to totals due to rounding.

— Signifies that data are not available or are not applicable.

* These Japanese data for 1975, for all industries and manufacturing, refer to the number of firms.

† Swedish data are for total assets, and the data for manufacturing are not comparable in magnitude with that for all industries.

^{1} These data are based on direct investment balance of payments transactions.

^{2} These data are based on a limited survey of firms with foreign interests and refer to the foreign share of nominal capital.

^{a} Denmark and Irish Republic are included in Other Europe.

^{b} Other Western Hemisphere is included under Latin America.

^{c} Africa included under Asia.

^{d} Belgium, Luxembourg, Italy, Denmark and Irish Republic included under Other Europe.

^{e} UK data for manufacturing, 1971, are not precisely comparable with all industry data as the latter has been subject to revisions.

SOURCE: See Appendices A and B.

Young and Hood (1980) argue that US relative ownership advantages have declined while locational advantages have improved. However, the motive apparently is not simple geographical diversification because an inspection of the identity of European firms entering the US market via takeovers shows that very few take place where the acquired firm's technology is unrelated to that of the acquiring parent (Buckley, 1981b).

The predisposition of UK firms to an acquisition to enter the US market suggests that their advantages lie in capital raising, because acquisition is a capital-intensive method of entering a market. In general entrants into the USA are both larger and more numerous than ever before (Buckley, 1981b), and even the Japanese presence has risen appreciably, though it is still biased away from manufacturing.

The only country with effective controls on inward DFI is Japan, where there has been regulation by government, particularly in those technology-intensive industries in which inward investment would be most likely. For the most restricted industries the definition of foreign ownership has been as low as 15 per cent, and the general effect has been to reduce significantly the volume of foreign participation in key technology industries, and strongly to discourage it in others. Relaxation of these formal regulations does, however, appear to have increased foreign ownership shares.

The US is by far the largest investor in Japan, and in 1975 the UK came a distant second, just ahead of Switzerland. The US occupies the same position in the UK market, although this has declined relative to European investment in the UK. This changing pattern may reflect the different industrial orientations of US and EEC DFI in the UK, added to which the US tendency seems to be to reallocate manufacturing investment elsewhere in the EEC than in the UK.

In Sweden the UK is the second largest investor after the US, but only fourth in respect of manufacturing alone. The strength of Swedish manufacturing industry seems to have a disproportionate effect on UK participation, all of which suggests that UK ownership advantages in manufacturing are not as robust as those of its European competitors.

Again, two sets of data are presented for Germany, with the first set based on balance of payments data, and the second set on limited survey values. Despite some variation, both sets agree that inward investment in Germany is mainly from Europe rather than the US, although the US remains the single largest investor.

Industrial Patterns of Inward Investment

The proportion of manufacturing inward investment is around, or just under, 50 per cent in the non-US countries. The trend was upward for Sweden and down for the UK, Japan and especially Germany, though this was from a higher figure of over 60 per cent in 1965. As a host country the US accepts a lower proportion of manufacturing than all the others, somewhere between 30 and 40 per cent. This may signify that the relative advantages of foreign entrants are in services, and indeed, around 45 per cent of US inward DFI is in banking, finance and other services.

We can summarise the importance of inward DFI in these countries by relating the estimates of foreign production to domestic manufacturing output. The figures we obtain in Table 3.8 are the percentages of output produced in each country owned by foreign MNEs, and are analogous to those presented earlier in Table 3.5 for outward DFI.

TABLE 3.8   *Direct foreign production as a percentage of host manufacturing, 1965–75*

	USA	Japan	UK	Sweden	FGR	All
1975	4.8	2.4	15.7	6.2	20.3	7.7
1970	3.1	2.3	12.1	5.2	14.0	5.3
1965	2.6	1.7	7.0	3.5	6.7	3.5

SOURCE: See Appendix A.

Inward direct foreign investment in manufacturing is very significant in the UK and Germany, where by 1975 it was accounting for between one-sixth and one-fifth of total manufacturing output. The degree of direct foreign penetration has risen substantially for all countries, and it seems evident that this direct internationalisation of major economies is a mutual process. Only for Japan is this proportion reluctant to rise. However, the rapid growth of Japanese domestic output in general may help explain this.

A comparison of Table 3.8 with Table 3.5 shows that only Germany had more foreign-produced manufacturing as a host than German MNEs produced abroad. This may reflect not so much low ownership advantages on the part of German firms, especially if there is a high degree of intra-industry production, but also strong locational advantages in the German economy for manufacturing industry.

This growing inter-penetration of economies also testifies to the increasing global nature of the MNEs engaged in direct foreign investment. Truly substantial proportions of their outputs and activities now lie outside their countries of origin. For non-US MNEs this means that they can attain what economies there are of large-scale production and scope previously only attainable by firms in a market as large as the USA. This can only point to further increases in our measures of inter-penetration.

Within manufacturing certain industries and types of industry are more strongly represented in inward investment. Table 3.9 shows the percentage distributions of inward direct foreign production for each country.

The absence of significant foreign penetration in the US transportation industry doubtless reflects the degree of indigenous strength. However, in certain technology-intensive industries, such as engineering and chemicals, there is a larger foreign presence in the US. While the absolute level of inward DFI is low in Japan, it is biased towards technology-intensive industries. Here foreign penetration is consistently highest in chemicals, which is the industry into which foreign firms were channelled in the 1950s and 1960s to build up Japanese capacity in this important heavy supplier industry.

While inward DFI is high in certain technology-intensive industries (though not in metals because of nationalisation), especially transportation, which has declined relatively, a large foreign presence is evident in UK food products. Again, mainly US-owned and a marketing-intensive industry, this may reflect the similarity in tastes between the USA and the UK. The UK invests abroad predominantly in food, drink and tobacco, so there is likely to be a large component of intra-industry DFI.

Comparing the inward investment patterns of Sweden and Germany, it is evident that the industrial distribution is rather more even for Germany. The argument that Sweden's indigenous manufacturing strengths are rather specialised has been met before, and is supported here by the low correspondence between the industrial pattern of inward and outward DFI for Sweden, whereas for Germany the correspondence is positive. Accordingly, Germany is likely to have a higher level of two-way investment, especially because of its attraction as a production base, though this appears to have declined relatively in transportation.

TABLE 3.9 Inward direct foreign production, percentage distribution by industry group

	USA	Japan	UK	Sweden	FGR	All countries
1975						
Food, drink and tobacco	14.18	2.69	17.32	21.44	12.50	13.55
Chemicals and allied products	26.29	41.23	15.46	20.10	18.14	21.76
Primary and fabricated metals	23.86	4.08	7.95	15.15	16.05	15.99
Mechanical and instrument engineering	12.16	17.28	15.43	14.93	12.85	13.51
Electrical engineering	10.54	14.20	11.08	14.44	16.96	13.46
Transportation equipment	0.15	14.86	18.87	3.13	14.71	10.78
Textiles, leather, clothing and footwear	2.15	0.54	2.84	2.69	2.20	2.22
Paper, printing and publishing	4.79	1.05	4.38	4.69	2.46	3.55
Other manufacturing industries	5.87	4.07	6.66	3.44	4.12	5.19
Total manufacturing	100.00	100.00	100.00	100.00	100.00	100.00
Value (US $bn)	(45.91)	(9.87)	(30.56)	(2.78)	(56.36)	(145.47)
1970						
Food, drink and tobacco	15.78	5.57	16.59	12.84	12.62	14.04
Chemicals and allied products	27.44	35.97	13.95	22.10	18.31	21.91
Primary and fabricated metals	20.20	8.74	8.98	15.18	9.71	13.15
Mechanical and instrument engineering	11.44	23.74	16.83	20.12	14.41	14.78
Electrical engineering	8.98	17.24	12.35	15.68	11.00	11.19
Transportation equipment	0.19	2.76	20.09	0.36	24.46	13.04
Textiles, leather, clothing and footwear	2.93	0.87	2.40	5.06	2.94	2.69
Paper, printing and publishing	5.94	1.08	1.70	7.28	1.46	3.12
Other manufacturing industries	7.08	4.04	7.12	1.36	5.08	6.07
Total manufacturing	100.00	100.00	100.00	100.00	100.00	100.00
Value (US $bn)	(19.16)	(4.43)	(12.59)	(1.03)	(18.89)	(56.10)

Table cont. p. 70

TABLE 3.9—continued

	USA	Japan	UK	Sweden	FGR	All countries
1965						
Food, drink and tobacco	13.51	4.68	19.83	15.30	13.01	14.40
Chemicals and allied products	29.09	40.66	13.49	26.10	13.95	22.70
Primary and fabricated metals	20.70	10.08	7.26	15.52	5.18	13.49
Mechanical and instrument engineering	11.18	23.29	13.28	9.79	17.67	13.73
Electrical engineering	9.82	12.72	8.90	18.33	7.22	9.34
Transportation equipment	0.22	0.75	24.41	0.28	31.49	12.78
Textiles, leather, clothing and footwear	3.08	1.50	5.37	5.96	3.70	3.71
Paper, printing and publishing	5.72	2.26	1.80	7.31	2.93	4.05
Other manufacturing industries	6.68	4.05	5.66	1.40	4.86	5.80
Total manufacturing	100.00	100.00	100.00	100.00	100.00	100.00
Value (US $ Bn)	(12.32)	(1.38)	(5.90)	(0.50)	(5.82)	(25.92)

NOTE: Figures may not sum precisely to totals due to rounding.
SOURCE: See Appendix A.

3.5 LICENSING

Data on international non-affiliate licensing is even less readily available than that on DFI. This section attempts to shed some light on this aspect of international business, which, while it does not match the scale of monetary flows recorded by trade and DFI, reveals rather more about the technical and technological capacity of each country.

What data there are cover transactions involving licences, patents, trade marks, design, copyrights, manufacturing rights, the use of technological know-how and technical assistance, plus royalties on printed matter, sound-recordings and performing rights. In practice, more so than is the case for DFI, licensing transactions are concentrated in manufacturing industries.

On average, between the mid-1960s and mid-1970s the proportion of manufacturing transactions by value was as follows (the figure for receipts is given first, followed by payments):

USA (87.8%, 93.0%)
UK (81.6%, 87.8%)
Japan (99.2%, 99.9%)
Sweden (100% and 100%)

Appropriate data are unfortunately not available for Germany. The lower proportions for the USA and UK result from transactions mainly in the petroleum industry, especially for payments in the earlier years.

The Geographical Distribution of Licensing Transactions

Tables 3.10 and 3.11 present the available data for all industries according to the geographical distribution (except petroleum, in the case of the UK). Again, suitable data for Germany are not available for such a comparison. For outward licensing (licensing receipts), it seems clear that most licensees are located in developed countries, confirming that licensing takes place predominantly between developed countries. The exception is Japan, which, according to the data for 1970, licensed Asian producers most intensively, confirming the special relationship with this region and the special nature of the technology concerned.

In turn the USA's largest single market is Japan, all of which

TABLE 3.10 *The geographical distribution of non-affiliate licensing receipts, percentage distribution for available years*

Licensee country	USA 1967	USA 1970	USA 1975	Japan 1970	UK 1965	UK 1970	UK 1975	Sweden 1965	Sweden 1969	Sweden 1975
North America	8.40	5.76	5.02	13.28	22.34	31.32	30.39	11.61	26.59	—
USA	—	—	—		21.28	30.22	29.08	11.40	26.08	13.90
Europe	48.35	43.11	45.44	28.27	39.36	32.42	32.03	41.95	43.08	52.74
EEC (9)	41.22[a]	31.17[a]	36.72[a]	—	31.92	23.63	23.53	29.81	32.52	—
FGR	—	—	—	—	13.83	9.89	7.84	5.86	9.21	8.84
UK	14.00	9.77	10.44	—	—	—	—	11.19	8.56	5.97
Other Europe	7.12	5.93	8.72	—	7.45	8.24	8.50	12.13	10.56	—
Sweden	—	—	—	—	—	1.10	1.31	—	—	—
Other Developed	30.28	39.27	34.21	2.47	17.02	15.93	17.32	—	—	6.32
Japan	24.17	32.35	29.83	—	12.77	10.99	11.76	5.65	3.74	—
Latin America	9.16	7.85	7.93	13.28	1.06	4.40	2.94	—	—	—
Middle East	—	—	—	—	—	—	2.94	—	—	—
Africa	—	—	—	2.09	0.00	0.55	1.63	—	—	—
Asia	—	—	—	40.61	2.13	2.75	2.61	—	—	—
Unallocated	—	—	—	—	—	12.64	10.13	40.80	26.59	27.03
Developed Total	87.02	88.13	84.68	44.02	93.62[b]	79.67	79.74	59.20	73.41	72.96
Developing Total	12.98[b]	11.87[b]	15.32[b]	55.98	6.38[b]	7.69	10.46	—	—	—
Total	100.00	100.00	100.00	100.00	100.00	100.00	100.00	100.00	100.00	100.00
(Value US $m)	(393)	(573)	(757)	(527)	(94)	(182)	(306)	(10)	(16)	(29)

NOTES:

Figures may not sum precisely to totals due to rounding.

— Signifies that data are not available or are not applicable.

0.00 Indicates a percentage of less than 0.005.

SOURCES: See Appendices A and B.

† UK data are adjusted to universal estimates for all industries but exclude petroleum.

a US data for the EEC excludes the Republic of Ireland and Denmark.

b Totals include unspecified detail.

TABLE 3.11 *The geographical distribution of non-affiliate licensing payments, percentage distribution for available years*

Licensing country	USA			Japan*			UK†			Sweden		
	1967	1970	1975	1965	1970	1975	1965	1970	1975	1965	1969	1975
North America	2.88	3.51	4.84	60.53	58.48	54.90	64.29	56.73	50.65	41.43	33.35	—
USA	—	—	—	59.24	56.90	53.36	64.29	53.35	50.00	41.02	33.23	37.88
Europe	89.42	86.84	85.86	37.33	39.91	43.87	26.79	28.85	40.26	27.31	48.91	44.40
EEC (9)	75.00[a]	76.32[a]	76.88[a]	27.16	30.80	34.28	17.86	16.35	24.03	22.12	41.04	—
FGR	—	—	—	11.60	12.76	12.55	7.14	5.77	3.90	2.49	3.81	8.39
UK	30.77	30.70	40.86	6.19	8.08	8.81	—	—	—	5.61	13.05	8.54
Other Europe	15.38	11.40	9.68	10.18	9.11	9.58	8.93	12.50	16.23	5.19	7.87	—
Sweden	—	—	—	1.46	1.24	1.58	1.79	0.96	0.65	—	—	—
Other Developed	3.85	3.51	5.38	0.19	0.44	0.62	1.79	—	1.30	0.42	0.62	0.79
Japan	3.85	3.51	4.84	—	—	—	—	0.00	0.65	—	—	—
Latin America	2.88	4.39	2.15	1.94	1.15	0.49	0.00	—	0.65	—	—	—
Middle East	—	—	—	0.00	0.01	0.03	—	—	0.00	—	—	—
Africa	—	—	—	0.00	0.00	0.02	0.00	—	0.00	—	—	—
Asia	—	—	—	0.00	0.00	0.08	0.00	—	0.65	—	—	—
Unallocated	—	—	—	—	—	—	—	14.42	—	31.05	17.11	16.83
Developed Total	96.15	93.86	96.77	98.06	98.83	99.39	100.00[b]	86.54	98.05[b]	69.16	82.89	83.07
Developing Total	2.88	6.14[b]	3.23[b]	1.94	1.17	0.61	—	—	1.95[b]	—	—	—
Total	100.00	100.00	100.00	100.00	100.00	100.00	100.00[b]	100.00	100.00	100.00	100.00	100.00
(Value US $M)	(104)	(114)	(186)	(3086)	(7286)	(12718)	(56)	(104)	(154)	(10)	(16)	(33)

NOTES:

Figures may not sum precisely to totals due to rounding.

— Signifies that data are not available or are not applicable.

0.00 Indicates a percentage of less than 0.005.

SOURCES: See Appendices A and B.

* Japanese data are for the number of agreements in the preceding ten years.

† UK data are adjusted to universe estimates for all industries and exclude petroleum.

[a] US data for the EEC exclude the Republic of Ireland and Denmark.

[b] Totals include unspecified detail.

suggests that Japan is continually upgrading its production structure. While Sweden's receipts are mainly from Europe, the UK's are consistently high from the North American market, and the US in particular. This testifies to the existence of technological strengths on the part of UK firms which are not so prominent elsewhere in the UK's international involvement.

The payments for technology are even more geographically concentrated than their receipts, as might be expected. For all non-US licensees the USA is universally the single largest supplier. Over the period the EEC share in supplying the USA has slowly risen. Again a most interesting testimony to UK firms' technological prowess is that the UK is the dominant licensor in the US market, accounting for 40 per cent by value in 1975.

As with inward DFI, Japan is the only country where formal control of foreign business has been in operation. The rationale for this government control of licensing is the 'failure' in licensing markets for agreements to reflect the external social policy goals of the recipient country (Ozawa, 1979), in which respect Japan's were for industrial development. In Japan controls were operated through the Foreign Exchange Control Law (1949) and the Foreign Investment Law (1950), and administered by the Bank of Japan and the Ministries of Finance and International Trade and Industry.

The effect of Japanese controls was to modify the prices, terms and conditions of agreements, to reduce the rent to the licensor – an element that some empirical work suggests can be very large (Contractor, 1980a) and to ration new technology to one selected Japanese firm, which prevented the raising of prices and the 'unnecessary' duplication of purchases of technology. The result was the creation of a Japanese monopolist in each particular product able to enjoy the benefits of a large domestic market size.

Ozawa (1979) notes that there has been no formal control of inward licensing since 1974, following the first substantial liberalisation of 1968. It is unclear how far informal control has subsequently been exercised.

The Industrial Distribution of Licensing

The above discussion naturally leads us to consider the importance of licensing for each country, and the industrial distribution of transactions. In a parallel fashion to earlier tables on DFI, Table 3.12

TABLE 3.12   *Licensed foreign production propensities, 1965–75*

	USA	Japan	UK	Sweden	FGR	All
Outward						
1975	1.4	1.0	2.7	1.3	2.1	1.5
1970	1.7	0.5	2.9	1.6	1.6	1.6
1965	1.4	0.3	1.9	1.4	1.6	1.4
Inward						
1975	0.4	2.7	1.6	1.5	1.2	1.1
1970	0.2	3.0	1.7	1.6	1.5	1.1
1965	0.4	2.8	1.1	1.4	1.1	0.8

SOURCE: See Appendix A.

conveys the importance of outward and inward licensing for the five countries.

Table 3.12 shows that while licensing is minor compared to production via direct foreign investment, it is a strategy which assumes a greater importance for some countries than others. For the UK outward licensing is appreciably higher than for the other countries, while for Japan in its role as a technology recipient, licensing is the main source of foreign technology.

Because the licensing propensities are derived from monetary flows, they are liable to fluctuate. The picture they convey is, however, fairly clear. Only Japan is a continuous net inward licensee, with Sweden on the borderline. Unlike the direct foreign production propensities presented in Tables 3.5 and 3.8, there is no marked general tendency for licensing to grow as a proportion of output over time. Instead it seems that it will, if anything, just about keep pace with the growth of production. Consequently the ratio of direct foreign production to licensed foreign production, will continue to rise (as indeed will the ratio of DFP to trade). The importance of multinational production is not likely to be superseded by contractual arrangements *en masse*. However, there are many novel international business relationships outside the scope of this study which are, and will become, far more important in particular industries and countries.

The aggregate propensities presented in Table 3.12 obscure the importance of licensing in particular industries. Although not shown here, licensing propensities of around 5 per cent of industrial production occur not infrequently, and are as high as 8 per cent for UK outward licensing in chemicals, and between 6 and 7 per cent in Japanese inward licensing in chemicals and engineering.

One way of appreciating the relative contribution of each industry to the countries' trade in technology is to inspect the percentage distributions. Table 3.13 reveals that each country has its own specialisation in outward technology licensing, although the chemical industry's share is consistently high for all countries except Sweden. As might be expected, the US proportions are highest for technology-intensive industries. Japan's high receipts in chemicals suggests that government policy of strengthening this industry has succeeded, although it does not represent a surplus in net receipts. Most of Japan's licensing in chemicals takes place mainly in Asia, where Japanese firms' knowledge is particularly appropriate.

A comparison of Tables 3.13 and 3.14 demonstrates the intra-industry nature of licensing, as the inter-penetration within industry groups is the highest of all the routes of international production. Licensing is without doubt most characteristic of technology-intensive industries, and there is every indication that while firms in each country may specialise in certain product technologies, the breadth of technological gaps between countries is closing.

3.6   GEOGRAPHICAL AND INDUSTRIAL PATTERNS: SOME TENTATIVE CONCLUSIONS

While the US is the dominant country by all measures in the world economy, it is at the same time the least open of the five countries. The argument encapsulated in the product cycle theory, to the effect that the high absolute and *per capita* incomes of the USA have been the root cause of its comparative advantage in technology-intensive industries, appears to describe the observed patterns.

With respect to US DFI, it is maintained that US firms gained experience of multi-plant operation and economies of firm size prior to first venturing outside the USA, conferring on them a considerable size advantage without the need for a large external sector. European firms, on the other hand have, as a matter of necessity, tended to prefix DFI with substantial international orientation.

Although Japan appears to be anything but an open economy it has, in its initial stages, traded intensively with certain areas, in particular with South-East Asian countries. Both Sweden and

TABLE 3.13 *Outward licensed foreign production, percentage distribution by industry group*

	USA	Japan	UK	Sweden	FGR	All countries
1975						
Food, drink and tobacco	1.62	0.99	3.34	1.26	0.28	1.57
Chemicals and allied products	17.99	42.54	33.14	14.67	42.08	28.72
Primary and fabricated metals	6.93	14.94	1.77	5.06	1.42	5.97
Mechanical and instrument engineering	19.76	8.78	10.54	39.89	12.96	15.68
Electrical engineering	24.48	8.88	11.74	22.95	20.08	19.19
Transportation equipment	8.41	7.74	1.48	0.42	14.39	8.10
Textiles, leather, clothing and footwear	0.88	3.86	1.26	2.10	0.51	1.30
Paper, printing and publishing	3.10	0.67	6.34	4.96	0.44	2.86
Other manufacturing industries	16.81	11.58	30.39	8.70	7.83	16.60
Total manufacturing	100.00	100.00	100.00	100.00	100.00	100.00
Value (US $bn)	(13.56)	(3.92)	(5.18)	(0.57)	(5.71)	(28.95)
1970						
Food, drink and tobacco	2.17	3.37	4.55	1.74	0.11	2.39
Chemicals and allied products	18.34	34.76	33.18	9.85	41.73	24.92
Primary and fabricated metals	6.71	12.54	1.52	11.46	0.79	5.44
Mechanical and instrument engineering	17.16	9.50	6.13	30.14	14.02	14.55
Electrical engineering	27.42	10.99	12.75	32.97	20.33	22.96
Transportation equipment	12.23	9.19	10.67	1.48	19.21	12.48
Textiles, leather, clothing and footwear	0.99	1.33	1.50	2.77	0.35	1.05
Paper, printing and publishing	2.37	0.83	4.50	3.74	0.35	2.42
Other manufacturing industries	12.62	17.48	25.21	5.86	3.11	13.80
Total manufacturing	100.00	100.00	100.00	100.00	100.00	100.00
Value (US $bn)	(10.14)	(1.01)	(2.98)	(0.31)	(2.19)	(16.63)

Table cont. p. 78

TABLE 3.13—continued

	USA	Japan	UK	Sweden	FGR	All countries
1965						
Food, drink and tobacco	2.40	0.65	3.59	1.57	0.40	2.25
Chemicals and allied products	20.96	66.91	45.39	11.51	39.23	28.23
Primary and fabricated metals	8.68	3.24	0.31	12.55	0.42	6.14
Mechanical and instrument engineering	17.96	2.77	10.31	29.29	11.48	15.72
Electrical engineering	23.05	4.81	10.07	22.38	20.05	20.16
Transportation equipment	8.98	17.74	6.48	7.43	23.69	10.83
Textiles, leather, clothing and footwear	8.38	0.65	12.73	4.18	0.85	7.76
Paper, printing and publishing	1.80	0.28	2.31	3.66	0.39	1.68
Other manufacturing industries	7.78	2.96	8.80	7.43	3.48	7.23
Total manufacturing	100.00	100.00	100.00	100.00	100.00	100.00
Value (US $bn)	(6.68)	(0.22)	(1.51)	(0.19)	(1.44)	(10.13)

NOTE: Figures may not sum precisely to totals due to rounding.
SOURCE: See Appendix A.

TABLE 3.14 *Inward licensed foreign production, percentage distribution by industry group*

	USA	Japan	UK	Sweden	FGR	All countries
1975						
Food, drink and tobacco	2.35	1.73	4.38	10.00	1.46	2.42
Chemicals and allied products	46.47	20.96	36.76	27.32	39.78	30.39
Primary and fabricated metals	1.76	6.85	2.63	12.38	4.15	5.19
Mechanical and instrument engineering	19.41	16.13	13.36	18.79	26.58	17.96
Electrical engineering	11.76	24.61	15.10	7.08	10.73	18.51
Transportation equipment	4.71	16.74	1.19	11.41	6.34	10.82
Textiles, leather, clothing and footwear	1.18	1.13	2.43	2.20	0.22	1.22
Paper, printing and publishing	3.53	0.75	9.58	3.23	1.07	2.59
Other manufacturing industries	8.82	11.10	14.57	7.59	9.66	10.90
Total manufacturing	100.00	100.00	100.00	100.00	100.00	100.00
Value (US $bn)	(3.40)	(10.98)	(3.08)	(0.66)	(3.34)	(21.46)
1970						
Food, drink and tobacco	4.04	0.90	3.09	6.18	2.47	2.16
Chemicals and allied products	56.57	24.71	31.85	25.48	43.57	34.26
Primary and fabricated metals	3.03	6.95	3.09	13.30	3.99	5.39
Mechanical and instrument engineering	7.07	17.46	22.52	21.86	23.79	17.67
Electrical engineering	4.04	27.18	17.45	15.12	8.73	18.44
Transportation equipment	10.10	14.82	5.70	7.87	9.54	11.57
Textiles, leather, clothing and footwear	3.03	1.00	3.86	1.81	1.19	1.83
Paper, printing and publishing	3.03	0.45	3.94	2.56	0.66	1.50
Other manufacturing industries	9.09	6.55	8.48	5.81	6.05	7.17
Total manufacturing	100.00	100.00	100.00	100.00	100.00	100.00
Value (US $bn)	(1.98)	(5.79)	(1.82)	(0.32)	(1.97)	(11.88)

Table cont. p. 80

TABLE 3.14—continued

	USA	Japan	UK	Sweden	FGR	All countries
1965						
Food, drink and tobacco	3.12	0.02	2.85	6.23	1.09	1.75
Chemicals and allied products	54.17	32.12	24.39	28.87	48.71	40.11
Primary and fabricated metals	9.38	8.72	2.24	17.86	2.60	7.28
Mechanical and instrument engineering	12.51	25.40	30.53	15.99	20.53	21.20
Electrical engineering	4.17	22.49	9.94	13.60	8.77	12.63
Transportation equipment	3.12	5.57	11.89	4.57	13.14	6.90
Textiles, leather, clothing and footwear	2.08	2.88	3.44	1.25	0.34	2.29
Paper, printing and publishing	3.12	0.09	4.84	6.44	0.48	1.99
Other manufacturing industries	8.33	2.72	9.88	5.19	4.35	5.84
Total manufacturing	100.00	100.00	100.00	100.00	100.00	100.00
Value (US $bn)	(1.92)	(2.26)	(0.95)	(0.19)	(0.96)	(6.28)

NOTE: Figures may not sum precisely to totals due to rounding.
SOURCE: See Appendix A.

Germany are open economies, especially Sweden in terms of trade, not least because of its small domestic absolute market size.

The degree of competition between US firms and their non-US rivals seems to have substantially increased, both in third markets and via DFI in the US itself. While foreign entry into the US appears to have been discouraged by US industry's ownership advantage strengths (see Section 2.7), if now non-US firms have also gained advantages of size deriving from internal economies, this may help explain their increasing competitiveness via DFI.

Consistent with this is the general observation that DFP has grown faster than trade, and that licensing has grown least of all. The increasing ratio of internalised forms of international competition cannot be explained by a general increase in ownership advantages. In theory, an increase in protectionism could be responsible, and in particular cases very likely is, but if this were widespread we would expect to see a significant rise in licensing. As it is, the average licensing propensity has virtually remained static, when expressed as a proportion of domestic production.

The most tenable explanation for the dramatic rise in DFP propensities is the continued increase in the efficiency of intra-firm transactions. Unless external markets are becoming more imperfect, this is the logical conclusion. The source of this efficiency gain is likely to be the increased scale of international operations. This is not mere tautology, because it is the acceleration in the shift towards DFP which must be explained.

This argument also suggests the likelihood of increased intra-industry DFI. The evidence of this study cannot directly assess this, but the increasing inter-penetration of DFI between countries points to this occurring.

At the very least, the changes in the patterns of DFI falsify the naive product cycle theory as a general theory of DFI. The example of DFI into the USA implies that much new investment must be coming from countries with lower *per capita* incomes than the USA. To this extent explanations are required for DFI that do not rest on high-technology alone. However, there is also some evidence that US firms' ownership advantages are not so marked over non-US firms as they once were.

The special nature of early Japanese manufacturing in LDCs has been noted, while new investment conforms more to the Western pattern and Japan's share of international licensing markets is also increasing. The effects of Japanese control of inward DFI are still very much in evidence despite these other changes.

The bias of earlier UK DFI towards non-manufacturing, especially in LDCs, has been giving way to increased manufacturing DFI in developed countries, and a shift from established hosts such as Canada, towards the USA. The UK's presence in foreign markets is substantial in both DFI and licensing, and this contrasts strongly with the problems of the UK economy and export performance.

The evidence of this chapter shows that national origins do have a large role in explaining the pattern of international competition. However, firms from countries other than the US tend to become multinational relatively early, and achieve very large size only later compared to US MNEs. The implications of this are that when they do attain large size and global operations there will be little to differentiate them from their US rivals, and the role of national origins may become less important.

4 The Determinants of International Competition

4.1 THE EXOGENOUS VARIABLES DEFINED

Exogenous Variables and Empirical Testing

In any statistical testing there is inevitably a gap between the data desired and the data available. So it is in this case. Certain aspects of the ideal model must be modified or omitted. These omissions relate to firm-specific factors and location-specific factors.

From theory it is known that those countries which record a particular level of foreign involvement do so partly on account of country-specific factors. Those industries which exhibit a particular level of foreign involvement, are accounted for by industry-specific factors, and the extent to which a firm is engaged in foreign involvement, in relation to its industrial compatriots, will be explained by firm-specific factors. In this study, firm-specific variables cannot be incorporated in the analysis, because of the aggregation of the data to industry groups.

The methodology nevertheless remains consistent with the theory of the firm as the agent of international competition, with country, industry, firm and location-specific factors acting so as to operate on the revenue and costs of the firm. Empirical work has suggested that one of the most frequently used firm characteristics, the size of the firm, may be superfluous if the appropriate ownership advantages are captured as variables (Horst, 1972b; Dunning, 1980; Owen, 1982). They cannot here be captured as firm-specific variables, but will be as industry-specific variables, and therefore the argument relates to the average firm. Other important firm-specific variables are absent, such as length of productional experience. However, if there is a systematic

83

difference in such variables across all firms in a country, they will be detected as country-specific differences.

Industry-specific factors are then measured by industrial variables, and country-specific factors, while they cannot be quantified *ex ante*, can be represented by dummy variables, to reveal international differences in the model, both as a whole, and in any of the coefficients obtained.

Location-specific factors, in their orthodox form of impediments to trade, do not appear in the statistical analysis. Locational variables have a chequered performance record in empirical work of this nature. Almost without exception ownership variables perform more successfully, and locational variables frequently never attain significance at all. This is unlikely to be because they are unimportant in the choice of location; it is more likely to be because they cannot be measured with sufficient accuracy, and that the level of inquiry is inappropriate, e.g., too aggregated. This is so with the present study. One good reason for this is the aggregation across host countries (and aggregation across source countries in the case of inward foreign involvement). Locational variables are most successful when host and home countries can be specified or grouped, as in studies of outward and inward international involvement respectively. When they are aggregated the individual effect of locational variables is lost, as the characteristics of heterogeneous host/source countries are summed. For example, Dunning (1980) found some evidence that his model was different between developed and developing hosts, and at least part of this observed difference will be due to locational factors.

Although they cannot be quantified, country-specific locational effects can be expected to show up as international differences between the regressions run for outward and inward involvement respecting the location of production, e.g. as differences in the equations for trade and direct foreign production. This will have to be borne in mind in interpreting the country-specific differences in the results.

The Explanatory Hypotheses

The empirical analysis begins with the premise that trade, direct foreign production and licensed foreign production are concurrent means by which firms exploit their ownership advantages. Thus our hypotheses have implications for each form of international competition, and in operational terms this requires that for each country the dependent variables must be regressed on the same set of independent variables.

The testable hypotheses, for which quantitative data are available for this study, cover a broad range of ownership advantages. There are, however, important differences between the hypotheses for outward and inward involvement. For the former, hypotheses relate to the industrial characteristics of the source country. For the latter hypotheses are constructed for host/recipient-industry characteristics. There is accordingly a distinction in interpretation between the exogenous variables when used in the outward equations and the inward equations.

For the outward equations, the exogenous variables represent source-country industrial advantages. For the inward equations they represent the host, and accurate inference is more problematic. If all DFI, for example, were inter-industry in nature, then strong host ownership advantages would, *ceteris paribus*, repel foreign entry. However, significant intra-industry DFI would lead to an observed positive relationship between the host advantage and foreign entry.

There are other recognised problems of interpretation which should be noted. Owen (1982), in his study of direct foreign investment in Canadian manufacturing, using host structural variables, argues that host data 'may be capturing both common cross-country industry similarities as well as characteristics which reflect either the vulnerability of the industry to foreign investment or the extent to which the industry is already dominated by such investment' (p. 224). This consideration is particularly appropriate to Canada, but may arguably extend to the UK and the Federal Republic of Germany, which in certain industry groups had inward direct foreign production of almost 30 per cent of total domestic production in 1975. By comparison the problem is almost non-existent for Japan.

The other noteworthy point is that the effect of government intervention is much more likely to be felt in statistical tests of inward involvement, because this is more frequently regulated as regards industry composition. Such intervention is particularly apparent in Japan.

Because the host country receives imports and inward direct foreign production from many source countries, it is not possible to infer that there is necessarily any relationship between them. However, it is possible to arrive at some hypotheses based on host-country ownership advantages. As the present sample countries are well developed we should in any event expect a high degree of inward licensing related in some way or another to host ownership advantages.

The following outlines some standard expectations, although some possible differences between the countries are considered and these are evidenced in Tables 4.1 and 4.2.

Technology Intensity

It would be unremarkable merely to hypothesise an increasing relationship between technological intensity and each dependent variable, although this must be the basic hypothesis. For the USA Lall's (1980) study suggests the product cycle hypothesis applies, with the US having a higher coefficient for this variable in the export equation than the DFP equation. For other countries, we have no expectation that their firms' comparative advantages lie so predominantly in technology.

The influence of the spatial transferability of ownership advantages should be considered. For the US the theory and empirical results have already been noted (Lall, 1980). Outside of the special circumstances of the product cycle model, it is only possible to anticipate that, unless there are strong reasons to the contrary, where a country's prowess is based on highly innovative technology, this will be exploited initially by trade rather than foreign production. The possible reasons militating against this include the possibility that a country's firms have a commensurately well developed ability to transfer even highly novel technologies abroad at low transmission cost. Such firms will be well developed multinationals from countries with an advanced international sector. Without the determinism of the product cycle, it is even possible that first commercialisation might take place in the host country. On the other hand, for a country at the earliest stages of international involvement, technology intensity should be expected not to favour direct foreign production at all, and it would be far more likely that exports and licensed foreign production would be used to service foreign markets.

The above argument applies to outward involvement. For inward involvement, the intra-industry nature of manufactures trade guarantees a positive association. Where DFI is intra-industry, or where source firms simply have technological superiority, a positive relationship is expected. Lall and Siddarthan (1982) found an absence of a relationship with the USA as the host. However this would be the one country where an exception is most likely, as foreign firms will not in general have a technological superiority over US firms. An auxiliary hypothesis might be that non-US firms base entry on other advantages, in particular on a capital advantage to buy into the US market.

Host technology intensity is expected to favour inward licensing. Empirical support from this comes from Oshima (1973) who noted that the cost of external transfer is reduced if the licensee has an existing research programme. The same point has been made theoretically by Buckley and Casson (1981), and there are no reasons to expect this hypothesis to differ between countries.

Capital Intensity

The role of capital intensity in explaining trade and direct foreign investment has a long pedigree, but mainly in US studies. There are two possible interpretations of its effect. The first is that capital intensity should favour direct foreign production more than exporting. This would be because capital represents an ownership advantage exclusive to large capital-endowed firms, and such a capital advantage enables the firm to cover the fixed costs of direct foreign investment more easily than other firms, given an imperfect capital market. Lall's (1980) empirical test of this hypothesis found no support on US data, a result surprisingly at variance with an essentially US-oriented theory.

An alternative interpretation is that capital intensity should favour exports more than direct foreign production. This would result from the savings on the deferral of fixed capital expenditure in expanding foreign markets. This would render capital intensity a location-specific factor favouring domestic production using existing plant, until foreign markets warranted direct foreign investments. This justifies the interpretation chosen by Swedenborg (1979) for Sweden. Sweden would be presumed to have relatively high labour costs, implying that direct foreign investment would be more characteristic of labour-intensive industries originating in Sweden. Though insignificant for export propensity, Swedenborg did obtain the expected negative and significant coefficient for direct foreign production.

It seems clear that the role of capital intensity is likely to depend on source country-specific factors. For countries with native firms expected to have favoured access to capital, despite Lall's result for the USA, in theory we should expect a positive relationship for direct foreign production and capital intensity, more so than for exports. It is for newer foreign investing countries that the Swedish type of result should be expected.

The effect of capital intensity on internalisation also has two possible interpretations. The first derives from a prediction of Buckley and Casson (1976) that it should favour direct foreign production and not licensing, because capital intensity is associated particularly with vertically integrated production processes, for which external markets are highly imperfect. The second interpretation is drawn from Buckley and Casson (1981), where capital intensity should favour externalisation (given foreign production), because licensing, if it is efficient, is a capital-saving mode of market servicing. The emphasis is on the capital-saving nature. However, there is no reason to believe that for source countries with higher capital accumulations that capital will be a constraint, and if there is significant existing direct foreign investment abroad, capital intensity may well be positively associated with direct foreign production, and at least this should show up in international comparison. Added to this, the high imperfections in licensing markets mean that licensing may often not be so efficient a mode of foreign market servicing for a mature foreign investing nation.

In fact, we can dispense with the first interpretation offered for capital intensity, because like most other studies of manufacturing, it has been assumed that generally direct foreign investment is horizontal, and the same factor combinations and output mixes usually apply at home and abroad. The second interpretation is chosen, with the amendment that it should be expected to favour internalisation for a country with substantial existing direct foreign investment.

Regarding inward involvement, and therefore a domestic characteristic, capital intensity would probably be interpreted as an entry barrier. However, it is precisely in such industries that multinationals generally have dominance. Thus the expected relationship with inward investment would arguably be positive. There are no obvious expectations for import penetration. Its effect on both inward direct and licensed foreign production may then be positive. For the latter the hypothesis is that a high domestic level of capital intensity represents existing capacity, lowering the cost of inward licensing.

Skills

The human capital approach to international trade is commonly applied to the United States. Here we have the opportunity to apply it to four other countries. As developed countries we would expect them all to be exporters of goods intensive in skills. However, when it comes to explaining direct foreign production the hypothesis is not obvious. As Lall (1980) has noted, the skills of production workers are not transferable to foreign plant, while the skills of managerial employees are more likely to be transferable. It therefore appears imperative to distinguish between the skills of these two groups of employees. Lall finds his measure of production workers' skills insignificant (except for multinationals' export propensity alone), however, the theory is well founded and should be tested on non-US countries.

Operatives' (production workers) skills should favour exports, as they can be exploited only from the domestic production base; conversely, they should exert an inverse effect on direct foreign production. The skills of non-operatives (management) constitutes an important test of a hypothesis not identified with the product life cycle. If such skills promote direct foreign production, this is substantiation of the hypothesis that ownership advantages other than technology can generate the continued expansion of direct foreign investment.

As for the hypothesis on internalisation, operative skills ought to be neutral as between either form of foreign production, i.e. substantially the same relationship for licensed foreign production as for direct, being an inverse one. Non-operative skills are not expected to be neutral. These skills represent existing investments in human capital, which lower the cost of setting up and running foreign operations. These will lower the cost of direct foreign production relative to licensing.

Domestic skills could exert more than due influence on inward involvement. Again, the distinction between productional and organisational skills is probably a crucial one. For the US, Lall and Siddarthan found average total wage (a measure of overall skills) insignificant for inward direct foreign investment. Their explanation was that local US skills are specific to US firms, not entrants. The question is, should this apply to operative skills, non-operative skills or both? As most inward direct investment originates from developed countries, it would seem reasonable to expect that multinationals will seek high skills in host industries, because their production functions would require a certain grade of labour input. However, remembering the hypothesis that for outward international involvement, high operative skills were expected to favour exports rather than direct foreign production, there appears to be an inconsistency.

If the structure of skills is similar between countries, but average skill levels are different, then entry patterns could feasibly be based on a set of skill requirements unrelated, or even negatively related, to the host skills. Unfortunately, testing this hypothesis requires data on precisely who the foreign firms are (i.e. the source country), which is not available in the present study. Nevertheless, this hypothesis could explain Lall and Siddarthan's result. Few countries have skill levels as high as the USA, so even a negative relationship is tenable. Here we are arguing that this hypothesis should apply to operative skills in particular.

Generally, average skill levels, as far as they can be gauged, are different between countries. However, there is a discernible degree of stability in the structure of skill levels (i.e. ranking) among industries and across countries. It is possible that where countries investing in the host have similar average skill levels (or even income levels by proxy), the relationship of entry pattern and host skills will be a positive one. This suggests a set of host-specific hypotheses; although these cannot be directly tested, they should generate country-specific differences in the models obtained in the statistical analysis.

The influence of operative skills on the level of externalisation is expected to be positive. This is because high skills in the host represent a high existing production capacity, and should reflect an ability to adapt to new technologies at low cost.

Managerial skills in the host measure the ability to manage competitively. Although to some extent the same arguments may apply to these as to operative skills, multinationals are expected to be concentrated in industries with higher managerial skills. Consequently, entry may be more common in industries with high managerial skills. We anticipate influence of these skills on the level of externalisation to be positive. This rests on the hypothesis that managerial skills reflect the capacity of management to organise the assimilation of new technology at low cost.

Complexity of Management

The last hypothesis offered is that the complexity of management influences the form of international involvement. This is a hypothesis which Caves (1974) considers theoretically weak, although as he points out, it is perhaps better suited to cross-country analysis. Nevertheless, it is possible to justify this hypothesis. It reflects not so much the skill of employees as the level of investment in managerial and production-coordinating infrastructure. This is a fixed investment, but its services are amenable to extension to foreign operations. Therefore it is expected to favour direct foreign production rather than exports. Lall (1980) found this hypothesis supported for the USA, and there are no strong reasons for believing the hypothesis is unsuited to the other countries.

The influence of management complexity on internalisation should be positive, and it is therefore thought to favour direct foreign production. The hypothesis is that such an investment will find more intensive use in direct foreign production, rendering licensing relatively inefficient. In his empirical work Lall found his proxy for this hypothesis significantly positively related to advertising intensity, an ownership hypothesis which it was not possible to include in the present study. If this association holds for non-US countries, it may affect the results, as no advertising variable is included. Unfortunately we cannot predict whether this is likely.

Lastly we consider the influence of the level of investment in managerial and production-coordinating infrastructure, as a host-country industrial characteristic. Lall and Siddarthan found this to be positive though insignificant for DFI in the USA. It may reflect structural similarities in industries across countries, and with the exception of Japan (noted later) there is a very strong correspondence in the average levels of managerial staff across countries. This would suggest, as it would for outward direct investment, that entry will typically be in industries intensive in managerial infrastructure. The argument is that foreign firms with such capacity can more easily expand operations into host countries in the same industries. This suggests an intra-industry pattern of entry, not necessarily related to technology intensity, once again a contrast with technology-oriented hypotheses.

The influence of host managerial capacity on the degree of inward licensing could be positive for two reasons. Firstly, as with the hypothesis on managerial skills, it may reflect host industries' assimilative capacity, thus reducing the total cost of licensing. Secondly, it may be structurally associated with marketing advantages, themselves the subject matter of licensing contracts, if the association reported in respect of product differentiation (advertising intensity) by Caves (1974), Lall (1980), and Lall and Siddarthan (1982) holds for other countries as well as the USA and Canada.

The Construction of the Exogenous Variables

The exogenous, or independent, variables have been chosen to afford the best opportunity to capture the hypotheses discussed above. The variables are expressed as follows:

RDEXP　　research and development expenditure divided by domestic industrial production, as a proxy for the degree of innovation and creation of technological ownership advantages.

RDEMP　　all employees engaged in research and development divided by total employment, as an alternative to RDEXP.

NTFA　　net tangible fixed assets at book values per employee, as a measure of capital intensity.

GFCF　　gross fixed capital formation per employee, as an alternative to NTFA.

WS　　wages and salaries per employee, as a measure of general skills.

WSOP　　wages and salaries per operative, measuring the skill level of production workers.

WSNONOP　　wages and salaries per non-operative, measuring the skill quality of managerial manpower.

NONOP　　non-operatives as a proportion of total employment, as a proxy for the complexity of management.

A few comments on these variables are in order. Firstly, their accuracy as measures of the hypotheses to be tested is sometimes a source of controversy. They all represent inputs or the payments for inputs of factors of production, rather than their outputs, which are the ideal measures. Thus they beg the question of the efficiency of use in production. Unfortunately, there is little scope for improvement of the data itself, but in certain circumstances justification can be given.

In the case of research and development inputs, these are the current levels of inputs, and may not necessarily accord with the actual generation of ownership of technology advantages at any one time. There is no clear evidence on the correctness of this measure, but for the industry groups used here it would seem reasonable to assume a strong relationship between inputs and the number and value of patents generated. One other feature of the research and development expenditure figures used here is that they include both current and capital expenditure. Sometimes capital expenditure is excluded, but this is not done here in order to keep the data comparable across countries.

Capital intensity is derived from the historic book value of plant and equipment. However, the preferred measure is the current or replacement value of capital, which is more likely to correspond to the actual input of capital services. Some support for NTFA as a measure can be derived from the generally high correlation between NTFA and GFCF, the latter being valued at current values. At least as a measure of capital intensity it is not contradicted by the additional information available.

With one exception, there are no reasons to fear any systematic incompatibility among countries in the data. The exception is the data for non-operatives in Japan. It is clear that the Japanese definition of non-operatives is appreciably wider than that of the other four countries, whose figures are very much in line with each other. The extent to which the inclusion of extra employees distorts the industry distribution unfortunately cannot be predicted.

The alternative specifications for research intensity and capital intensity are useful as a check on the consistency of different sources of data as measures of the same hypotheses. The correlation between RDEXP and RDEMP is so high that they are effectively the same variable and, in the results reported later, RDEMP is dropped as it adds nothing to our understanding above that of RDEXP. Similarly, GFCF is omitted from now on, because as a measure of capital intensity it is theoretically inferior to NTFA. The general skills variable, WS, is not systematically reported in the results because it represents a less demanding hypothesis than either WSOP or WSNO-NOP. However, it was included in other regressions not reported here, and on occasion can be instructive in comparison with other studies using this variable.

A final comment on the quality of the exogenous variables and the hypotheses they represent is required. The disadvantages of the selection must include the omission of some theoretically important hypotheses, particularly on the influence of advertising intensity and industrial concentration. These data could only be included for one or two countries, and therefore not in the present comparison. The advantage of this selection, however, is the exclusive use of own-country data, that is, no data from one country has been used to stand for another country; to do this would have defeated the very basis of this study. Additionally, this procedure reduces the proliferation of errors in the data, and avoids the 'washing out of international differences in the range of values' (Hufbauer, 1970, p. 152).

4.2   REGRESSION SPECIFICATIONS

Although two full models were used in the final set of regressions, as noted in the previous section, the variable WS is not included in the main reported results. The justification for this is that the distinction between WSOP and WSNONOP is a meaningful one in both theoretical and empirical terms, and the correlations between WSOP and WSNONOP demonstrate that they do not behave as proxies for each other. The reported regressions therefore include RDEXP, NTFA, WSOP, WSNONOP and NONOP as exogenous variables.

The regressions are run on three pooled cross-sectional sets of data for the years 1965, 1970 and 1975, and the regression equations are in double logarithmic transformation. This involves the conversion of both the data for the dependent and independent variables into natural logarithms. This transformation was chosen because it substantially reduces the curvature in the data when plotted on natural scales, both improving the goodness of fit and permitting the use of linear regression. This is a transformation employed by many similar studies. As a consequence the estimated coefficients are elasticities.

In the statistical analysis, each dependent variable is regressed on the same set of independent variables, for each country, an approach which is justified below.

Methodology

There are several econometric considerations present in any work of this nature. It is the purpose of this section to consider their implications for the present study.

Concerning the properties of the error term certain explicit assumptions are essential:

(i) that the constant term incorporates the mean of any omitted variable.
(ii) that the disturbances are not correlated across countries. Therefore for each country there are two systems of four equations, considered separately.
(iii) that the disturbances are not autocorrelated. A reasonable assumption as autocorrelation is not commonly a problem with cross-sectional data.
(iv) that the disturbances are independent of the date of observation

and of the country. This assumption concerns the absence of heteroscedasticity, and can be defended on both counts. Firstly the relevant data are rendered into constant (1970) dollars in the regressions, using a US price index (United Nations, 1977). This is necessary for the pooling of the data for the three years. Secondly, the data for each country are standardised by dividing by data appropriate to the size of each domestic industry. This is necessary in the context of pooling the data for the five countries.

(v) that for any single country the disturbances corresponding to different dependent variables are contemporaneously correlated, implying that the set of equations for each country should be considered jointly.

(vi) that the independent variables are independent of the error term, i.e. are exogenous. This is a requirement that no independent variable depends on any dependent variable, otherwise an identification problem arises. This is not expected to be a problem here, particularly because of the level of aggregation used in the industry groupings.

Because the independent variables are exogenous (assumption vi) and the disturbances are contemporaneously correlated across equations (assumption v), the model is in the form of Zellner's Seemingly Unrelated Regressions (Zellner, 1962). For such a system, ordinary least squares estimations would give unbiased but generally inefficient estimates. However, in the present study ordinary least squares is optimal, i.e. gives efficient as well as unbiased estimates. This is because each equation includes the same set of explanatory variables and there are no restrictions imposed on the parameters either within or across equations in the system. This implies that the regression system is in the form of a 'multivariate classical linear regression model' (Goldberger, 1964 pp. 246–8). In Section 4.5, there is some discussion of the correlation of the disturbances across equations, however these do not have to be taken into account when estimating the model.

Some consideration will now be given to the issue of correlation between the independent variables.[1] Multicollinearity is frequently present in data, and this study is no exception. This correlation is often significant, and while any significance is generally stable over time for one country, it is by no means stable across countries.

There are no clear guidelines for identifying when multicollinearity becomes a problem, which is a different consideration from the existence of multicollinearity *per se*. Standard analysis suggests comparison of the correlation (squared) between any two regressors and the multiple correlation coefficient of the equation (Koutsoyiannis, 1977). However, this is only unambiguous when there are exactly two independent variables.

By such criteria, it is evident that, as there are eight dependent variables for each country regressed on each country's set of independent variables, multicollinearity might be indicated as a problem in as few as one equation or as many as eight, assuming it is a problem at all.

In the present study the procedure has been adopted of maintaining the same model for all equations and countries, on theoretical grounds. However, some opportunity to monitor for problems of multicollinearity is afforded by checking the reported results against 200 preliminary regressions run on each independent variable, and 240 using varying sets of independent variables. The symptoms of such problems would include the insignificance of truly significant variables, or possibly the reversal of signs. While the chosen procedure concerning multicollinearity is distinct from the argument based on assumptions (v) and (vi) presented above, both support the application of a common model for each country.

Expected Signs of Exogenous Variables

We make a brief summary here of the expected signs for the independent variables, by equation and by country. The discussion of hypotheses established that there are good reasons for believing the independent variables may in some cases exert differential effects between countries. Dunning (1981) found marked country-specific differences in his model determining net outward investment, although this was for a very large number of countries with a wide range of levels of development. The five countries used here are, by comparison, at very similar stages of development, nevertheless we foresee some pronounced differences.

In so far as comparison is possible, the relationships obtained are expected to conform with the previous empirical works noted already. In the outward equations the United States is expected still to be characterised by a model resembling the product cycle over this period. Japan, however, is the most likely to reveal a distinctive model in both outward and inward equations, because of the earlier stage of its international involvement. The UK is anticipated to have features peculiar to a very open economy, with a mature pattern of outward and inward involvement, and to show some marked contrasts with the US model. Sweden is the country thought most likely to resemble the USA in certain respects, with its very high GNP *per capita*. The Federal Republic of Germany is a country which, like Japan, has been rapidly expanding its international involvement from a low base, and is still at an earlier stage than the countries other than Japan.

Tables 4.1 and 4.2 show the expected signs of the independent variables for each dependent variable for the five countries. The number of uncertain signs principally results for the overall dependent variables INTPRODOUT and INTPRODIN, not because of any failure in theory, but because of conflicts in expectations between

TABLE 4.1   *The expected directions of the relationships between the dependent and independent variables, outward equations*

	RDEXP	*NTFA*	*WSOP*	*WSNONOP*	*NONOP*
USA					
INTPRODOUT	+	+	?	?	?
EXP	+	+	−	+	+
DFPOUT	+	+	−	+	+
LFPOUT	+	+	?	−	−
Japan					
INTPRODOUT	?	?	?	?	?
EXP	+	−	+	+	−
DFPOUT	−	−	−	+	+
LFPOUT	+	+	?	−	−
UK					
INTPRODOUT	+	?	?	?	?
EXP	+	?	+	+	−
DFPOUT	+	+	−	+	+
LFPOUT	+	+	?	−	+
Sweden					
INTPRODOUT	+	?	?	?	?
EXP	+	+	+	+	−
DFPOUT	+	−	−	+	+
LFPOUT	+	+	?	−	−
FGR					
INTPRODOUT	+	?	?	?	?
EXP	+	+	+	+	−
DFPOUT	+	−	−	+	+
LFPOUT	+	+	?	−	−

TABLE 4.2   *The expected directions of the relationships between the dependent and independent variables, inward equations*

	RDEXP	NTFA	WSOP	WSNONOP	NONOP
USA					
INTPRODIN	?	?	?	?	?
IMP	+	?	−	?	?
DFPIN	?	+	−	+	+
LFPIN	+	+	+	+	+
Japan					
INTPRODIN	+	?	?	?	?
IMP	+	?	−	?	?
DFPIN	+	+	+	+	+
LFPIN	+	+	+	+	+
UK					
INTPRODIN	+	?	?	?	?
IMP	+	?	−	?	?
DFPIN	+	+	+	+	+
LFPIN	+	+	+	+	+
Sweden					
INTPRODIN	+	?	?	?	?
IMP	+	?	−	?	?
DFPIN	+	+	+	+	+
LFPIN	+	+	+	+	+
FGR					
INTPRODIN	+	?	?	?	?
IMP	+	?	−	?	?
DFPIN	+	+	+	+	+
LFPIN	+	+	+	+	+

their sub-dependent (i.e. constituent) variables. It cannot be predicted what the net effect will be, and so these are left unsigned. The following sections report the results of these statistical tests.

4.3   RESULTS FOR THE OUTWARD EQUATIONS

This section reports the results obtained from separate regressions for each country. To the extent that this exercise treads the same ground as any previous studies we should expect substantial agreement with them. Where there is material disagreement, the contrasts are fully discussed. Naturally, many equations are presented for which there are no precedents, and these also require careful interpretation.

Overview of the Results

Table 4.3 reports the results for the outward equations. Certain general comments can be made. The incidence of sign and significance of variables is by no means consistent across countries, although the explanatory power of RDEXP is usually high, the notable exception being the UK equations. Of the hundred regression coefficients, excluding the constants, forty-six are significant, although not all of these are anticipated. More than anything else, the pattern of significance confirms the country-specific nature of the results.

Some interesting results, however, do commend themselves from Table 4.3, with respect to particular equations and to the hypotheses represented by the independent variables. In particular, comparison of the influence of each variable between equations reveals whether the variable promotes each form of international competition, or has a differential effect. The structure of such influences is by no means stable across countries.

The first equation, INTPRODOUT, for the USA exhibits a higher coefficient of determination than any of the constituent routes taken individually. This reproduces the results obtained by Horst (1972a), Wolf (1977) and Lall (1980), in respect of research intensity. However, here, the result extends to the model as a whole, together with the inclusion of outward licensing (it also obtains for a regression on RDEXP alone, with very similar results). This corroborates the conclusion of partial substitutability, suggesting that all three routes are part alternatives as means of exploiting advantages.

This result is, however, not a general one, and is shared only with the Federal Republic of Germany. Here, as for the US, the significance of the total equation is highest. If the same credence is attached to these results as to the original finding, it suggests that only the US and Germany have technologies capable of generating substitute means of involvement. Why this should not apply to the other countries is not immediately obvious. If the argument is restricted to technology intensity alone, as in the original work by Horst and subsequent studies, then we can note that the coefficient of RDEXP is more significant for Sweden's INTPRODOUT equation as well, though not higher. The finding of partial substitutability was not obtained by Swedenborg (1979) either, and so the present results confirm that there is a genuine country-specific difference, compared to the US.

Of the specific hypotheses on ownership advantages, the most

TABLE 4.3 Multiple regression results for the outward equations

	RDEXP	NTFA	WSOP	WSNONOP	NONOP	Constant	R^2	F. Stat.
USA								
INTPRODOUT	0.512	0.568	−1.850	−0.604	0.064	4.232	0.764	13.590[a]
	(3.784)[a]	(2.768)[a]	(−1.626)[c]	(−0.282)	(0.110)	(1.271)		
EXP	0.473	0.284	−0.853	0.032	−0.308	−0.472	0.680	8.920[b]
	(2.814)[a]	(1.116)	(−0.604)	(0.012)	(−0.422)	(−0.114)		
DFPOUT	0.479	0.735	−2.320	−0.372	0.406	4.073	0.701	10.027[a]
	(2.935)[a]	(2.974)[a]	(−1.693)[c]	(−0.144)	(0.574)	(1.015)		
LFPOUT	0.848	0.516	−1.265	−1.569	−1.149	2.508	0.688	9.260[b]
	(3.467)[a]	(1.393)[c]	(−0.615)	(−1.615)	(−1.083)	(0.417)		
Japan								
INTPRODOUT	−0.063	−0.762	3.205	−1.867	−2.968	−4.313	0.709	10.229[a]
	(−0.537)	(−3.290)[a]	(3.088)[a]	(−1.616)[c]	(−4.901)[a]	(−3.652)[a]		
EXP	0.293	−0.988	5.842	−5.272	−4.828	−2.914	0.762	13.434[a]
	(1.822)[b]	(−3.100)[a]	(4.088)[a]	(−3.314)[a]	(−5.790)[a]	(−1.791)[b]		
DFPOUT	−0.749	−0.803	0.390	2.675	0.378	−8.885	0.764	13.636[a]
	(−3.982)[a]	(−2.155)[b]	(0.234)	(1.438)[c]	(0.388)	(−4.673)[a]		
LFPOUT	1.170	0.618	3.705	−3.940	−0.277	−0.060	0.739	11.913[a]
	(4.384)[a]	(1.169)	(1.562)[c]	(−1.493)[c]	(−0.200)	(−0.022)		
UK								
INTPRODOUT	0.080	0.165	−1.170	2.100	0.361	−1.954	0.350	2.264
	(0.950)	(1.109)	(−1.173)	(1.461)[c]	(0.776)	(−1.493)[c]		
EXP	0.298	−0.237	0.146	1.511	−0.416	−2.933	0.528	4.698[c]
	(2.837)[a]	(−1.281)	(0.118)	(0.834)	(−0.718)	(−1.798)[b]		
DFPOUT	−0.141	0.442	−3.430	4.628	1.049	−4.330	0.394	2.730
	(−0.949)	(1.681)[c]	(−1.946)[b]	(1.821)[b]	(1.277)	(−1.872)[b]		
LFPOUT	0.145	0.403	−4.195	3.905	2.701	−1.220	0.296	1.768
	(0.513)	(0.806)	(−1.251)	(0.807)	(1.727)[b]	(−0.277)		

	RDEXP	NTFA	WSOP	WSNONOP	NONOP	Constant	R^2	F. Stat.
Sweden								
INTPRODOUT	0.716	−0.294	1.317	−0.539	−1.122	0.343	0.513	4.430[c]
	(2.953)[a]	(−0.753)	(0.575)	(−0.218)	(−0.921)	(0.129)		
EXP	0.709	−0.294	1.951	−1.062	−1.795	−0.910	0.440	3.296[c]
	(2.820)[a]	(−0.726)	(0.822)	(−0.415)	(−1.422)[c]	(−0.331)		
DFPOUT	0.796	−0.036	0.634	0.789	0.158	−1.164	0.622	6.919[b]
	(2.770)[a]	(−0.078)	(0.234)	(0.269)	(0.110)	(−0.370)		
LFPOUT	0.583	−0.199	−5.054	3.641	0.497	−0.389	0.441	3.310[c]
	(1.760)[b]	(−0.373)	(−1.614)[c]	(1.078)	(0.298)	(−0.107)		
Federal Republic								
of Germany								
INTPRODOUT	0.287	−0.408	0.491	0.738	−0.289	−1.384	0.867	27.395[a]
	(6.335)[a]	(−2.404)[b]	(0.590)	(0.849)	(−0.855)	(−1.567)[c]		
EXP	0.305	−0.658	1.870	−0.708	−0.664	−1.167	0.811	17.985[a]
	(5.184)[a]	(−2.984)[a]	(1.731)[b]	(−0.628)	(−1.512)[c]	(−1.019)		
DFPOUT	0.272	0.114	−3.437	5.327	−0.431	−6.731	0.709	10.255[a]
	(3.021)[a]	(0.339)	(−2.079)[b]	(3.087)[a]	(−0.642)	(−3.841)[a]		
LFPOUT	0.921	0.023	−0.319	0.572	−0.526	−1.709	0.717	10.619[a]
	(5.485)[a]	(0.037)	(−0.103)	(0.178)	(0.178)	(−0.522)		

NOTES: Figures in parentheses are t statistics.
Significance levels are denoted by: a(1%), b(5%) and c(10%).

consistently supported is that of the role of research intensity. Total international involvement is promoted by research intensity for countries other than Japan and the United Kingdom. The same applies for all three routes, again with the exception of Japan and the United Kingdom. This attests to country-specific differences for these two countries, and these are discussed in Chapter 5. With these exceptions, the general hypothesis that all the means of international competition are promoted by research intensity is confirmed.

The generally strong relationship between licensing and research intensity is as expected. Only for the UK is research intensity not significant, which is a result requiring some explanation. The inference one might draw from the more standard finding for other countries is that licensing is predominantly incident in high-technology industries. Whether countries' firms are in a position to exploit these technology advantages via direct foreign investment is another matter, and as expected this varies substantially among these countries.

The basic hypothesis for the role of capital intensity rested on the principle that for countries new to international competition it should lead to a greater promotion of exports than direct foreign production. This has not been borne out by any of the countries. For Japan a negative coefficient is obtained in the direct foreign production equation, but this is accompanied by a markedly more negative coefficient for the export equation. The basic hypothesis is most clearly refuted by the USA and UK, however these are precisely the two countries whose large, and capital-endowed, multinational firms would be expected to enjoy capital advantages.

It is now easier to appreciate the prevalence of the belief, based on observation of a majority of US and UK multinationals, that capital intensity is an advantage of all multinationals from all countries. The finding for the capital advantage theory clearly has country-specific foundations.

The discovery that this theory does not apply to countries other than the USA and UK may be explained as follows. These countries have notably large and well-established multinational firms, for whom the cost of capital is lower than for firms from more recent foreign-investing nations, because of their own internal funding and their size, commanding lower interest charges. As such, they will be relatively advantaged in capital-intensive industries. This may be support for the firm-specific reinterpretation of Aliber's (1970; 1971) country-specific currency area hypothesis, which was proposed by Dunning (1971).

Only for the US is licensing found to be related to capital intensity, although as expected, to a lesser extent than direct foreign production. It was argued that this should be the case because licensing is a capital-saving means of international involvement. That a plus sign is obtained probably reflects the fact that US firms have generated more technology in capital-intensive industries, and these are consequently the technologies they are most likely to have for sale. This does not apply to the UK (and in no preliminary equation). We can draw the conclusion that the UK licenses fewer capital-intensive production processes, and characteristically such processes are mostly internalised.

The theoretical effect of skills was argued to be dependent on their type. Operative skills were expected to promote exports and not to promote direct foreign production. For all the countries, except perhaps Sweden, this relativity is maintained, i.e., the WSOP coefficient is higher for exports than direct foreign production. However, country-specific differences mean that its coefficient for exports is only significantly positive for Japan and the Federal Republic of Germany, and significantly negative for direct foreign production in the case of the USA, UK and Federal Republic.

Nevertheless, the direction of the differential effect of the skills variables is supported generally, and therefore suggests that Lall's inference from the USA is one that might apply to developed source countries as a rule. The fact that for the USA, the coefficient obtained for WSOP is not significant in the export equation, does not deny that it may be significant for US multinational exports alone, as Lall found in further regressions. The stronger result obtained here, regarding the negative influence of WSOP in DFPOUT, may arise again because of aggregation. This would suggest that the hypothesis applies more to larger direct foreign investing industries (and firms), and may explain why it is not obtained for Japan and Sweden, where the average extent of direct foreign investment is generally smaller. Larger multinationals are able to base their foreign expansion on other, more readily, transferable, ownership advantages which may in some way be related to their size.

There has been little prior empirical work concerning the effect of operative skills on licensing. However, a significant result is obtained for Japan, and – in an opposite direction – for Sweden. These are stable results and require some explanation. In the case of Japan, it is known that a large volume of licensing receipts are from less developed countries (in contrast with the other four countries). It would appear that Japan's licensing is in technologies associated with high operative skills in Japan. It may therefore be that Japanese firms have pursued a policy, through licensing, of relocating production abroad in these countries (Asia and, to a lesser extent, Latin America). Thus both home and host country-specific effects come into play, with Japanese firms gaining access to markets via licensing, where these markets cannot be serviced from Japan.

The explanation for the negative sign of WSOP for Swedish licensing will be in the nature of its industrial profile. This would imply that Swedish technology-licensing takes place in industries other than those with the highest domestic non-operative skills. This is not to deny that such licensing takes place in high skills industries, indeed, as measured by WSOP, Sweden has skill levels in manufacturing second only (and very close) to the US. The result simply suggests that other Swedish industries not involved in licensing have relatively higher non-operative skills. The likely cause for this is a country-specific attribute such as the importance of domestic resource-based industries.

The hypothesised role of managerial skills was that it should favour direct foreign production rather than exports. It seems to fit this relative expectation for all countries, except the US and Sweden. Again country-specific differences in the model mean that its coefficient for direct foreign production is significantly positive only for Japan, the UK and Federal Republic, and negative for exports only for Japan. This result is surprising for the US, but is repeated in other regressions. Moreover, taking an overview of the US equations, it has not achieved any significance. We might conclude cautiously that there is some evidence for the hypothesised relationship in general.

Managerial skills were believed to favour direct foreign production over licensing, and the results indicate this is the case, wherever significance is attained for either of the equations (Japan, the UK and the Federal Republic of Germany).

The last variable measured the complexity of management. Again the hypothesis was that it should favour direct foreign production over exports, and it is found to do so whenever it is either significant in the DFPOUT or EXP equation (Japan, Sweden and Federal Republic). Its coefficient in the DFPOUT equation for the UK does not quite attain significance. The lack of significance for the US has no precedent and conflicts with the result obtained by Lall. Although not finding a significantly positive coefficient for his NONOP in the direct foreign production equation, a negative coefficient was obtained for exports. However, it should be remembered that the significance of this was lost when US multinationals' exports alone were substituted as the dependent variable.

The result we obtain here, therefore, resembles this second insignificant performance for exports, and a possible reason may again be aggregation. If this is so it suggests that US multinationals typically export goods using more managerially complex production than non-multinational US firms; a feasible conclusion given that non-multinationals are in general likely to be smaller firms.

The effect of NONOP on externalisation was hypothesised to be negative, as it should capture the ability to use internal markets more effectively than external markets. The only significant result obtained runs counter to this hypothesis. This is for the United Kingdom, and is always a stable result. The only explanation that can be offered is that we may be seeing the effect of a similar structural association between NONOP and advertising intensity to that reported by Lall using US data. This would imply that UK firms may have particular licensing ownership advantages in marketing – such as trade marks and brand names – compared to foreign producers. If this is so it is clearly a country-specific peculiarity of the UK.

The above discussion has shown that there has been mixed support for the hypothesis put forward for each of the explanatory variables. Amongst the statistical findings there are inevitably a substantial number of insignificances. These are difficult to explain away without additional knowledge. Similarly, there are results that run counter to expectations. Attempts to explain these types of findings can prove rewarding and provide valuable insights into the true complexities of international competition. This is best approached on a country by country basis, and we now turn to a more searching appraisal in the light of each country's experience and the results of previous empirical studies.

Analysis of the Results by Country

The power of the innovation and capital intensity hypotheses, together with the negative influence of the operative skills variable (principally on direct foreign production), are our major results.

The question is, does the present configuration of findings agree with the product cycle account, as presented by Lall? Comparisons have already been made with this study, but not with Lall's own major conclusion. This was that for the US mobile ownership advantages should explain direct foreign production to a greater extent than exports, and *vice versa* for less mobile or immobile factors, given the US has a comparative advantage in the export of technology-intensive exports. The logic behind this has already been discussed. Our own results here just narrowly fall short of reproducing Lall's result for research intensity, the central variable. The coefficient for exports is marginally lower and less significant than for direct foreign production, and indeed what difference there is, is unlikely to be significant.

Some possible reasons for differences with Lall's study have already been cited. One further difference is in the definition of the research intensity variable. Lall uses data on current expenditures, whereas the data used here include capital expenditures. In fact, this is not likely to be the cause of any material difference. It is more likely to arise from the definition of the model.

Up until now we have defended the use of the full model on theoretical grounds, to avoid the introduction of bias inherent in using a partial theoretical model. It is possible for the data used in this study to reproduce Lall's results quite closely if used in the same way. The coefficients Lall reports are based on a selective procedure appropriate to a single country study, and certain of Lall's reported equations include as few as one independent variable. Two of these are for research intensity and average total wage (cited in Chapter 2). The equivalent regressions using our present data yield coefficients with respect to DFPOUT of 0.343^a and 1.767^c for RDEXP and WS respectively, and with respect to EXP, 0.384^a and 1.826^c, with significance denoted as in Table 4.3. Thus, if the data are used in this way, the findings do not conflict. This is only worth stressing because of the strong *prima facie* similarities between the two studies. The conclusion is clearly that the US has the archetypal neo-technology configuration of international competition over the period studied.

One further apparent conflict is that Lall found no evidence for the capital advantage theory in his US study. Some relatively minor differences in procedure, for example, Lall's selection of twenty-five industries, cannot account for this, as the data base for the dependent variables is substantially the same. The likely explanation is the effect of industrial aggregation used in the present study, leading to a stronger result. In aggregation it is likely that the largest US direct foreign investing industries, being more capital-intensive than smaller industries, dominate. A useful way of viewing this is that the capital advantages of US direct foreign investors are primarily those of its leading multinational firms in major capital-intensive industries. This interpretation implies that it is perfectly feasible that non-US firms may increasingly come to have these characteristics although not necessarily in the same industries.

There is a general insignificance in the skills variables of the US equations. It is possible to attribute these to some multicollinearity, a problem which may be introduced by specifying two skills variables: WSOP and WSNONOP. However, the latter of these two, WSNO-NOP, is not significantly correlated with the complexity of management variable, NONOP, and so it is evident that they do not duplicate each other.

The Japanese equations are the most distinctive of the five countries, and many of the effects exerted by the independent variables are as hypothesised. There are no previous empirical studies of a similar nature with which to draw comparisons. However, there is a strong body of theory associated with Japanese economists such as Kojima (1973; 1977; 1978; 1982), already reviewed in Chapter 2. This literature predicts that the type of production transferred abroad as DFI should contrast markedly with production located in Japan for export. This is deemed to reflect the reorganisation of the location of production in line with the Japanese economy's comparative advantage in trade.

Thus, we are led to expect that if Japan's comparative trade advantage is in high-technology exports, then its firms' DFI will be in low-technology industries. The significant and opposite signs for RDEXP between the EXP and DFPOUT equations bear this prediction out.

Although the above account provides a plausible description of Japan's pattern of international competition, it does little more than that. As argued in Chapter 2, it certainly does not follow that the normative conclusions of the Kojima hypothesis are proven as a result. The embryonic nature of Japan's DFI over this period is far more likely to account for these observations.

The negative relationship between capital intensity and DFPOUT is likely to derive from the character of the firms involved in Japanese DFI over this period. These are typically small firms in standardised-product and labour-intensive industries. The nature of this DFI could not contrast more with that of most developed countries. From this it does appear that such small firms are in no way exploiting a general capital advantage. However, Japanese DFI has not remained static, and there can be no presumption that these characteristics will continue to dominate. The appropriate test of this argument is to investigate any changes in the Japanese pattern and that is carried out in Chapter 5.

For the present, however, there is no doubt at least that Japan's DFI has characteristically been in low-technology industries, consistent with observation in Chapter 3.

The finding for capital intensity is equally noteworthy in both the EXP and DFPOUT equations. It is consistent with the argument given above, that Japanese DFI should be in low capital-intensity industries, but more interestingly that this should apply with even more force to exports. The inference from this is that, as we are looking at export propensities, exports as a percentage of domestic output are characteristically in the lower range of capital intensity of Japanese industry as a whole. The implication of this is that Japan's export comparative advantage, in so far as it is reflected here, is based on advantages other than capital.

Apart from research intensity, an appealing explanation of Japan's performance in exports might be Japanese skills. Indeed, the significantly positive influence of WSOP seems to support this. However, the reverse relationship applies to WSNONOP, while this variable explains Japanese DFI. Unfortunately, it is important not to place too much credence in these particular results, as the problems of multicollinearity seem to interfere with our interpretation of the Japanese skills variables. These problems arise possibly because of the definitions of the two groups of employees, as noted in Section 4.1.

It has already been remarked that the Japanese definition of non-operatives is clearly out of line with that of other countries, and it may well be that the definitions of skill classifications can cut across those of the other countries. If we discard model two, and adopt model one (specifying only average total wage skills) it is found that general skills promote direct foreign production over exports. The relevant statistical findings are that the effect of average skills, WS, is estimated as 2.937[a] for DFPOUT and 1.190[a] for EXP (cf. Table 4.3).

This result is also obtained when WS is the only regressor. From separate equations it is, however, possible to say with some confidence that managerial skills do promote Japanese direct foreign production, and the skills of operatives just fail to attain significance as a determinant of exports, a result more in line with that for other countries. Other than this the indications are that, as far as these data can be considered correct, Japanese licensing is predominantly in high operative skills industries.

The regressions for the UK are consistently among the least significant of all the countries. This suggests that the hypotheses and the general approach of this study are at least appropriate to outward UK involvement. Thus it may be enlightening to discuss what the UK equations tell us about the likely character of omissions from the hypotheses we have applied. Foremost amongst the possible candidates is the effect of advertising intensity as a measure of the marketing prowess of UK firms. In particular such an advantage should transfer to DFI, and so the absence of this hypothesis is likely to be a significant one from the approach of this study.

The special relationships over long periods which UK firms have had, both as exporters and foreign investors, in Commonwealth markets are impossible to capture *ex ante* in the present study, but have no doubt played a very large part in the extension of UK international competition abroad.

A result unique to the UK is the complete lack of any association between research intensity and DFPOUT, and most surprisingly to LFPOUT. The implications of this latter finding are that UK firms' ownership advantages in technology seem to have been exploited primarily via exports, at least over the period studied. The association between NONOP and LFPOUT, however, provides an indication that UK firms' non-affiliate licensing may contain a significant marketing-related component, if the structural association between NONOP and advertising intensity extends from the US (Lall, 1980) to the UK.

Because of the low significance of the UK equations, it is likely that the problems of multicollinearity are invited and we now check for these. The most striking result obtained for the UK, that its direct foreign production is unrelated to research intensity, is supported in every equation run. A regression of licensing on research intensity alone yields a statistically significant coefficient for 0.361^b (cf. Table 4.3). However, this is still a lower coefficient than for any other country. The only other instability is that the negative coefficient for operative skills in the DFPOUT equation drops below significance, otherwise the results are confirmed.

We have already noted the interpretation of the capital intensity finding in the case of the US model. This is a result shared only with the UK, in kind, though not degree. It is, therefore, suggested that the advantageous access to capital of UK MNEs has a significant role in explaining the UK's direct foreign investment.

Swedenborg (1979) concluded that Sweden enjoyed a 'relative advantage' in direct foreign production involving skill-intensive activities, as the coefficient on average total wage was significant for this and not for exports, while the reverse applied to research intensity in the relevant two equations. How far do the present results agree with these findings? The first impression is that research intensity not only promotes both exports and direct foreign production, but is actually slightly stronger for the latter. As for skills, both operative and managerial, these are insignificant in both equations for Sweden. Data for Swedish direct foreign production are taken from the Swedish study and its ultimate source, the Swedish Industrial Institute, so at least a confirmation of Swedenborg's results ought to be obtained.

The conflict is likely to derive from the way in which the data are used, and again, the problems of aggregation. Swedenborg's results were obtained from regressions across firms, while in the present study the regressions are across industries. The result of this, as argued in the case of aggregation of US industries, is likely to be an upward bias of the effect of characteristics of large firms. Here the characteristics of larger Swedish multinationals would be a higher than average research intensity. If this is so, the reverse argument would seem to apply to skills. Accordingly the smaller direct foreign investing firms may have a relative skills advantage although this effect is lost in the equations in Table 4.3. The issue of international comparisons is pursued further in Chapter 5.

The Federal Republic of Germany appears as a country where total international involvement is strongly determined by research intensity. As for the United States, this is stronger for the total than the component routes of international involvement taken individually, including licensing (Table 4.3).

To this extent the Federal Republic's international involvement resembles the stylised product cycle. However, there are differences with the product cycle model and with the US model found in this study. Firstly, the skills variables are better behaved in the Federal Republic's equations, and do indicate a meaningful distinction between managerial and operative skills. High operative skills promote exports and high managerial skills promote direct foreign production (these results are obtained also when they are single regressors). If these skills variables are replaced by the single average total wage, we find the now familiar result that overall skills promote direct foreign production more than they promote exports. It does appear that in comparison to the USA, German DFI and exports are more skill intensive, but this applies *a fortiori* to skills.

At least for the Federal Republic, it seems that the sort of skills which favour direct foreign production are managerial, and those that favour exports are the skills of operatives, as theory would predict. Thus, we have some indication of how a non-US country might extend direct foreign production based, at least relatively, more on skills.

The Federal Republic's exports are negatively related to capital intensity, and this is a stable result in all other equations. This is a little puzzling, and it is a result shared only with Japan, although in comparison with the USA, the exports of all countries would seem to be less capital-intensive. The absence of a positive association between capital intensity and exports has been met before and it seems to be a general result. Swedenborg found it an insignificant (or negative) variable in her export propensity regressions across firms. Attention can be drawn to the observation that countries other than the USA base their international involvement relatively more on skills. This applies more to direct foreign production, but still obtains for exports. Thus, it seems that especially for non-US countries exports are based more on skills than capital intensity.

It may well be that we are seeing the effect of a generally lower level of domestic capital accumulation, particularly in non-US countries, associated with a comparative advantage in skill-intensive activities, very much as the spirit of the original Leontief hypothesis for the US would imply for non-US countries. However, our present data are not designed, nor are appropriate, to test this.

Lastly, attention can be drawn to the now familiar result for countries other than the USA and UK, that DFI is not positively associated with capital intensity. This is found to apply to Germany's MNEs, and the interpretation that has been attached to this is that access to capital is not yet an advantage of German firms as a notable characteristic of their DFI.

4.4　RESULTS FOR THE INWARD EQUATIONS

Overview of the Results

This section reports the results for the inward involvement hypotheses in an analogous format to that for outward involvement in the previous section. Thus, the findings are in the form of a model presented for each country. There is a less coherent body of statistical work on the determinants of inward involvement, and not surprisingly, the most relevant work originates from research on US data, such as Lall and Siddarthan (1982).

The first notable feature of the inward equations is their generally lower success, as measured by the levels of statistical significance. This is not altogether unexpected. Owen (1982) found that by replacing US home-industry characteristics with Canadian host characteristics to explain US involvement (by far the principal source) in Canada, the general level of significance dropped appreciably. Here we find that, of the hundred regression coefficients, excluding the constants, thirty-four are significant, although as with the outward equations, not all of these were anticipated. Despite this it is possible to gain some insight into the host (or recipient country) determinants of inward involvement, and particularly in the present study, into those differences which exist among countries (this is given special attention in Chapter 5). Given the generally lower significance of the equations, the problems of multicollinearity are more likely to appear, and so caution must be exercised in our interpretation. Again, results can be checked for stability in the many equation runs.

From a first inspection of the results reported in Table 4.4 the construction of different hypotheses for variables commonly used in outward analysis, when used in inward analysis, seems justified. There are a number of contrasts with the influences exerted in outward regressions. For the specific ownership advantage hypotheses, research intensity promotes imports of manufactures, where significance is obtained, except for the notable exception of the United Kingdom. This is a clear indication of a country-specific difference, although all these results are subject to the later discussion and confirmation in the context of the models for each country. There is no unanimous finding for research intensity and inward direct foreign production. The basic hypothesis of a positive association applies only to Japan, the UK and Federal Republic of Germany, and is rejected by a reverse finding for Sweden. Research intensity invites

TABLE 4.4 Multiple regression results for the inward equations

	RDEXP	NTFA	WSOP	WSNONOP	NONOP	Constant	R^2	F. Stat.
USA								
INTPRODIN	0.119	0.814	-2.634	1.798	-0.001	-2.895	0.539	4.917[b]
	(0.966)	(4.364)[a]	(-2.546)[a]	(0.924)	(-0.001)	(-0.956)		
IMP	0.035	0.202	-1.127	1.760	-0.426	-5.904	0.216	1.154
	(0.207)	(0.783)	(-0.788)	(0.654)	(-0.577)	(-1.410)[c]		
DFPIN	-0.205	1.812	-8.735	5.385	2.641	-0.979	0.446	3.386[c]
	(-0.480)	(2.806)[a]	(-2.440)[b]	(0.799)	(1.430)[c]	(-0.094)		
LFPIN	0.825	1.422	-2.259	-3.679	-1.052	5.590	0.548	5.097[b]
	(2.952)[a]	(3.357)[a]	(-0.962)	(-0.832)	(-0.868)	(0.828)		
Japan								
INTPRODIN	0.741	0.012	-0.506	0.388	1.179	2.087	0.744	12.189[a]
	(5.851)[a]	(0.048)	(-0.450)	(0.310)	(1.797)[b]	(1.530)		
IMP	0.256	0.136	-0.231	0.103	1.674	-0.877	0.262	1.490
	(1.618)[c]	(0.433)	(-0.164)	(0.066)	(2.042)[b]	(-0.548)		
DFPIN	1.419	0.434	-1.021	-0.090	3.322	5.849	0.741	12.027[a]
	(6.597)[a]	(1.019)	(-0.534)	(-0.042)	(2.979)[a]	(2.689)[a]		
LFPIN	1.586	-1.029	8.040	-7.959	-3.539	4.406	0.800	16.752[a]
	(5.550)[a]	(-1.818)[b]	(3.166)[a]	(-2.816)[a]	(-2.389)[b]	(1.062)		
UK								
INTPRODIN	0.061	0.073	0.380	1.162	0.034	-3.052	0.423	3.082
	(0.814)	(0.547)	(0.427)	(0.904)	(0.082)	(-2.608)[a]		
IMP	-0.259	0.016	-1.161	2.534	0.533	-4.720	0.371	2.473
	(-2.607)[a]	(0.091)	(-0.986)	(1.492)[c]	(0.971)	(-3.054)		
DFPIN	0.411	0.220	1.657	0.501	-0.517	-3.801	0.636	7.341[b]
	(3.716)[a]	(1.125)	(1.264)	(0.265)	(-0.847)	(-2.210)[b]		
LFPIN	0.022	0.041	-3.020	1.807	3.326	0.729	0.418	3.013
	(0.108)	(0.113)	(-1.228)	(0.510)	(2.902)[a]	(0.226)		

TABLE 4.4—*continued*

	RDEXP	NTFA	WSOP	WSNONOP	NONOP	Constant	R^2	F. Stat.
Sweden								
INTPRODIN	0.448	−0.135	−6.182	6.782	−0.734	−3.606	0.761	13.341[a]
	(3.394)[a]	(−0.636)	(−4.958)[a]	(5.042)[a]	(−1.108)	(−2.496)[b]		
IMP	0.588	−0.242	−6.040	6.622	−1.496	−3.942	0.741	12.006[a]
	(3.810)[a]	(−0.975)	(−4.145)[b]	(4.212)[b]	(−1.932)[b]	(−2.334)[b]		
DFPIN	−0.366	0.560	−11.530	13.290	3.578	−9.640	0.625	7.010[b]
	(−1.367)[c]	(1.297)	(−4.555)[a]	(4.867)[a]	(2.660)[a]	(−3.286)[a]		
LFPIN	0.574	0.681	−4.150	3.801	0.138	−3.858	0.706	10.084[a]
	(3.564)[a]	(2.626)[a]	(−2.729)[a]	(2.316)[a]	(0.170)	(−2.189)[b]		
Federal Republic of Germany								
INTPRODIN	0.068	−0.056	−0.444	1.470	−0.389	−3.320	0.710	10.276[a]
	(1.980)[b]	(−0.433)	(−0.698)	(2.216)[b]	(−1.508)[c]	(−4.928)[a]		
INP	−0.048	−0.233	−0.818	1.749	−0.688	−4.745	0.505	4.286[c]
	(−1.089)	(−1.419)[c]	(−1.019)	(2.086)[b]	(−2.108)[b]	(−5.571)[a]		
DFPIN	0.144	0.014	1.589	−0.362	0.676	−2.005	0.693	9.469[b]
	(1.974)[b]	(0.051)	(1.186)	(−0.259)	(1.244)	(−1.412)[c]		
LFPIN	0.534	0.086	5.458	−6.094	1.713	3.281	0.737	11.768[a]
	(4.522)[a]	(0.195)	(2.516)[b]	(−2.692)[a]	(1.945)[b]	(1.427)[c]		

NOTES: Figures in parentheses are *t* statistics.
Significance levels are denoted by: a(1%), b(5%) and c(10%).

inward licensing, but not for the UK, a result clearly requiring some investigation.

The basic hypothesis for capital intensity argued that it should promote both forms of inward foreign production. In only three cases is significance attained, and one of these is contrary to expectations. Only for the Federal Republic of Germany does it reveal a relationship with imports, and this is a negative one.

As with outward involvement, a distinction was drawn between managerial skills and operative skills. However, their expected effects are not the same as for outward involvement. It was proposed that for the highest income and highest skill level countries, such as the US, inward foreign entry might be expected to avoid the indigenous industries most strongly based on high operative skills. This argument is apparently supported not only for the US, but also for Sweden, where domestic skill levels are second only to the US itself. No other such relationship or different pattern emerges for the other countries. Operative skills show a consistently negative relationship to all international production in Sweden. Other than this, a positive relationship with licensing is found for Japan and the Federal Republic of Germany, in support of the hypothesis that operative skills represent an ability to assimilate new technologies into production, and are particularly appropriate to these countries.

Our expectations about managerial skills were not generally borne out. The basic hypothesis put forward was that inward direct foreign investment should be expected in managerial skill-intensive industries. Only for Sweden does this hypothesis receive support. The externalisation hypothesis contended that inward licensing should be positively related to managerial skills. This receives support only in Sweden, and seems contradicted in Japan and Germany.

The last hypothesis concerned the complexity of management variable. It was argued that inward direct foreign production would take place in such industries because it is in precisely these managerially complex industries that multinationals have structural advantages. This result is supported only in Japan (where doubt has already been expressed over the definition of these data) and Sweden. This variable appears to promote inward licensing, as hypothesised in the UK and Federal Republic of Germany. The next section looks at the results for each country, and where appropriate, considers the relationship between our present findings and previous empirical works.

Analysis of the Results by Country

There are few strong results in the inward equations for the United States, and indeed the import equation does not attain general significance (Table 4.4). From the total equation INTPRODIN, it appears that inward competition into the US market is usually capital-intensive (although this is not so for imports), and is negatively related to operatives' skills in the US. The inward direct foreign production equation does return two clear results: that inward direct entry is related to domestic capital intensity, but is apparently negatively related to operative skills.

If we compare these results to those of Lall and Siddarthan (1982), the general results are in agreement. There are, however, some differences in the details between the two sets of findings. Both studies employ a double logarithmic transformation, so all coefficients reported are elasticities.

In line with Lall and Siddarthan's own results, foreign direct investment in the USA is found to be unrelated to US technology intensity. This suggests that foreign firms make their entry into the USA, as a rule, based on ownership advantages other than technology. This is probably because in many major industries US absolute technology advantages are superior to those of potential entrants. This results in a picture of low intra-industry foreign investment into the US where intra-industry investment is normally based on firms' technology advantages. Perhaps because of this US superiority, foreign firms' technology advantages are generally licensed to US firms in the most technology intensive industries, in the absence of a strong enough basis for direct entry. This is suggested by the positive coefficient on RDEXP for inward licensing, and agrees also with our general hypothesis proposed earlier.

Table 4.4 shows DFPIN to be negatively related to operative skills (though not non-operatives). Lall and Siddarthan reported an insignificant relationship with general skills. However, the equivalent variable, WS, when replacing the two skills variables in this study, still produces a significant negative coefficient (-7.050^a). Both studies agree that US domestic skills do not attract inward DFI, but we find here that they actually repel entry.

The difference, however, may be due to the effect of higher aggregation across industries than in Lall and Siddarthan's study. This is likely to amplify any negative association between inward DFI and average skills, where this association is characteristic of dominant industries. While this suggests that, in terms of volume, most DFI in the USA is in lower (US) skills industries, we may nevertheless be overstating the cross-sectional disincentive effect of high average skills.

The above discussion has centred around the effect of average skills. However, Table 4.4 presents the two skills variables WSOP and WSNONOP. Unfortunately, it appears that the correlation between these variables interferes with the sign of WSNONOP. It is clear only that WSOP is negatively signed. The meaning attaching to this may be that foreign MNEs have operative skill requirements at the lower end of US industries' skills ranking, possibly because foreign entrants do not have the production technology to enter the leading and most (operative) skill-intensive US industries.

On what basis then is entry via direct foreign production made into the US? The capital advantage hypothesis has the strongest support. Inward direct foreign production is positively related to capital intensity in the USA, indicating that to enter these industries foreign multinationals must have some ownership advantage based on capital.

Additionally, there is some support for the hypothesis that inward DFI is in industries with complex organisational structure, suggesting that a strength in this respect is a characteristic of incoming firms. This reasoning is supported by the variable NONOP in the DFPIN equation. This variable may also be registering marketing advantages, but this can be no more than speculation.

One last result of interest for the USA is that inward licensing is not only into research-intensive US industries, but into capital-intensive ones also. This may be because potential foreign entrants with ownership advantages in technology and capital are deflected from entry, not on account of any inadequacy in US market size, but because in some industries US ownership advantages in technology or capital are simply too great. This is a plausible conclusion because our variables measure host-industry characteristics, and these do not directly measure foreign firms' advantages. However, the basic externalisation hypothesis that indigenous technology intensity favours licensing is supported.

The most striking result for Japan is the role of research intensity in total inward international production. It is evident that host research intensity encourages both inward direct and licensed foreign production. It is also evident that this is a peculiarly Japanese phenomenon. The cause of this distinctive result is most likely the extensive domestic industrial policy in Japan, the effect of which, as was intended, has been to ensure that only high-technology production is located in Japan. While this applies to both licensing and direct foreign production, the empirical significance of the former has been greater.

Because of the regulated nature of foreign involvement in Japan, we might expect the role of ownership advantages other than technology to have a very low explanatory power. This is true as far as host capital intensity is concerned, which has an insignificant effect on foreign entry via direct foreign production. Capital advantages are, therefore, not advantages enabling direct entry into Japan, given, as seems likely, that foreign investment is required more for the technology it transfers than for capital. This argument would seem to apply *a fortiori* to inward licensing into Japan, to which host capital intensity appears as negatively related.

We have already expressed some reservations about Japanese skills variables, based on a questionable classification of employees into operatives and non-operatives. In Table 4.4 both variables appear to be generally insignificant apart from in the inward licensing equation. In separate regressions where the two skills variables are replaced by the one average skills variable, they perform insignificantly. The problem which shows itself most clearly in the LFPIN equation seems to be the result of collinearity between WSOP and WSNONOP, probably caused by the imprecise definition of operatives and non-operatives. The general conclusion is that for all inward involvement into Japan there is no support for any skills hypothesis (including that for general skills) where both types of employee are combined.

The influence of the managerial complexity variable appears positive on imports and inward direct foreign production, but negative on inward licensing. Again there must be reservations about the accuracy of these results because of the definition of the data. That for the inward direct foreign production accords with the basic theory, but in the case of Japan there are no strong reasons to believe that this basic theory should apply. The effect of this variable on inward licensing is negative. This could arise, arguably, if a structural association between managerial complexity (or this variable in Japan) and marketing intensity, existed in Japanese data. It would suggest that vetting of technology agreements results in the rejection of those not purely associated with technology. However, this is not an entirely satisfactory answer, as it begs the question of how the positive influence of this variable on DFPIN arose. Clearly, more detailed and accurate data are required to address this issue successfully.

Of all the inward equations for the United Kingdom, only the inward direct foreign production equations record any significance as a whole. The only clear results are for the technology intensity hypothesis, that is, the presumed positive influence of technology intensity on manufactures trade. However, we are using host-country data to measure this and it could be reasoned that while UK exports are promoted by UK technology intensity (as seen in Table 4.3), this should not necessarily apply to imports. Here we are assuming that if we classify UK trade according to technology intensity, then the UK appears to be engaged in rather more inter-industry trade in manufactures than intra-industry trade. It may well be that the resource intensity of imports generates this result, as the UK is in certain areas a country lacking in resources.

Inward direct foreign production is found to be characteristic of UK research-intensive industries. It may be argued that there are statistical problems interfering with this conclusion, in that if the colonisation of UK industry by foreign affiliates is sufficiently high we may be effectively using their own research intensity to explain their penetration. This would constitute a breakdown of assumption (vi), put in Section 4.2, that the independent variables are exogenous. However, this would require the strong expectation that inward penetration is high enough to cause this. There are two considerations arguing against this expectation, using the present data. Firstly, there are no reasons to believe that affiliate research expenditure actually located in the UK itself, and therefore recorded in UK host statistics, should be markedly high on average (Lall, 1979), or at worst materially different from that of indigenous UK firms. Secondly, that at the level of industrial aggregation used here the highest levels of inward penetration are unlikely to be attained which might result in the general breakdown of this assumption.

Given this, the result obtained suggests that research intensity is the basis for entry into the UK. The UK has been seen to not be a leader in research intensity, and it is certainly tenable that foreign firms are endowed with higher technological advantages than indigenous UK industry.

In the DFPIN equation no further significant results emerge. The two skills variables are not, on their own, of any significance. If combined as the single overall skill intensity hypothesis, the average total wage variable does significantly promote foreign entry (significant at the 5 per cent level). This contrasts markedly with the result for the United States, showing a negative influence. However, UK skills are third in the international ranking in 1965, and fifth – or lowest – by 1975. Thus foreign firms would not find the grade of UK skills unassailably high for their production techniques, and would likely be producing in UK skills-intensive industries. Unfortunately, we cannot differentiate between the two specific skills hypotheses, on operative and managerial skills.

The results for UK licensing reveal the remarkable fact that it is unrelated to UK research intensity. However, the equation as a whole does not attain even the lowest threshold of significance and in fact in an equation where RDEXP is the single regressor it does just attain significance at the 5 per cent level. However, this is still a notably lower result than for other countries and is the subject of international comparison in Chapter 5. The interpretation of this finding could be that UK firms are buying in technology in areas unrelated to their own specialities. However, our additional result, that of the positive (and stable) effect of the UK managerial complexity variable, might indicate another possible factor. We have already noted the US structural association between management intensity and advertising intensity (marketing intensity). Again, if this is extended to the UK finding, it suggests that licensing may have a higher marketing component. If this is so it is remarkable, because it seems to apply (though with less force) to outward UK licensing. This may have something to do with the mature nature of the UK market, but this can be no more than speculation.

The Swedish equations generate a larger number of statistically significant results than do the equations for the other countries. Total inward involvement is characterised by Swedish research intensity, though strangely this does not apply to inward direct foreign production. The import equation shows a positive relationship between the dependent variable and research intensity, suggesting the likelihood of research-based intra-industry trade in manufactures.

The research intensity hypothesis is rejected in the DFPIN equation, which is completely unexpected. Furthermore, our present finding appears to be contradicted by a very much more disaggregated study by Samuelsson (1977) for the year 1970. Samuelsson's conclusions, from a regression across 120 Swedish industries, were that the foreign-owned share of output was positively related to high technical-personnel intensity and high capital intensity. Samuelsson used host industry characteristics, and this ought to minimise the difference from the present results. As it is, there is little agreement between the two studies.

Samuelsson's inward direct foreign production hypotheses are, in principle, very similar to the hypotheses put forward here: that to enter a host industry, the incoming firms must have ownership advantages. The identity of these ownership advantages can then be inferred from the characteristics of those industries in which inward foreign production is highest. Apart from a relatively minor difference between the definition of the variables (e.g. the proportions of technicians as opposed to research intensity) testing the same hypotheses, the major source of the conflict seems likely to reside in the effect of aggregation across countries investing in Sweden. This explanation also sheds light on the nature of differences between source countries.

The argument put forward here is that the aggregation of investing countries has given enhanced weight to European affiliates' characteristics, compared to those of the US. In 1970 over half of DFI in Sweden came from other European countries (Table 3.7).

Samuelsson himself found European affiliates to be concentrated in high-advertising industries, and by contrast US affiliates to be concentrated in those intensive in technical personnel. This may provide a reason for the significance of the NONOP coefficient in the DFPIN equation if the structural association between this variable and advertising intensity holds good in Sweden.

From Table 4.4 we find that capital intensity narrowly fails to meet the significance level as a determinant of Sweden's inward direct foreign production. Again, capital intensity was a host characteristic reported by Samuelsson, although, as with the measure for technology intensity, this was a dominant feature for US affiliates not European ones. It seems again that the meaning of these results is lost through mixing source-country data, where source countries have different foreign production models. This is not too surprising, given that within the confines of our own present study, we have found capital-intensive outward direct foreign production to be characteristic of the USA (and the UK) but not the other European countries.

There is some ground for reservation about the stability of the skills variables in these equations. Run in regressions on their own they show only low, if any significance, yet here they show some pronounced effects. The cause does not appear to be simple collinearity between the two skills variables. It is also true that the general skills variable, WS, is generally not significant (and never in the DFPIN equation) when replacing the two skills variables.

Without additional information, and if taken at face value within the theoretical model, the equations suggest a strong differential effect between WSOP and WSNONOP. WSOP appears to act against each dependent variable. As Sweden has very high average skill levels in this respect (second only to the USA), it seems likely that both Sweden's comparative (trade) advantage *vis-à-vis* foreign competitors and its absolute production advantages lie in very high operative skills activities. This reduces imports because the domestic competition is stronger, and also reduces inward foreign production because only the lower range of skills attract foreign entry (as argued previously in the case of the USA).

The reverse argument would then apply to the managerial skills variable, with foreign firms competing in the Swedish market revealing strengths in this respect. In addition to the argument offered previously for NONOP in the DFPIN equation, managerial complexity does seem to characterise direct investment in Sweden.

The Swedish inward licensing model reveals some comparatively straightforward results. As hypothesised, inward licensing is into Swedish research-intensive industries. Furthermore, these are capital-intensive Swedish industries, a result similar only to the US finding on capital intensity and inward licensing. The structure of the effects of the skills variables are the same as in the import and inward direct foreign production equation. It would be reasonable to deduce that the same factors are causing this, and it is possible to speculate as to their nature.

In Sweden the importance of natural resource-based activities is very marked, and these are associated, in Sweden, with high worker skills, plus technology and know-how specific to those industries. It does appear that the 'learning by doing' explanation (Swedenborg, 1979) has particular relevance to Sweden, and here to explaining why operative skills deflect all forms of inward competition. What competition from abroad there is, then appears based on managerial skills, particularly for inward direct foreign investment.

The final set of results to be reported are for the inward equations of the Federal Republic of Germany. In Table 4.4, as for Sweden, all the equations are significant, although the import equation is the least successful. The Federal Republic is a country for which both total outward and inward involvement is expected to be positively related to research intensity. This expectation is fulfilled. The first unexpected result is that federal imports are not research-intensive, according to domestic data.

With developed markets there has been a presumption of research-intensive trade in manufactures, in both directions. This has broken down for imports on three occasions. If our countries are truly representative of highly developed national characteristics, then we might expect these imports to originate from less developed countries. There is no evidence for this. Table 3.3 shows that the Federal Republic has, in 1975, the second lowest percentage of imports of manufactures from less developed countries. It seems that when we classify imports according to home research intensity we get rather more inter-industry type trade, as far as these data can detect, and assuming they are positively related to research intensity in the exporting country. This may well again have some relationship with the pattern of domestic resources or demand, and it is apparent that, as is generally the case, the import equations perform worst, suggesting much of the explanation for the dependent variable lies outside these specifications.

However, German imports are related to domestic managerial skills, but not managerial complexity. These results have been met before in the Swedish import equation, and it might seem more reasonable to assume that they reflect the quality of the goods. It is rather more straightforward to interpret the inward direct foreign production equation. It seems to be a requirement, in terms of host characteristics, for inward investment to be based on a technology advantage, as measured by research intensity. To be consistent in our reasoning, this suggests that incoming foreign multinationals are generally able to compete directly in Germany's most research-intensive industries. To this extent, indigenous firms in Germany do not appear to possess the degree of technological unassailability which we have assigned to US firms.

It does not seem that incoming firms require capital advantages to a marked degree. Direct penetration into German industry may, therefore, be characterised as that of research-intensive firms, possibly with modest capital advantages. The influences of the skills variables are both insignificant. If we substitute the total skills variable average total wage for the two, it is found that skills are significant at 1 per cent, yielding a coefficient of 0.843.

This does give some credence to the hypothesis that foreign firms in Germany required ownership advantages appropriate to these industries, but it does not tell us if their advantages lie in managerial skills or production processes requiring relatively high grades of workers. In separate regressions, where the coefficients may well not be accurate, there is no notable difference in the results for the two variables, other than an indication that the operative skills coefficient may be a little more important (i.e. in magnitude) than that for managerial skills. However, this is insufficient to base a conclusion on. Managerial complexity just fails to attain significance as a host entry characteristic.

German inward licensing, apart from research intensity, does seem associated with skills, where these are indicated to be in processes appropriate to high production worker skills. The two skills variables have differential influences here (but the opposite pattern to that found for Sweden). Unlike Sweden, there are no special reasons why high operative skills should not represent a demand for foreign technology. Licensing is evidently normal in Germany's high worker productivity sectors.

4.5   THE METHOD OF MARKET SERVICING: INSIGHTS FROM THE CORRELATIONS OF THE RESIDUALS

The last set of statistical tests in this chapter are based on assumption (v) in Section 4.2, that the disturbances corresponding to different dependent variables are contemporaneously correlated. We might find such a correlation if there is a significant omitted independent variable, which influences more than one dependent variable. If the residuals in different equations are correlated, the direction of the correlation and any pattern revealed between regressions will give some indication of the identity of the omitted variable or variables.

According to our theoretical approach, some pattern of correlation is expected not simply because it is possible that we have not included all relevant independent variables, but also because the theoretical theme of this study is that each of the routes of international production should be considered in a unified framework.

Tables 4.5 and 4.6 present the correlations of the residuals for outward and inward equations respectively. Of the fifteen correlations in each table, five are significant between the outward equations and five also between the inward equations. A positive correlation implies that the unexplained variances in the two dependent variables concerned, have a common cause, therefore leading the two dependent variables to be higher than can be predicted on the basis of the specified equations. A negative correlation would indicate the omission of a factor, causing the dependent variables to be affected in opposite directions, and therefore resulting in a substituting relationship. The general nature of the omitted variables likely to cause this will probably be country-specific and locational factors, which we have been unable to specify *ex ante*.

Outward Equations

The positive correlation between the residuals in the US DFPOUT and EXP equations (Table 4.5) suggest an omitted common factor. This could be a country-specific influence causing both trade and DFI to be affected. The paired residuals of three US industries seem central to this result, namely mechanical, electrical engineering and transportation equipment. For each of these the positive correlation is strongest, furthermore the residuals move (rise) together over the period 1965–75.

One compelling reason why the US should have such correlated residuals is due to its special relationship with Canada. The high penetration of the Canadian economy by US firms (Canada accepted 30 per cent of US DFI over the period) leads to a large amount of US DFI being recorded in precisely the industries which US exports are noted for. The rise over the period in the residuals may reflect the growth of trade barrier-related DFI, where this will be part of a strategy to retain world markets by production within markets. Notable here would be the EEC market. The interesting consequence is that trade and DFI, under these circumstances, are induced to form part of a complementary strategy.

For Japan, two types of influences, both related to Japan's indigenous resources, seem to be at work. The first is the country-specific and location-specific influence of the lack of indigenous resources related to food products and to paper. Location advantages are low for both, thus explaining low exports, but this generates a lowering country-specific influence on Japanese firms' ownership advantages, thus DFI is lowered.

The second influence inducing a positive correlation, derives from those industries where the paired residuals between the equations have been high or rising. Foremost here is electrical engineeering and textiles, which have recorded increasing DFI over the period due to

TABLE 4.5   *Correlations of the residuals between outward equations*

	EXP	DFPOUT	LFPOUT
USA			
EXP	1.000		
DFPOUT	0.480[b]	1.000	
LFPOUT	0.202	−0.055	1.000
Japan			
EXP	1.000		
DFPOUT	0.410[b]	1.000	
LFPOUT	0.115	0.153	1.000
UK			
EXP	1.000		
DFPOUT	−0.254	1.000	
LFPOUT	0.326[c]	0.227	1.000
Sweden			
EXP	1.000		
DFPOUT	0.625[a]	1.000	
LFPOUT	0.418[b]	0.769[a]	1.000
FGR			
EXP	1.000		
DFPOUT	−0.221	1.000	
LFPOUT	0.250	0.129	1.000

NOTES: Values shown are t statistics.
Significance levels are denoted by: a(1%), b(5%) and c(10%).

locational shifts. Electrical exports have continued to rise from Japan while certain production has been located abroad, especially in South East Asia, following cost and other locational considerations. In textiles, the servicing from Japan has remained unusually high because of production in the low-skilled labour sector of Japan's 'dual economy'. At the same time rising Japanese labour costs have necessitated increased low-wage oriented DFI, again especially in Asia. The result is that both exports and DFI are unusually high.

The UK positive correlation for LFPOUT and EXP derives from some country-specific factors influencing particular industries. The paired unexplained variances of food and transportation are negative together. Exports from the UK are unusually low for food, probably owing to locational disadvantages, while licensing is unusually low because UK firms prefer to internalise their ownership advantages. Accordingly the food residual for DFPOUT is highly positive. So here the significant size and capacity to internalise by UK MNEs in this industry seems to account for part of this finding.

In transport, a similar argument can be made out on locational grounds, but not on grounds of ownership advantages, and so licensing is unusually low because of lack of supply. Of further interest is that the paired residuals of chemicals and mechanical engineering are positive, suggesting UK locational and certain ownership advantages have both been higher than average, but have not been significantly exploited via DFI. This may be because of the position of the UK in the world economy and we might speculate that the unidentified advantages may result from productional know-how, so that an export and licensing strategy may be preferred to DFI to service a large number of geographically dispersed foreign markets.

Sweden is the only country for which the residuals are cross-correlated. The most plausible argument to explain this general result is the very narrow industry specialisation by Sweden in international competition. Thus, the omitted factors would explain the existence of simultaneously high or low residuals for the same industry in each form of competition.

This specialisation appears to be a consequence of the concentration of manufacturing industry according to Sweden's natural resource advantages. Thus the residuals (in each three equations) are high for mechanical engineering (resource advantages in ferrous metals) and particularly for paper and other industries (mainly wood-based, such as furniture) owing to Sweden's forestry resources. This pattern of competition clearly demonstrates the significance of an omitted locational variable for natural resources (in the export equation) and the omission of country-specific factors which generate ownership advantages (the foreign production equation). This latter point is the same as the 'endogenous technical progress' argument put by Swedenborg (1979).

There are two Swedish industries where residuals are simultaneously negative across equations. These are food and transportation equipment. Food is not an international industry for Sweden. However, in vehicles the residuals are negative, particularly in the foreign production equations. This suggests that locational factors favour Swedish production.

Inward Equations

In the inward equations correlations presented in Table 4.6, the first significant result is for Japan's DFPIN and IMP equations. Here a variable is implicated which causes inward direct foreign production and imports to be simultaneously high. A possible cause could be a combination of the large Japanese domestic market size and resource requirements with Japanese industrial policy. In particular, two industries' residuals are instructive. Chemicals shows high residuals, for imports this will reflect the shortage of domestic resources, while inward investment will result from industrial policy encouraging the import of technology to build up domestic capacity. Both electricals residuals are negative, and here this probably derives from captive domestic markets and policy barriers to inward investment.

For the United Kingdom, there is a correlation between LFPIN and IMP. Country and location-specific factors again appear to be at work. For example, negative residuals for food manufactures suggest that the UK market may be serviced in another way, and indeed the residual is accordingly high for DFPIN. The manufacture within the UK by foreign MNEs would account for this, and the cause is likely to be the extensive UK market size, and similarities in tastes with the

TABLE 4.6   *Correlations of the residuals between inward equations*

	IMP	DFPIN	LFPIN
USA			
IMP	1.000		
DFPIN	− 0.105	1.000	
LFPIN	− 0.160	0.311	1.000
Japan			
IMP	1.000		
DFPIN	0.457[b]	1.000	
LFPIN	0.279	0.129	1.000
UK			
IMP	1.000		
DFPIN	0.305	1.000	
LFPIN	0.480[b]	0.192	1.000
Sweden			
IMP	1.000		
DFPIN	0.077	1.000	
LFPIN	0.606[a]	0.569[a]	1.000
FGR			
IMP	1.000		
DFPIN	− 0.393[c]	1.000	
LFPIN	0.130	0.226	1.000

NOTES: Values shown are *t* statistics.
Significance levels are denoted by: a(1%), b(5%) and c(10%).

US. In electricals the residuals have risen together, and this may reflect both growing locational disadvantages, and an increasing technological dependence.

Sweden's inward equations reveal two instances of residuals correlation. The omitted factor, or factors, appear to cause LFPIN and IMP to be high, and LFPIN and DFPIN to be high together, but not DFPIN and IMP to be so related. The reasons for this pattern seem to largely result from the narrow specialisation of Swedish industry; Sweden's specialised competitive strengths repel inward competition in its major industries. Thus, Sweden's international competition is characteristically inter rather than intra-industry in nature. The origins of this pattern are country and location specific, as argued earlier. Negative residuals in transportation and paper are notably in evidence in each equation.

In the Federal Republic of Germany, a negative correlation between residuals in the DFPIN and IMP equations suggests that the omitted variable concerned is negatively related to one dependent variable and positively to the other, inducing an inverse relationship. There is general presumption that the Federal Republic is a favourable market to produce within, and given that it is also the market for sale, such locational advantages as a growing market and a skilled labour force would tend to raise inward direct foreign investment and lower imports. The pattern of residuals, particularly for food and transportation, accord with this, that is, investment is unusually high and imports unusually low. Other industries play their part in producing this finding. However, the cause does seem to be country- or location-specific.

One particularly compelling explanation of this German result is that the tariff protection afforded by the EEC's common external tariff (CET) has acted so as to favour increased DFI in Germany. It may be that the CET has the same effect in other EEC countries. However, it is likely that this import substitution within Germany also captures its attractiveness as a production base from which to service the EEC market as a whole.

From the correlations of the residuals, whatever the precise cause of the observed patterns, there is indirect evidence that these equations should be considered as a system vindicating the approach used in this study. It is an important finding to confirm that the methods of market servicing do bear relationships to each other which are explicable by theory, even when certain data cannot be explicitly included in the equations.

4.6   SOME PRELIMINARY CONCLUSIONS

The results reported in this chapter are on the basis of separate regressions for each country, not unlike the single-country studies predominant in the empirical literature. However, here the hypotheses tested are represented by the same variables for each country. In certain instances agreement with previous works is obtained, and in others contrasts are reconciled.

In the outward equations, the hypothesis of research intensity is the most consistently supported supposition. This implies that countries' international competition is higher in their more technology-intensive industries. The exceptions seem to be Japan and the UK, both of whose direct foreign investment is characteristically not research intensive, and indeed for Japan actually negatively related to research-intensity.

The role of capital intensity in its product cycle interpretation (favouring exports over DFI) is rejected by all our results. This is not too surprising, as the circumstances necessary for it to fulfil this role are highly restrictive, and it was not expected to behave in this way, especially for the major foreign investing countries – the USA and UK. For these two countries, this variable promotes DFI, and we have interpreted this as confirming that the MNEs of the US and UK have advantages in terms of access to capital, resulting in the high capital intensity of foreign investment. This advantage may itself be correlated with the large size of MNEs and the efficiency of internal capital markets.

There is an indication that the general tendency of operative skills is to favour exports over DFI, although significance is not always obtained. This effect is plausible because such skills are the least transferable to DFI, and are largely location-specific.

The conclusion of Horst (1972a) on the partial substitutability of US DFI and exports is here extended to licensing. This result also applies to Germany, but not the other countries.

The product cycle description of US DFI and trade is given some confirmation by the research intensity of both foreign propensities, but we do not reproduce fully Lall's (1980) result of research intensity favouring exports. Here this result is only obtained for Germany, where it is tenable that German industry has a comparative advantage in technology-intensive activities. We might expect the product cycle to apply most to Germany because it fulfils the requirement of the theoretical model, with much of its DFI being of a more recent nature than other countries considered.

Although Japan's DFI is also recent, it does not conform to a Western-style product cycle because of the special conditions under which it took place, discussed in Chapter 3. However, it does represent, in many ways, the Japanese equivalent; the difference is that the technology transferred abroad is very much more standardised and labour-intensive than the US equivalent. This episode in Japanese DFI is unlikely to continue, and Chapter 5 investigates this further. As the Kojima hypothesis is also largely descriptive of this early Japanese DFI, it is hardly surprising that the equations give support to it, at least as a historical account.

The evidence on the skills hypotheses is very mixed across countries, although for Germany the classic result is obtained of operative skills favouring exports and non-operative skills favouring DFI. Perhaps again this result would be most expected for Germany, as its DFI is recent, and the relative transferability of the two skills should then show most clearly.

The Swedish equations all suggest a large role for research intensity, but little else as the skills variables fail to attain significance. However, the UK equations, more than those of any other country, suggest the omission of significant variables, and in particular advertising intensity is likely to be a crucial omission for the UK.

The inward equations followed the same statistical methodology as the outward equations, but not with respect to interpretation. The use of host proxy variables to infer the advantages of foreign firms is a less robust procedure, and this was confirmed by the generally lower level of significance in the equations.

With the research intensity and skills hypotheses there seems to be an indication that the influence the variables exert on inward DFI depends on the absolute level of the host intensities. This becomes noticeable for the USA and Sweden, whose average industrial research and skills intensities are higher than the other countries. Thus, the host industries into which most DFI takes place will be those where foreign firms are not at an absolute disadvantage, but have comparable expertise. This will explain the finding of inward DFI unrelated or even negatively related to host characteristics.

The negative effect of Swedish research intensity on DFI is not that found by Samuelsson (1977) but may be reconciled with it. His finding for a positive relationship held for inward DFI from the USA, and we might expect that US firms in particular are relatively advantaged compared to Swedish firms. This argument can also be extended to capital intensity, also found to be significant by Samuelsson. The skills variable found to repel foreign DFI in the US and Sweden is operative skills, which would be the main issue for a foreign manufacturing firm considering competing in the same location against local producers adapted to high skills.

Evidently, the UK and German environments do not have local standards of technology that are systematically in excess of foreign firms, thus host research intensity is related to inward DFI. This result is also obtained for Japan; to an extent the same logic may apply, but the regulated nature of inward competition dominates the pattern.

Capital intensity explains inward DFI only in the USA, and our conclusion on this is that the distinguishing advantages of those firms entering the US is an advantage in access to capital, indeed they are found to be advantaged in no other respect here. We have also inferred that such firms will be among the largest non-US MNEs, and therefore best equipped to compete in the US environment.

Licensing was found, as expected, to be related to research intensity, both in the outward and inward equations for all countries except the UK. Only in partial model regressions on research intensity alone was significance obtained. The possibility of statistical problems is particularly suggested by the insignificance of the equations. For all other countries the general hypothesised result is that licensing is primarily of a high-technology nature and – as classified by research intensity – of an intra-industry nature.

The final statistical results for the correlations of the residuals confirmed that, first, the methodology of treating countries' equations as part of a system is correct, and secondly that we can infer that there are country- and location-specific influences in the form of competition. Trade, DFI and licensing are related strategies and both policy and location-specific factors were implied by the correlations.

5 International Differences in Competition and Evolution over Time

5.1 TESTING FOR DIFFERENCES BETWEEN MODELS

Two sets of explicit tests are made concerning the stability of the model. These are tests of two assumptions, which the eclectic theory suggests are open to question.

The first test is of the stability of the model between countries. The results reported in Chapter 4 refer to regressions for each country separately, and thus the assumption of a common model for all five, or any sub-set of countries, has not so far been imposed. This assumption is now investigated.

Regressions are run on the data for all five countries, and each combination, with respect to each dependent variable. This enables formal tests of exactly how far, and in what way, the model varies across countries. Chow tests of the country-specific nature of the equations are followed by more detailed tests on the stability of each coefficient, using dummy variables, representing an investigation of the stability of each hypothesis.

The second test arises for an assumption which has been imposed previously, without question. This is the assumption of a stable model in the case of each individual country for each of the three years. General stability between the three cross-sections would vindicate the procedure of pooling the time periods. However, the opportunity to identify any changes over time is valuable as it may provide insights into the dynamic nature of international competition.

There are possible reasons for such changes. The enlargement of the EEC, or the rapidly changing conditions in countries such as

133

Japan are each possible causes. Again Chow tests are conducted on the general stability, followed by more detailed tests for each coefficient as required.

5.2 INTERNATIONAL DIFFERENCES IN THE OUTWARD EQUATIONS

Chow tests are reported in Table 5.1 for the outward equations. These test for equality between sets of coefficients in two regressions. Here the data are pooled across combinations of countries and two regressions are run, a restricted and a completely unrestricted form, and the statistic calculated from the sum of the squared residuals.

From Table 5.1 it is evident that in thirty-four of the forty-four tests we have to reject the hypothesis that there are no international differences in the models for the four outward dependent variables.

The hypothesis of similarity (no significant difference) between all five countries is rejected in each of the four cases presented in the 'All countries' cell. This means that we have not found a model able to describe successfully for the total, or any of the three routes of outward involvement of the five countries taken together. The values in the other cells are for bilateral tests between countries, and enable us to distinguish which countries are the most similar, or least dissimilar, in terms of the results obtained.

Of the ten instances where the hypothesis of similarity is not rejected, six are for the outward licensing model. This suggests that, as was anticipated in Chapter 4, there is a greater similarity in the international determinants of outward licensing than for the other means of competition. The one model for which no case of international similarity at all is found, is for DFPOUT. The outward direct foreign production model is highly country-specific, endorsing the caution of those authors who obtained results for single countries without suggesting their results had wider applicability. That said, there is some general similarity between Sweden and the Federal Republic of Germany. However, the source of any similarity cannot be determined at this stage.

International Differences in Hypotheses

The Chow test reported above is a useful general guide to the overall stability in the regression equations. However, if general instability is found, as it is here, then further investigation is required.

TABLE 5.1 *Chow tests of international stability in the outward equations*

Tests in the total outward production equations (INTPRODOUT)

	All countries	US	Japan	UK	Sweden
All countries	5.906[a]				
US					
Japan		7.612[a]			
UK		4.144[a]	6.545[a]		
Sweden		3.554[a]	2.251[c]	2.913[b]	
FGR		13.719[c]	4.851[a]	5.979[a]	1.226

Tests in the export equation (EXP)

	All countries	US	Japan	UK	Sweden
All countries	8.227[a]				
US					
Japan		5.129[a]			
UK		2.401[b]	5.248[a]		
Sweden		7.923[a]	1.981[c]	0.594	
FGR		18.994[a]	5.601[a]	1.063	0.684

Tests in the outward direct foreign production equations (DFPOUT)

	All countries	US	Japan	UK	Sweden
All countries	7.763[a]				
US					
Japan		7.042[a]			
UK		2.824[b]	8.520[a]		
Sweden		2.659[b]	4.002[a]	6.220[a]	
FGR		3.232[b]	5.829[a]	9.450[a]	3.209[b]

Tests in the outward licensed foreign production equation (LFPOUT)

	All countries	US	Japan	UK	Sweden
All countries	2.245[a]				
US					
Japan		2.360[b]			
UK		1.356	2.709[b]		
Sweden		0.883	3.131[b]	0.886	
FGR		0.930	0.757	1.996[c]	0.870

NOTES: Values shown are F ratios.
Significance levels are denoted by: a(1%), b(5%) and c(10%).

TABLE 5.2   *Tests of international stability in the coefficients for the outward equations*

Test of the total outward production equation (INTPRODOUT)

	RDEXP	NTFA	WSOP	WSNO-NOP	NONOP	Constant
Japan	− 2.505[a]	− 3.329[b]	2.554[a]	− 0.408	− 2.790[a]	− 1.910[b]
UK	− 2.119[b]	− 1.238	0.349	0.818	0.308	− 1.362[c]
Sweden	0.913	− 2.481[a]	1.602[c]	0.021	− 1.147	− 0.868
FGR	− 1.215	− 2.604[a]	1.197	0.442	− 0.386	− 1.269

Test of the export equation (EXP)

	RDEXP	NTFA	WSOP	WSNO-NOP	NONOP	Constant
Japan	− 0.680	− 2.762[a]	2.933[a]	− 1.485[c]	− 3.607[a]	− 0.473
UK	− 0.745	− 1.390[c]	0.444	0.388	− 0.097	− 0.470
Sweden	0.915	− 1.442[c]	1.230	− 0.309	− 1.246	− 0.085
FGR	− 0.787	− 2.179[c]	1.207	− 0.215	− 0.337	− 0.136

Test of the outward direct foreign production equation (DFPOUT)

	RDEXP	NTFA	WSOP	WSNO-NOP	NONOP	Constant
Japan	− 3.838[a]	− 2.765[a]	0.983	0.706	− 0.018	− 2.079[b]
UK	− 2.182[b]	− 0.648	− 0.408	1.086	0.479	− 1.328[b]
Sweden	1.018	− 1.594[c]	1.073	0.271	− 0.172	− 0.839
FGR	− 0.802	− 1.189	− 0.410	1.348[c]	− 0.656	− 1.752[b]

Test of the outward licensed foreign production equation (LFPOUT)

	RDEXP	NTFA	WSOP	WSNO-NOP	NONOP	Constant
Japan	0.666	0.121	1.192	− 0.364	0.381	− 0.273
UK	− 1.636[c]	− 0.166	− 0.713	0.786	1.898[b]	− 0.390
Sweden	− 0.564	− 0.978	− 0.911	0.806	0.756	− 0.307
FGR	0.187	− 0.625	0.230	0.335	0.323	− 0.453

NOTES: Values shown are t statistics.
Significance levels are denoted by: a(1%), b(5%) and c(10%).

As a means of enquiring into these international differences more fully, Tables 5.2 and 5.3 report the formal tests of international differences in individual coefficients. These can be viewed as a more detailed breakdown of the Chow tests already reported.

The sets of results for each dependent variable reported in Table 5.2 are analogous to the 'All countries' cells presented in Table 5.1. These are the results of a completely unrestricted regression on the data of the five countries. Here the United States provides the general model under the null hypothesis, and so it is with respect to the US coefficients that the restriction is applied, so the US is the country of comparison.

The statistics represent the significance of dummy variables for each coefficient. As such they indicate whether we are justified in

TABLE 5.3   *Bilateral tests of the international stability in the outward equations*

INTPRODOUT
(a) Compared with Japan

	RDEXP	NTFA	WSOP	WSNO-NOP	NONOP	Constant
UK	0.993	3.375[a]	−3.040[a]	2.149[b]	4.367[a]	1.338[c]
Sweden	2.832[a]	0.934	−0.750	0.481	1.314[c]	1.610
FGR	2.958[a]	1.244	−2.045[b]	1.818[b]	3.997[a]	2.005[b]

(b) Compared with the UK

	RDEXP	NTFA	WSOP	WSNO-NOP	NONOP	Constant
Sweden	2.675[a]	−1.155[c]	1.004	−0.840	−1.196	0.750
FGR	2.246[a]	−2.468[a]	1.278	−0.834	−1.144	0.368

(c) Compared with Sweden

	RDEXP	NTFA	WSOP	WSNO-NOP	NONOP	Constant
FGR	−2.096[b]	−0.252	−0.342	0.498	0.727	−0.642

EXP
(a) Compared with Japan

	RDEXP	NTFA	WSOP	WSNO-NOP	NONOP	Constant
UK	0.025	2.081[b]	−3.012[a]	2.795[a]	4.405[a]	−0.008
Sweden	1.372[c]	1.261	−1.403[b]	1.385[b]	1.960[b]	0.629
FGR	0.074	0.864	−2.220[b]	2.367[b]	4.619[a]	0.888

(b) Compared with the UK

	RDEXP	NTFA	WSOP	WSNO-NOP	NONOP	Constant
Sweden	1.609[b]	−0.132	0.678	−0.762	−1.035	0.615
FGR	0.060	−1.428[c]	1.047	−1.071	−0.344	0.899

Table cont. p. 138

(c) Compared with Sweden

	RDEXP	NTFA	WSOP	WSNO-NOP	NONOP	Constant
FGR	−1.841[b]	−0.749	−0.031	0.129	0.921	−0.089

DFPOUT
(a) Compared with Japan

	RDEXP	NTFA	WSOP	WSNO-NOP	NONOP	Constant
UK	2.501[a]	2.684[a]	−1.571[c]	0.626	0.521	1.529[c]
Sweden	4.433[a]	1.211	0.076	−0.540	−0.124	2.108[b]
FGR	4.872[a]	1.824[b]	−1.628[c]	1.045	−0.682	0.832

(b) Compared with the UK

	RDEXP	NTFA	WSOP	WSNO-NOP	NONOP	Constant
Sweden	3.031[a]	−0.925	1.262	−0.940	−0.553	0.796
FGR	2.408[a]	−0.757	−0.003	0.230	−1.420[c]	−0.833

(c) Compared with Sweden

	RDEXP	NTFA	WSOP	WSNO-NOP	NONOP	Constant
FGR	−1.956[b]	0.254	−1.287	1.352[c]	−0.393	−1.584[c]

LFPOUT
(a) Compared with Japan

	RDEXP	NTFA	WSOP	WSNO-NOP	NONOP	Constant
UK	−2.484[a]	−0.273	−1.913[b]	1.480[c]	1.361[c]	−0.229
Sweden	−1.367[c]	−1.047	−2.230[b]	1.760[b]	0.353	−0.073
FGR	−0.715	−0.712	−1.030	1.070	−0.126	−0.384

(b) Compared with the UK

	RDEXP	NTFA	WSOP	WSNO-NOP	NONOP	Constant
Sweden	0.992	−0.817	−0.187	−0.045	−0.958	0.146
FGR	2.397[a]	−0.466	0.850	−0.581	−1.620[c]	−0.090

(c) Compared with Sweden

	RDEXP	NTFA	WSOP	WSNO-NOP	NONOP	Constant
FGR	0.908	0.269	1.077	−0.657	−0.490	−0.270

NOTES: Values shown are *t* statistics.
Significance levels are denoted by: a(1%), b(5%) and c(10%).

treating any two or more countries as having the same coefficient on a variable; a statistically significant value indicates that no justification for this exists. The sign of the statistics indicates the direction of the deviation with respect to the country of comparison.

Results indicating the absence of significant differences are as interesting as those suggesting their presence. Table 5.2 verifies that all five countries export products which are similar in terms of research intensity, while the most striking contrasts arise in the DFPOUT equations.

Direct foreign investments by Japan and the UK are significantly less research-intensive than those of the USA, and in turn, DFI by Japan is less research-intensive than the UK (Table 5.3(a)). Only Sweden and Germany resemble the USA in this respect.

The causes of differences from the US model are rather varied across equations. In particular, the capital intensity of US exports exceeds that of the other countries. This finding agrees *prima facie* with the traditional factor-proportions stylisation of US trade. However, to a certain extent this same contrast also applies for US imports, as found in Section 5.3.

Meaning is rarely attributed to the constant terms in statistical tests. However, the significance tests in the DFPOUT equation suggest that (with the exception of Sweden) outside the US the degree of direct foreign production has a lower starting point than the US. The dependent variable, DFPOUT, is expressed as the proportion of DFP to domestic production. Consequently, it can be inferred that the average effect of omitted variables is to cause this proportion to be significantly less for countries other than the US and Sweden.

From the regression results in Table 4.3 in Chapter 4, it appears that for the other three countries the constants are negative, whereas for the US and Sweden they are zero. This suggests a proportionality between domestic production and DFI abroad for these two countries. The cause of this is likely to be the proximity to and integration with neighbouring countries – Canada in the case of the USA, and the Scandinavian countries in the case of Sweden – added to which will be the effect of Sweden's small domestic market size, leading firms to venture abroad at an earlier stage.

In a number of instances the formal international comparisons add to our understanding of the country-specific nature of international competition. In particular, the structure of differences between the equations provides some valuable insights. The INTPRODOUT equations evidently only summarise the character of the overall pattern; this character originates in the EXP, DFPOUT and, to a lesser extent, LFPOUT equations.

So far we have seen that exports are of comparable research intensity regardless of source country; perhaps this is not too surprising as all are well-developed economies. The research intensity of direct foreign investment patterns is clearly another matter, and it is evident that differences according to capital intensity are also appreciable. The hypothesis for international differences in capital intensity suggests that these will follow the pattern of access of each country's firms to capital. This access to capital has appeared to be related to the degree of extension of the MNE, which seems highly correlated with country of origin. Here the differences in the NTFA coefficient with the US are significantly negative for Japan (being the most marked) and Sweden. Bilateral tests (Table 5.3) confirm the ranking seen in Table 5.2.

The incidence of significant differences across the skills and managerial complexity variables is very low, most likely as a consequence of insignificant coefficients in the original regressions. In particular, the skill intensity variables performed poorly in the US model estimated in Chapter 4. Lall's (1980) study used the single measure of average total wage, and attempts here to analyse the differential effects of operatives' and non-operatives' skills have not always met with success.

This measure of general skills was found by Lall to be a better explanatory variable for exports than direct foreign production, and this finding was reproduced in this study on the inclusion of the variable WS. Further light can be shed on the distinctiveness of the skill intensity of US direct foreign production and exports by substituting WS for the two skills variables in the international comparisons, analogous to the stability tests for the US in Table 5.2. The results are presented in Table 5.4.

There is some evidence that general skills are not only more characteristic of non-US international involvement, but that this is more pronounced for direct foreign production than exports, although the UK narrowly fails to conform to this. To this extent it does appear that skill intensity is generally more important as a basis for DFI from countries other than the USA. The UK resembles the USA, however, and for both these countries there is added similarity in the value of the explanatory power of the capital hypothesis. The importance of the present finding is that the skills identified clearly relate to ownership advantages as they not only enable but also

TABLE 5.4   *International comparison for general skills (WS), outward equations*

	DFPOUT	EXP
Japan	3.802[a]	1.723[b]
UK	1.384[c]	1.509[c]
Sweden	2.737[a]	1.522[c]
FGR	3.029[a]	1.771[b]

NOTES: Values shown are *t* statistics.
Significance levels are denoted by: a(1%), b(5%) and c(10%).

favour direct foreign production. This is a noteworthy contrast to the US stylisation, and verifies that the experience of one country cannot be assumed to apply to others.

In order to highlight the possible causes of these country-specific differences, the findings are now briefly appraised on a country-by-country basis. Before finishing with the USA, however, the implications of the US model itself can be summarised.

It appears that the US pattern of foreign involvement is technology-based, and this may extend to a comparative advantage in research-intensive trade (as in the product cycle) compared to direct foreign investment. This is emphatically different from the UK and Japanese models, but not from Sweden and Germany.

The USA does appear to be advantaged in capital-intensive industries, in terms of its direct foreign production. This result is shared with the UK. It would also be common to Germany. However, the relevant German regression coefficient in Table 4.3 was itself insignificant. For skills we have seen that for the US general skills appear to favour export over DFI, but that this does not apply outside the USA, other than to the UK.

The models which emerge for Japan are assuredly ones of contrast with the other countries. Sections (a) of Table 5.3 demonstrate that Japanese international involvement is consistently different. Most notable of all is that Japan's direct foreign production is by far the least research-intensive. It is also the least capital-intensive, together with Sweden. Indeed, Japan is the only source country for which capital intensity is negatively signed in the DFPOUT equation, indicating that Japanese firms have been producing abroad in industries where domestic labour intensity is highest. These are the sort of results which might be identified with the Kojima hypothesis.

However, there is an important difference between the Kojima hypothesis as a statement based on observation at a particular point in time, and a more complete theory based on a dynamic analysis. These results could equally be consistent with a theory which says that Japan's international involvement is at an early stage of development, and that its model should become more similar to other countries as its international involvement expands, and its firms grow. If this is the case, we should expect Japan's model to be in disequilibrium. Time stability tests to detect precisely this are reported later, in Section 5.4.

Because of the practical problems of interpreting the Japanese skills definitions, it can only be suggested that operative skills are more important for Japanese DFI as compared with the UK and Germany.

In Chapter 4 we noted the interpretation of significance in the capital-intensity variable for both US and UK DFI. These two countries stood apart from the others in this respect, and here the bilateral tests confirm this finding for the UK. The capital hypothesis was based on the proposal that large multinationals enjoy advantages in raising capital, and this is thought to apply to UK MNEs. This furnishes one tenable explanation for the continued expansion of UK direct foreign production; there is nowhere in these data any suggestion that a product-cycle type of technology advantage is in operation for the UK, although UK exports do show the normal result of a significant relationship with research intensity. However, there is some role played by managerial skills (Table 4.3), although this does not appear any more pronounced than for most other countries (Tables 5.2 and 5.3).

The higher skill intensity of non-US direct foreign investment has been noted above. Swedenborg (1979) in particular argued that Sweden's 'comparative advantage' lay in skill-intensive rather than capital-intensive activities, and indeed her own capital intensity variable was either insignificant or negatively signed. This assertion concerning Sweden's 'comparative advantage' can be formally tested here by using the general skills variable, and making a comparison to the US model. The differences in the coefficients are found to be as presented in Table 5.5.

Although we find no significant difference between the RDEXP coefficients for the US and Sweden, we do find that Swedish skills are more characteristic of Sweden's direct foreign production. It is true also that they are more characteristic of exports. However, this is not as marked. Swedenborg advanced that this was because 'endogenous technical progress' generated mobile intra-firm skills, which characterised Swedish direct foreign production. This might have been

TABLE 5.5   *Comparison of Sweden with the US for general skills (WS)*

	DFPOUT	EXP
RDEXP	0.982	0.996
WS	2.553[a]	1.552[c]

NOTES: Values shown are *t* statistics.
Significance levels are denoted by: a(1%), and c(10%).

expected to show in the managerial skills variable, as this reflects the ability to organise production. However, there was no evidence of this in Chapter 4. Although strictly we cannot infer the desired result, from separate regressions managerial skills were found to exert a significant and stronger effect on Swedish direct foreign production than operative skills.

The Swedish model which emerges here is one where international involvement is clearly based on technology and skills. There is no doubt that Swedish exports are research-intensive, and in international comparison a further finding is that they are more so than for other non-US countries (Table 5.3). It is possible to conclude from this appraisal that Swedish direct foreign production is indeed relatively more skill-intensive than it is for the US.

The Federal Republic of Germany is compared with the other countries in Table 5.3, where it is seen that Sweden alone has a higher research intensity for exports and DFP. While Chapter 4 established that German DFI does not appear to be based on a capital advantage, in the international comparisons in Tables 5.2 and 5.3, it seems to be the least far behind the USA and the UK. German multinationals may then be one of the next national groups to obtain the advantages of international extension, as reflected in access to capital.

Table 5.4 presented comparisons for general skills, and Germany is confirmed as a country for whom skills promote direct foreign production more than exports. Tables 5.2 and 5.3 give an indication that relative to the USA and Sweden, the German skills responsible are managerial in nature.

5.3   INTERNATIONAL DIFFERENCES IN THE INWARD EQUATIONS

The Chow tests in Table 5.6 show that the absence of concordance in the inward equations is even more pervasive than it was for the

TABLE 5.6 *Chow tests of international stability in the inward equations*

Tests in the total inward production equations (INTPRODIN)

	All countries	US	Japan	UK	Sweden
All countries	23.063[a]				
US					
Japan		7.664[a]			
UK		8.174[a]	11.125[a]		
Sweden		22.450[a]	4.622[a]	9.202[a]	
FGR		34.439[a]	6.769[a]	1.763	8.381[a]

Tests in the import equations (IMP)

	All countries	US	Japan	UK	Sweden
All countries	16.488[a]				
US					
Japan		1.534			
UK		4.596[a]	8.109[a]		
Sweden		17.571[a]	7.420[a]	9.015[a]	
FGR		13.413[a]	3.970[a]	3.071[b]	9.716[a]

Tests in the inward direct foreign production equations (DFPIN)

	All countries	US	Japan	UK	Sweden
All countries	11.557[a]				
US					
Japan		6.065[a]			
UK		5.012[a]	12.251[a]		
Sweden		1.575	6.381[a]	10.116[a]	
FGR		9.273[a]	9.479[a]	1.035	14.256[a]

Tests in the inward licensed foreign production equations (LFPIN)

	All countries	US	Japan	UK	Sweden
All countries	6.926[a]				
US					
Japan		9.924[a]			
UK		2.732[b]	7.902[a]		
Sweden		7.375[a]	6.564[a]	1.055	
FGR		5.968[a]	6.886[a]	1.887	3.152[b]

NOTES: Values shown are F ratios.
Significance levels are denoted by: a(1%), b(5%) and c(10%).

outward equations. The *F* ratios are generally high, and the hypothesis of similarity is rejected in all but six of the forty-four tests. Neither is there any higher degree of stability in the licensing model than in the other equations.

This increased lack of international stability probably arises because for inward involvement a number of (host) country-specific factors assume an importance not applicable to outward involvement. For example, government policy is more likely to impinge on inward rather than outward competition, and this applies equally to trade, DFI and licensing.

International Differences in Hypotheses

Table 5.7 reports the stability tests with respect to the general US model. For the most part the other countries show no consistent pattern of deviation from the US model. The exception is for the capital-intensity hypothesis. Here it is found that inward direct foreign investment in other countries is consistently less capital-intensive than DFI into the USA. This finding reinforces the conclusions arrived at in Chapter 4, that foreign multinationals producing in the US would tend to be those with capital advantages.

The same enhanced capital intensity of production in the US applies to inward licensing there, as this is also higher than for other countries. This tells us that the quality of technology licensed to the US market is probably the most capital-intensive there is, which would agree with our expectations about the nature of US production. Clearly this represents the technology matching the recipient country characteristics.

There are few compelling comparisons to be made for the skills variables, especially WSNONOP, because of the general lack of significance for these variables in the US regressions in Chapter 4. Nevertheless, it does appear that the other countries, except Sweden, received inward DFI in industries where the host's operative skills are highest. In Chapter 4 the negative association of operative skills and inward DFI was attributed to the high absolute level of indigenous skills; this argument was also applicable to Sweden. These international comparisons formally show that for the other countries, inward DFI is not associated with the lower range of host skills. Because the separate analysis of skills into operatives and non-operatives proved in some cases to be problematic, Table 5.9 reports the results of the

TABLE 5.7   *Tests of international stability in the coefficients for the inward equations*

Test of the total inward production equation (INTPRODIN)

	RDEXP	NTFA	WSOP	WSNO-NOP	NONOP	Constant
Japan	3.672[a]	−2.723[a]	1.457[c]	−0.617	1.472[c]	1.510[c]
UK	−0.382	−3.089[a]	2.093[b]	−0.261	0.049	−0.047
Sweden	1.997[b]	−3.704[a]	−2.433[a]	2.200	−0.961	−0.215
FGR	−0.369	−3.148[a]	1.518[a]	−0.146	−0.575	−0.130

Test of the import equation (IMP)

	RDEXP	NTFA	WSOP	WSNO-NOP	NONOP	Constant
Japan	0.713	−0.265	0.218	0.657	2.755[a]	0.905
UK	−2.509[a]	−0.311	0.738	0.293	1.374[c]	−0.033
Sweden	2.024[b]	−2.292[b]	0.223	1.154	−0.513	1.233
FGR	−1.975[b]	−1.837[b]	1.002	1.230	0.482	−0.164

Test of the inward direct foreign production equation (DFPIN)

	RDEXP	NTFA	WSOP	WSNO-NOP	NONOP	Constant
Japan	4.281[a]	−2.088[b]	2.359[a]	−1.070	0.379	0.924
UK	1.827[b]	−2.961[a]	3.222[a]	−0.894	−1.984[b]	−0.376
Sweden	−0.438	−2.181[b]	−0.856	1.557[c]	0.548	−1.169
FGR	1.138	−2.904[a]	3.195[a]	−1.146	−1.299[c]	−0.140

Test of the inward licensed foreign production equation (LFPIN)

	RDEXP	NTFA	WSOP	WSNO-NOP	NONOP	Constant
Japan	2.018[b]	−3.735[a]	3.167[a]	−0.841	−1.393[c]	−0.221
UK	−2.394[a]	−2.581[a]	−0.237	1.010	2.765[a]	−0.655
Sweden	−0.685	−1.296[c]	−0.582	1.482	0.700	−1.296[c]
FGR	−0.956	−2.168[b]	2.402[a]	−0.484	1.837[b]	−0.331

NOTES: Values shown are *t* statistics.
Significance levels are denoted by: a(1%), b(5%) and c(10%).

TABLE 5.8   *Bilateral tests of the international stability in the inward equations*

INTPRODIN
(a) Compared with Japan

	RDEXP	NTFA	WSOP	WSNO-NOP	NONOP	Constant
UK	−4.752[a]	0.222	0.620	0.422	−1.511	−2.930[a]
Sweden	−1.596[c]	−0.442	−3.379[a]	3.474[a]	−2.041[b]	−2.952[a]
FGR	−5.877[a]	−0.248	0.049	0.781	−2.420[a]	−3.826[a]

(b) Compared with the UK

	RDEXP	NTFA	WSOP	WSNO-NOP	NONOP	Constant
Sweden	2.636[a]	−0.849	−4.299[a]	2.901[a]	−1.005	−0.294
FGR	0.092	−0.658	−0.752	0.223	−0.884	−0.205

(c) Compared with Sweden

	RDEXP	NTFA	WSOP	WSNO-NOP	NONOP	Constant
FGR	−3.221[a]	0.304	4.127[a]	−3.598[a]	0.523	0.185

IMP
(a) Compared with Japan

	RDEXP	NTFA	WSOP	WSNO-NOP	NONOP	Constant
UK	−2.716[a]	0.031	0.776	0.376	−1.540[c]	−1.356[c]
Sweden	1.498[c]	−0.940	−2.869[a]	2.937[a]	−2.806[a]	−1.318[c]
FGR	−2.118[b]	−1.070	−0.365	0.947	−2.908[a]	−2.184[b]

(b) Compared with the UK

	RDEXP	NTFA	WSOP	WSNO-NOP	NONOP	Constant
Sweden	4.718[a]	−0.861	−2.611[a]	1.724[b]	−2.168[b]	0.337
FGR	2.090[b]	−0.975	0.240	−0.437	−1.958[b]	−0.015

(c) Compared with Sweden

	RDEXP	NTFA	WSOP	WSNO-NOP	NONOP	Constant
FGR	−4.532[a]	0.031	3.157[a]	−2.775[a]	1.031	−0.437

Table cont. p. 148

DFPIN
(a) Compared with Japan

	RDEXP	NTFA	WSOP	WSNO-NOP	NONOP	Constant
UK	−4.374[a]	−0.487	1.161	0.200	−3.143[a]	−3.414[a]
Sweden	−5.150[a]	0.200	−3.312[a]	3.847[a]	0.145	−4.251[a]
FGR	−6.156[a]	−0.845	1.123	−0.108	−2.254[b]	−3.070[a]

(b) Compared with the UK

	RDEXP	NTFA	WSOP	WSNO-NOP	NONOP	Constant
Sweden	−2.861[a]	0.749	−4.661[a]	3.563[a]	2.891[a]	−1.670[c]
FGR	−2.009[b]	−0.615	−0.036	−0.366	1.458[c]	0.804

(c) Compared with Sweden

	RDEXP	NTFA	WSOP	WSNO-NOP	NONOP	Constant
FGR	2.116[b]	−1.022	4.610[a]	−4.518[a]	−2.150[b]	2.413[a]

LFPIN
(a) Compared with Japan

	RDEXP	NTFA	WSOP	WSNO-NOP	NONOP	Constant
UK	−4.428[a]	1.588[c]	−3.129[a]	2.153[b]	3.666[a]	−0.769
Sweden	−3.133[a]	2.912[a]	−4.121[a]	3.627[a]	2.227[b]	−2.331[b]
FGR	−3.542[a]	1.564[c]	−0.775	0.518	3.120	−0.213

(b) Compared with the UK

	RDEXP	NTFA	WSOP	WSNO-NOP	NONOP	Constant
Sweden	1.973[b]	1.370	−0.388	0.540	−2.189[b]	−1.275
FGR	2.197[b]	0.076	2.585[a]	−1.915[b]	−1.126	0.652

(c) Compared with Sweden

	RDEXP	NTFA	WSOP	WSNO-NOP	NONOP	Constant
FGR	−0.177	−1.192	3.611[a]	−3.503[a]	1.248	2.414[a]

NOTES: Values shown are *t* statistics.
Significance levels are denoted by: a(1%), b(5%) and c(10%).

substitution of WS into the DFPIN and LFPIN equations, which yielded significant results in these comparisons.

Table 5.9 verifies that inward DFI into the USA is averse to high host-country skills compared to the other countries. Sweden finds itself grouped with the other countries here because the repulsive effect of Swedish operative skills on inward DFI is lost in aggregation with managerial skills.

The dramatically high explanatory power of research intensity for both inward DFI and licensing in Japan is confirmed in the stability tests in Tables 5.7 and 5.8. For Japan research assumes an importance far in excess of that for the other countries. This strong country-specific result has a country-specific cause, as argued in Chapter 4. This cause is the government regulation of inward DFI and licensing to build up high-technology industries in Japan, and as evidenced by our statistical results, this policy has been very successful.

Inward DFI into Japan is no more capital-intensive (by Japanese standards) than inward DFI in the European countries. However, inward Japanese licensing is by comparison into less capital-intensive industries. This probably reflects the disassociation of technology from capital and the emphasis in the industrial policy of successfully developing key industries.

The inward UK equations reported in Chapter 4 were distinguished by their general lack of significance. This reduces the scope for illuminating comparisons between countries. However, certain observations can be made.

Tables 5.7 and 5.8 demonstrate that inward DFI into the UK is second only to Japan as ranked by host technology intensity. This probably reflects the attractiveness of the UK for production by US multinationals. The unusually low research intensity of inward licensing into the UK is confirmed in the comparisons as is the distinctive-

TABLE 5.9   *Comparison to the US inward equations with general skills (WS)*

	DFPIN	*LFPIN*
Japan	2.845[a]	2.941[a]
UK	3.856[a]	1.198
Sweden	3.535[a]	2.025[b]
FGR	4.088[a]	2.375[a]

NOTES: Values shown are *t* statistics.
Significance levels are denoted by: a(1%), and b(5%).

ness of the association with the managerial complexity variable, NONOP, which we have argued may be associated with advertising.

By international standards Sweden is characterised as having high income *per capita*, an advanced manufacturing industry based on high productional expertise and a strength in resource-based activities. How far does this explain our observations? In the import equation we note that Swedish imports of manufactures are more research-intensive than those of any other country. At the same time the capital intensity of Swedish imports is the lowest, at least in comparison to the USA. This suggests that imports to Sweden are likely to be high value added with a low natural resource content, on the grounds that research intensity is characteristic of manufactures, and, in trade, capital intensity tends to be positively associated with natural-resource content. The lower coefficient on operative skills compared to other countries also tends to support this interpretation.

The distinctiveness of Sweden's industrial base, very much influenced by the availability of indigenous natural resources, has carried through to the ownership advantages of firms (Swedenborg, 1979). The comparisons in Tables 5.7 and 5.8 show that Swedish host research intensity has the lowest relationship with inward DFI of the other countries, and that this finding is not significantly different from the result obtained for the USA. The regression results in Chapter 4 showed that US research intensity had an insignificant effect on inward DFI, whereas it was found that for Sweden a negative relationship existed. It seems clear, therefore, that Swedish specialisation has produced indigenous firms capable of deflecting certain foreign entry. The argument, which is again supported, is that country-specific attributes have been responsible for the pattern of specialisation in both production and technology creation. This same technology and skills are firm-specific, and in turn can help explain Swedish outward competition in world markets.

The Federal Republic of Germany does not manifest any strong idiosyncrasies in comparison with the other countries. Like the other countries, inward DFI is not capital-intensive, as it is for the US. In comparison to Sweden, German inward DFI is found to be related to host technology intensity, but this is a more standard result, with Sweden being considered a little exceptional because of its narrow specialisation. It does appear, therefore, that DFI into Germany is at least rather more intra-industry.

German inward licensing does seem particularly related to operative skills, and this is highlighted in comparison with the USA, UK and Sweden. To this extent German licensing resembles the Japanese; though there has not been the regulation of licensing, German firms appear to have selected foreign technology suitable for high labour-skills manufacturing industry.

5.4 EVOLUTION OF INTERNATIONAL COMPETITION OVER TIME

Up until this point we have retained the assumption of stability in the equations over time. The assumption of stability in the model across countries was unequivocally rejected at an early stage, and the inquiry had to proceed on the basis of country-specific models. The general rejection of the time stability assumption would, however, be more serious as it would suggest that the pooling of data over the three years has been in error, and that a single equation for each country and each dependent variable does not truly exist. Table 5.10 reports Chow tests of this assumption, in the context of the model as a whole, for those countries where significance was attained. While a general rejection of the assumption of time stability across equations would be a serious matter, a limited number of changes would provide a valuable insight into how country-specific parameters may develop over time, without calling into question the procedure of pooling.

There are only three equations where instability is indicated in the general model. The first is for the US in the DFPOUT equation, for the period as a whole from 1965 to 1975. The second instance is the US import equation for all years, including each of the two sub-periods. The third is for the Japanese inward licensing model, for all years, and particularly between 1975 and 1970. In order to analyse

TABLE 5.10   *Chow tests of time stability*

	US (DFPOUT)	US (IMP)	Japan (LFPIN)
1975 1970 and 1965	2.414[c]	7.864[b]	2.904[c]
1975 and 1970	0.873	4.576[b]	5.000[b]
1970 and 1965	1.768	4.061[c]	1.852

NOTES: Values shown are F ratios.
Significance levels are denoted by: b(5%), and c(10%).

these changes more fully, detailed tests for individual coefficients are reported in Table 5.11. In addition, a few coefficients have changed in other equations which do not generate instability in the context of the model as a whole. Again these can provide some insights into country-

TABLE 5.11   *Selected tests of time stability in the coefficients of US and Japanese equations*

USA
Outward direct foreign production (DFPOUT)

	RDEXP	NTFA	WSOP	WSNO-NOP	NONOP	Constant
1975 and 1965 *1970*	0.664 −1.212	0.030 −0.235	0.055 −1.270	−0.484 1.307	−0.961 0.963	0.636 −1.186
1975 and 1970	1.770^c	0.217	1.039	−1.536^c	−1.632^c	1.628^c
1970 and 1965	−1.496^c	−0.290	−1.568^c	1.614^c	1.189	−1.465^c

Import (IMP)

	RDEXP	NTFA	WSOP	WSNO-NOP	NONOP	Constant
1975 and 1965 *1970*	1.153 1.765^c	−0.860 −1.135	0.212 1.464^c	−0.321 −1.184	−0.433 −1.506^c	0.631 1.126
1975 and 1970	−1.012	0.705	−2.530^b	1.763	1.906^c	−0.995
1970 and 1965	1.513^c	−0.973	1.255	−1.015	−1.292	0.965

Japan
Outward direct foreign production (DFPOUT)

	RDEXP	NTFA	WSOP	WSNO-NOP	NONOP	Constant
1975 and 1965 *1970*	2.816^b 0.964	1.488^c 1.057	−0.944 −1.058	−0.157 0.559	0.917 0.824	2.464^b 0.729
1975 and 1970	1.565^c	0.285	0.169	−0.565	0.044	1.494^c
1970 and 1965	1.271	1.394	−1.396	0.738	1.087	0.962

Inward licensed foreign production (LFPIN)

	RDEXP	NTFA	WSOP	WSNO-NOP	NONOP	Constant
1975 and 1965 *1970*	−2.299^b −1.982^b	1.508 0.920	−2.793^b −1.581^c	2.279^b 1.448^c	2.651^b 1.451^c	−0.687 −0.932
1975 and 1970	−0.691	1.670^c	−2.984^b	2.048^b	3.567^a	0.685
1970 and 1965	−1.653^c	0.768	−1.319	1.208	1.210	−0.778

NOTES: Values shown are t statistics.
Significance levels are denoted by: a(1%), b(5%) and c(10%).

specific developments, in particular for Japan, which is included in Table 5.11.

These results can be viewed, as with the country stability tests, as more detailed versions of the relevant Chow tests in Table 5.10. They test for significant differences in the coefficients between two regressions, a restricted form imposing the coefficients of a selected year and a completely unrestricted form, permitting all coefficients to vary. Thus the test for all years investigates differences in the coefficients in 1975 and 1970 as compared to 1965, and is the most general test on the data for all three years. The sign of the change indicates the direction with respect to the reference year. The two other tests are run on pooled data for just two years: the first test is for changes in 1975 compared to 1970, and the second for changes in 1970 compared to 1965.

The Chow tests indicate that the US direct foreign production model was unstable to some degree. Table 5.11 shows that this instability arose in several coefficients. Firstly, the research-intensity coefficient appears to have been higher in 1975 than it was in 1965. Thus the change is not a consistent one. If a single regression is run on the data for 1970 alone then the coefficient on research and development is estimated to be 0.410 ($t = 1.212$), which is insignificantly different from zero. However, it does provide some circumstantial evidence that the data for 1970 agree more closely with the coefficient reported by Lall (1980) in his work on 1970 data alone. It seems that the model has changed, and this casts some doubt over the accuracy of the coefficient reported for US research intensity in Table 4.3. As a matter of record, if a time stability test is run for average total wage rather than the two skills variables, there is no significant change for this variable, so our previous conclusions on it need not be modified.

Because of the general instability in the US model, affecting at various times operative and non-operative skills, managerial skills and the constant term, it is difficult to put any clear interpretation on any one change. But for the inconsistent nature of the changes over the two sub-periods, an argument citing the influence of the enlargement of the EEC might have been tenable. As it is, there is no clear indication about whether a meaningful cause is at work. We can note that certain coefficients in the licensing equation are similarly affected, although they are not reported here. The next questionable finding concerns the US import equation. Instability influences several coefficients, but again the pattern suggests no clear reason why this should have occurred.

The last instability indicated by the Chow tests is the inward licensing model for Japan. Instability occurs in several coefficients in the equation. The most noticeable change is the decline in the research and development coefficient. Although it might seem unlikely that Japanese firms are becoming less interested in licensing the most advanced technologies, this change might possibly result from relaxation of Japanese government control over the type and content of inward licensing, and permitting a greater diversity in terms of subject matter. This contention is given some modest support by the increase in the coefficients of the managerial skills and complexity variables, and the decline in that of operative skills.

There are a few other coefficients which exhibit instability, while the model as a whole remains stable. One interesting exception is obtained in respect of the Japanese outward direct foreign production equation. There seems to be some empirical evidence in Table 5.11 for the proposal put earlier, that Japanese direct foreign investment has become more technology-intensive, and the corollary that it can be expected to continue to become more so in the future. There has been a significant increase in the research-intensity coefficient, both in 1975 on 1970 and the period as a whole. Coupled with this, the coefficient on capital intensity has increased over the period. All this suggests that the direct foreign investment of Japanese multinationals as a group is becoming more technology- and capital-intensive. This must call into question the explanatory power of the Kojima hypothesis as a general theory of Japanese direct foreign investment. Such developments can really only be investigated by a theory which explains how country-specific advantages, generated within firms, can develop over time. It should be said that, at least in part, this increasing research intensity of direct foreign investment will be due to relative locational advantages deteriorating for Japan as a production base. However, it can also be noted that Japanese exports have not become any less research-intensive over the period.

5.5 CONCLUSIONS

The formal tests of country-specific differences have demonstrated that, in general, the models for each country are distinctive. This chapter has been concerned with providing some explanations for this.

Theory suggests that we should expect country-specific differences in the equations for total outward and total inward competition if ownership advantages are themselves country-specific in nature, that is, related to country of origin. This would unequivocally seem to be the case, and it confirms much of the empirical work noted in Section 2.8 of Chapter 2 on the extent of variation between countries.

Differences between countries in the trade, DFP and licensing equations are also most likely to result from country-specific differences in ownership advantages. However, locational advantages, which are omitted, could also influence the dependent variables, and cause differences between countries. Nevertheless, we retain the conclusions made here because locational effects in this form of study are not widespread, and because we do not wish to exclude the possibility that differences in indigenous resource advantages have actually generated country-specific differences in ownership advantages.

Many of the country-specific contrasts established in this chapter confirm conclusions based on observation of the equations in Chapter 3, for example, the negative research intensity of outward Japanese DFI is clearly a unique result for Japan. Further conclusions are suggested by the present systematic tests.

The DFPOUT equations are the least similar across countries, of the three methods of outward competition. This implies two things, firstly that the structure of ownership advantages is different between countries, and secondly that because of their nature their use is more frequently internalised.

The outward DFI of the UK, though more research-intensive than Japan's, is less so than the other three countries. Clearly, UK DFI abroad does not, relative to other countries, derive its competitiveness from research intensity. The capital intensity of UK DFI seems to provide a relative source of advantage. This is correlated with national origin. However, the argument has been made out that the large size and intra-firm efficiency of UK MNEs has enabled the exploitation of this as an advantage. This argument suggests that other national groups of MNEs will increasingly resemble the USA and UK far more in this respect, as the size of their MNEs increases. The argument is, therefore, that firm-specific efficiency in capital-raising and allocation increases with the geographical extension of the MNE, as noted in Chapter 2.

It was found that average skills were significantly more important for outward DFI and exports for the four countries compared to the USA. In this comparison a bias seemed to exist for skills to favour DFI, but this is only with respect to the US coefficient. There is at least some evidence that skills are more important in explaining competition by countries other than the USA.

It was argued that the USA and Sweden have a generally higher level of DFI abroad because of peculiarities of their economies. For the US the proximity to Canada was put forward, and for Sweden the small domestic market was believed to be the factor explaining an earlier venturing abroad by Swedish MNEs.

The greater dissimilarity between the inward equations of countries was believed to derive from the increased weight given to host factors, which seem to influence the import equations the most. The comparison of inward equations largely confirms findings in Chapter 4, in those cases where the variables were significant.

Of particular interest was the marked capital intensity of US inward DFI. Foreign MNEs in the US probably required capital-access advantages, and would tend to be large. This was a characteristic of US DFI abroad and of the UK, and it may be that UK MNEs contribute to the significance of this result in the US.

It appears that high average skills in US industry repel foreign firms, by comparison to other host countries. The explanation for this was argued to be that US industry on average has higher skills than other countries' industry, therefore incoming MNEs will tend to concentrate in the relatively lower-skill indigenous US industries. Furthermore, there is evidence that the same explanation applies to operative skills in Sweden, i.e. on average they are higher than in countries other than the USA. We might reason that this result is not found for Germany because of its high pre-existing degree of foreign penetration before the period studied here, implying that much new DFI in Germany represents extensions to existing investments, to which the US and Swedish argument would not apply.

The tests of time stability generally supported the procedure of pooling. The most interesting results were those anticipated for Japan. The pressure of other countries on Japan to liberalise industrial policy seems to have had a perceptible effect on the character of inward licensing permitted. However, this effect had not appeared to extend to DFI, where informal controls may be easier to continue.

It is found that Japanese outward DFI has become more research-intensive over time, supporting the view put earlier in Chapter 3, that the Kojima description of Japanese DFI is an obsolete account of new investment patterns. We anticipate that the country-specific differences of Japanese outward DFI compared to other countries will continue to diminish, as larger Japanese MNEs compete more extensively in the US and European markets.

6   Policy Implications

This chapter attempts to draw some policy implications from the findings in this study. However, this is not to endeavour to generate policy prescriptions; this would be unwise and presumptuous on the basis of an essentially aggregative investigation. Neither does this constitute a systematic review of actual policy options or their objectives,[1] although the principal examples are noted.

The main value of the conclusions found in this type of study is that they can clarify certain basic facts about actual international competition. By doing so welfare issues are not directly tackled, but some of the assumptions on which welfare analysis is based can be verified or falsified.

This discussion will concentrate on those implications for policy indicated by the findings of this study alone. Necessarily, therefore, it must remain silent on perfectly feasible policy options which another sort of investigation might suggest.

The most important general observation about policy is the substantial increase in the degree of integration of the five economies into the international economy over the period analysed. Not only has total inward and total outward competition as a proportion of the domestic economy risen (in manufactures), but within that, production through DFI has grown faster than trade, which in turn has grown faster than licensing.

For particular countries the existing pattern is striking – by 1975 DFP into Germany had a higher value than German imports. For the USA and UK the value of outward DFP exceeded the value of exports from the home country.

For all of the countries then, the degree of interpenetration has risen, and this may have had the effect of increasing competition. There are two main consequences with implications for policy. The first is the consequence for national commercial policy on trade, DFI and licensing. The second is the issue of attempting to control the behaviour of MNEs. In particular, this argument is about the two countries whose DFI is most extensive, and whose MNEs compete on a global basis, the US and UK. Accordingly, the first issue is dealt with from the perspective of host or recipient countries, and the second mainly from that of home countries.

The only real scope for extending the use of non-equity related technology transfers is for industrialising less developed countries. These countries may try to follow the Japanese example since the 1950s. As noted in Chapter 3, Japanese policy discriminated strongly against inward DFI, and increased licensing while also intervening in the terms and conditions of contracts to make the transfer even more favourable to Japan.

To do this, a country must have the necessary bargaining power to follow the Japanese example. A large home market is an advantage which itself implies a sufficient level of industrialisation. Retaliation is always a possibility, by governments on behalf of their MNEs and licensor firms. However, if the major trading partners of the LDC are not the same as the technology-supplying nations, then there is little that can be done. In the 1950s Japan's major export markets were in its own Asian 'zone of influence'.

It is, therefore, not feasible for a developed country which, because of the effects of intra-industry trade and DFI (and licensing too) tends to have substantial dealings with a wide range of other developed countries, to institute such a policy on licensing or DFI. The increased integration of the world economy makes independent actions such as this virtually impossible.

Nevertheless, for those LDCs who do have the bargaining strength, such policies are feasible, in particular Asian countries show a preference for the Japanese model of technology importation. While few countries can expect to follow Japan's example so successfully, it is difficult to agree with the argument that national industrial development is never best served by treating indigenous markets as infant industries, and that any such reasoning is essentially based on 'extremely weak theoretical (and empirical) underpinnings' (Teece, 1981, p. 15).

The issue of DFI substituting for trade (exports) has its roots in the work of Horst (1972a) and has been thought as a result to apply especially to technology-based trade and to the United States. The dilemma that this poses appears again in the discussion below.

However, can this substitution be turned to advantage from the point of view of the host economy? Chapter 4 found an indication that the common external tariff (CET) of the EEC has encouraged

DFI into Germany. As was argued there, this strong result probably owes as much to the attractiveness of the German economy within the EEC as it does to the CET *per se*. In other words, tariff protection by itself will not guarantee inward DFI into a particular country within the context of an integrated market.

As the data assembled in this study show, the major economies are becoming more integrated through the process of trade and DFI. This is in some ways a departure from the historical pattern. The traditional pattern of inter-industry DFI does not have the same implication for policy as intra-industry DFI. The inter-DFI pattern does not produce large volumes of two-way DFI between developed nations. Rather it tends to follow a hierarchical pattern where the leading country invests in less advanced countries who in turn may invest abroad, but they will not have significant investments in countries higher up the hierarchy. This means source countries may be integrated into the world economy, but typically only parts of it, and different parts at that, according to political and cultural ties.

The implications of intra-DFI are analogous to those of intra-trade for commercial policy. The growth of intra-trade in manufactures where trade becomes two-way and most intensive between the same partner countries, follows because countries manufacture the same range of products. To this extent, they have a common interest in trade liberalisation. In tariff negotiations this resulted in across-the-board tariff reductions rather than reciprocal bargaining. The 'most favoured nation' principle was a means of widening the benefits of a bilateral system, but inter-industry trade did not introduce the same mutual dependence between countries as intra-trade does.

As DFI becomes increasingly intra-industry the possibility of a country maintaining formal or informal discrimination against foreign firms becomes very much reduced, as its own firms may suffer from retaliation. The same would apply to any unilateral attempts to control inward DFI.

Intra-industry DFI has not been directly investigated here, but apart from the suggestion of increasing similarity in industrial patterns of DFI, Chaper 3 noted the key inter-penetration of DFI between developed countries geographically, which is the trademark of similar industrial tendencies.

Thus, developed country policy on DFI is likely to become more liberal for this reason and a developed country such as Japan now attempting to embark on a policy of discrimination would face effective opposition.

Simultaneous with the interpenetration of DFI is the increase in size of MNEs. Many MNEs, especially those of the US and UK are truly global in nature, and in certain cases it is difficult to maintain the fiction that they are based in one source country when the major proportion of their operations may lie abroad. The functional integration of these firms does pose some policy dilemmas.

For example, as noted in Chapter 2, the existence of established MNEs can cause a shortening of the product cycle, that is, the more rapid transfer of production abroad. This is seen by the US government to pose particular strategic problems for the US, because the US comparative advantage is in technology-intensive industries. Pressure by the government on firms not to transfer high-technology production abroad can lead to the perverse result of the MNEs transferring the research activity itself abroad, in order to evade such controls. While this may bring positive spillovers for the hosts (themselves developed countries), the USA feels that it is faced with an even more rapid loss of technology advantage.

The presumptions of this analysis are that the US is not replacing its lost technology at the rate it is losing it, and also that a decline in relative US ownership advantages would not have occurred anyway. Over the period studied here, we did find that US DFI abroad is comparatively research-intensive by international standards, although this also applies to Swedish DFI. However, increasing European DFI into the USA does not appear to be related to US technology, and therefore the increased intensity of competition may have other sources, more likely related to the country-specific ownership advantages of non-US firms.

A related issue is US anxiety that the transfer of its technology abroad through means other than DFI, which are seen as less secure, such as licensing, could have a similar effect as above on the USA's competitive position. However, there is no evidence that the general tendency towards licensing is increasing faster than DFI. Indeed, our estimates suggest it is increasing slower than the growth of trade.

One alternative way to increase the security of licensing, that exists on a supra-national level, is to extend the duration of patents from the fifteen to twenty years currently common. However, a policy such as this would probably not be welcomed by technology-recipient governments and firms.

The relatively poor economic performance of the UK economy, and the contrast this makes with the record of outward DFI and licensing, was noted in Chapter 3. The question is, does this have an

implication for UK policy? UK outward DFI and licensing propensities are appreciably higher than the average, and are mainly
directed at developed hosts. However, this would probably not
translate into an opportunity to force more production to locate in
the UK. The most likely outcome would be a more rapid evacuation
of existing production.

The UK problem may derive from poor locational advantages
rather than weak ownership advantages on the part of its firms
(Dunning, 1979a). The evidence here would seem to agree with this.
Under these conditions the implication is that a policy aimed at
making the UK a more attractive production location is required. But
it is important to stress that this includes a policy on research and
education because the process of innovation is synonymous with the
generation of ownership advantages. It may also have to be recognised that the UK could not generate a comparative advantage in
certain activities, in which case economic restructuring would be
indicated.

There are many specific policies governments may choose to suit
their particular circumstances. Because our five countries are developed, while it is possible that, under certain circumstances, tariff
(or non-tariff) protection might be considered to encourage import-
substitution (for various reasons), it is highly unlikely that the
ultimate motive would be to bring about a capital import. Only a
newly industrialising country would be likely to insist that foreign
firms service the local market by DFI rather than licensing.

On the other hand, it is plausible, because DFI is a package, that a
developed country might prefer the direct transfer of another component or components. The UK, for example, would prefer inward DFI
from Japan, rather than licensing, because management and marketing expertise would accompany the technology transfer. These other
components may not be so readily available on their own.

The existence of global MNEs is a focal point for both home and
host countries alike. In the case of the USA, the argument that
technology is transferred abroad prematurely is based on the view
that the speed of such MNEs' adjustment processes can exceed those
of the home economy if MNEs in general have truly world-wide
operations. In such instances the home country is really in a position
little different from any host country.

This does not seek to suggest that MNEs are the cause of structural
disequilibrium; because of the competitive nature of the international
economy such adjustments as are necessary in the home economy

would probably also have arisen as a result of rivals' actions, where the rival may be an industrialising country.

Indeed, the argument could be made that MNEs would be the first to identify opportunities for production wherever they arose, either naturally, or as a result of government incentives. From the point of view of national policy on encouraging inward DFI, theory suggests that improving locational advantages is a sensible course, through fiscal incentives for example. Our study has nothing to add to this. However, what the results do suggest is that the long-run national policy on research, education, etc., will make an environment more attractive for MNEs and non-MNEs alike, perhaps obviating the need for a series of short-term measures to increase locational appeal.

This study has been unable to address certain interesting aspects of this process of DFI, one in particular is intra-firm trade. The empirical evidence only implies that this will have increased, in particular through the growth of DFI itself. The presence of intra-firm trade may have some implications for adjustment policy, if it can be presumed that such trade is less price-elastic than external trade. Were this the case it might be found that imports or exports responded less to exchange rate changes, in particular products. The issue of the actual pricing of intra-firm trade is, of course, another matter and outside the scope of this study.

We have argued that the scope for negative measures by developed countries is very small. Positive measures may have a role to accelerate restructuring in particular sectors, but cannot deal with the problems of widespread restructuring. Here there is no substitute for a long-run policy of improving the capacity of the economy to originate advantages, similar to those that first enabled its firms to compete internationally. Thus, in an integrated international economy, non-discriminatory policy is probably optimal for a developed economy.

7 Conclusion

International competition is a considerably more complex subject than the process of international trade alone. The branches of trade, direct foreign investment and licensing are not only the principal means by which firms may compete against each other, they are also the means by which any one firm can simultaneously compete in international markets. The multinational enterprise is the form of international firm that unites these various means of market servicing, and this study has viewed the role of the MNE as central to explaining actual behaviour in world markets.

In this study we have traced the development of the theory of the MNE as a process originating with the industrial organisation approach. Despite the major step foward that this analysis represented, it was over-influenced by the experience of a single source country, the USA, and was committed to the explanation of the MNE as the product of concentrated market structure alone.

The fact that multinationals also act as licensors of technology and exporters of products gave rise to a search for a more comprehensive account of actual behaviour. The growth of the firm itself, to the point where it qualified as an MNE, was another question not addressed by the industrial organisation account.

To explain these phenomena it has to be recognised that firms are rarely single product units. Typically firms represent the vertical and horizontal integration of many and multiple stages in the process of producing final output. These stages of production are the internalised analogies (because they are under common ownership) to external markets. The theory of internalisation uses transactions-cost analysis to explain and predict the circumstances which characterise the creation of firms, and in particular the creation of firms across national boundaries, in other words, MNEs.

The transactions costs of conducting business in external markets do vary with industry as industrial organisation theory suggests, but not with industry alone. Indeed, even within a single industry some firms may choose a higher degree of integration than others. This is

164

because, *inter alia*, the capacity to internalise itself depends on complementary inputs in the firm, such as management expertise, capital and so on.

If the business of a firm is internationally oriented, then it operates in international markets where the transactions costs of doing business can vary according to the partner country. This explains the fact that a firm can license in one foreign market and yet choose to produce directly within another, in any given industry. This sensitivity in firms' behaviour can be exploited by governments, through raising the cost of one form of business activity compared to the other through policy.

Internalisation commonly takes place in activities when the external costs of transferring knowledge or intermediate products are high. As it is more correct to say, the rights to such items are traded. These rights can be termed 'ownership advantages', and it then becomes clear that the owner is the party initiating internalisation. The concept of the ownership advantage is introduced by the eclectic theory to determine the direction of international competition.

While the internalisation theory of the MNE emphasised the firm as a generator of knowedge, it did not directly address the question of why different countries seem to specialise in different activities. Here the eclectic theory links the national origin of the firm to the generation of ownership advantages. Thus, the eclectic theory represents an integration of internalisation theory into international economics, and with the addition of location advantages, determining the least cost location of production, predictions about trade flows can be added to those on DFI and licensing. Again, governments can exploit the sensitivity of the firm in locating production by various policies designed to affect relative location costs.

Theory suggests that the parameters of international competition are liable to change over time, not least because government intervention will seek to influence the location of economic activity. An added reason for such change is that as firms, and MNEs in particular, expand, internal markets frequently become more efficient for the firm's purposes, relative to external markets.

The result of this process should be a general increase in the proportion of DFI in international competition. Although such firms will retain characteristics inherent from their national origins, the subsequent growth of the firm should increasingly result from the efficiency of its internal markets. Such firms will become global in their activities.

While much empirical work has vindicated the industry-specific argument on the form of international competition, the essentially international aspects of transactions-cost theory were rarely investigated, and yet it is these that make the forms and patterns of international competition so diverse, in terms of the different strategic options open to firms.

Data presented in this study clarifies and confirms many of the predictions of theory. An overview of the information available for a comparison across five major developed countries, covering trade, DFI and licensing, revealed the distinctive and country-specific nature of international patterns of competition. All the data indicate that the international sectors of each country are continually increasing, and that indeed the proportion of DFI is rising the fastest, as theory predicts.

We find that the intensity of international competition is at its peak between developed countries, although Japan adheres a little less closely to this pattern. Furthermore, the indications are that intra-industry penetration through all routes of competition appears to be rising.

Despite these common trends, each country begins from a different starting position; the range runs from the least open, but largest economy, the USA, to the most open and smallest economy, Sweden.

We find some interesting developments in the geographical pattern of competition. Non-US firms have intensified direct competition via DFI within the US market itself, and especially within manufacturing industry. By contrast, US DFI in Europe has risen most in non-manufacturing, and the suggestion was that this reflected both the rise in labour costs and in European market size relative to the USA.

New European DFI in the USA is inexplicable using the US product cycle model, proving that a more general theory is needed to account for the clear evidence that DFI can and does increase in all directions simultaneously.

That trade patterns are a very incomplete account of total international competition, vindicates the thesis that trade, DFI and licensing should be estimated side by side in statistical analysis.

The results of this analysis show that while a product cycle type of account might provide a basic model of international production for the USA, to the extent that the US pattern is characterised by product innovation, the structure of the US model is not shared by the other countries. Yet despite this, non-US countries continue to increase their competition abroad, and in the US itself. The clear inference from this is that different countries base their international competition on a different mix of ownership advantages. Evidence on competition within the five economies tends to confirm this.

Formal tests of the differences in the mix and importance of ownership advantages between countries reveal that successful international competition has a markedly country-specific flavour, and that, for example, leading innovation intensity is not a necessary prerequisite for such success.

The sources of these country-specific variations are held to be the indigenous environment and resource advantages of countries, and also its institutions, government policy and the maturity of its firms in international involvement. Ownership advantages remain the property of firms, however it is a major confirmation of the theoretical perspective that they vary in a systematic manner between countries.

In respect of hypotheses omitted from the analysis, such as locational variables, these omissions, where significant, show up in correlations of residuals across equations, confirming that locational factors can also cause one form or another of competition to be extraordinarily high.

We find that the shifts in the Japanese model over time are explained by locational factors influencing Japanese trade and the improvement in Japanese firms' ownership advantages. Coupled with our knowledge of Japanese industrial policy and the extent of the inward transfer of technology in the inward equations, this suggests some scope for national policy.

However, on the issue of policy the argument is made that policies of the Japanese kind can only feasibly be pursued by the industrialising less developed countries. For developed countries the scope for decisive national policy on international competition is limited by the integration of their economies with each other, via trade and especially via their own MNEs. Non-discriminatory national policies directed at research and education would appear to be optimal.

IMPLICATIONS FOR FUTURE RESEARCH

It is clear from the observations made in this study that certain data on additional forms of international business linkage are desirable. Here we have extended economic analysis to international licensing, and this has afforded valuable insights. There are many other flows internationally, particularly within internal markets, for which data are still required. International economics has a tendency to concentrate on real (physical) factors. There is every indication that research on the extension of international competition should involve previously neglected flows such as services and finance. A more complete representation of the multinational firm may greatly assist our understanding of the rapid expansion in new direct foreign investment by existing multinationals.

A call for improved data is worth very little unless it recognises the practical problems. Most official data reach the economist in a secondary manner, that is, the researcher often uses data in a way for which it was not designed. Greater contact between academic economists and the official agencies which already collect data from firms, often on a universe basis, should result in more appropriate information being gathered. Additionally, and this need not be exclusive, those surveys by academic economists themselves could then extend their enquiries still to more searching areas of theoretical interest.

The important point is that it now matters more not that data are collected, but which data are collected. Theory has an increasingly important role to play in directing applied research to the correct empirical questions which logically begin at the firm level.

Appendix A
Statistical Sources

Data used in the construction of the dependent and independent variables employed in the statistical analysis are taken from the sources detailed below. These are grouped according to the variables and series they principally contribute to, and by country, where apposite.

Exports and Imports (Direct Trade)

OECD (various years) *Trade by Commodities,* Statistics of Foreign Trade, Series C, January–December, Paris: OECD.

Direct Foreign Production (Outward)

United States

US Department of Commerce (1977) 'Sales of Majority-Owned Affiliates of US Companies 1975', *Survey of Current Business*, February.
US Department of Commerce (1974) 'Sales by Majority-Owned Foreign Affiliates of US companies, 1966–72', *Survey of Current Business*, August, Part 2.
US Tariff Commission (1973) *Implications of Multinational Firms for World Trade and Investment and for US Trade and Labor*, report to the Committee of Finance of the US Senate and its Sub-Committee on International Trade, 93rd Congress, 1st session, Washington, DC: US Government Printing Office, February.
US Department of Commerce (1976) *US Direct Investment Abroad, 1966, Final Data*, Social and Economic Statistics Administration,

169

Bureau of Economic Analysis, Washington, DC: US Government Printing Office.

Japan

Ministry of Finance, *Zaisei Kinyu tokei Geppo* (various issues).
Ministry of International Trade and Industry, *Japan's Direct Overseas Investment*, News from MITI (various issues) and various materials in Japanese.
Export–Import Bank (1972) *Japanese Private Investment Abroad. The Summary of the Third Questionnaire Survey*, October. International Monetary Fund (Various years) *Balance of Payments Yearbook*, Washington, DC.

United Kingdom

UK Department of Industry (1977) 'Book Values of Overseas Direct Investments', *Trade and Industry*, 25 February.
UK Department of Industry (1978) *Business Monitor 4: Overseas Transactions 1975*, Business Statistics Office, London: HMSO.
UK Department of Industry (1977). *Census of Overseas Assets 1974. Business Monitor M4, 1974 Supplement*. Business Statistics Office, London: HMSO.
UK Department of Industry (1973) 'Book Values of Overseas Direct Investments', *Trade and Industry*, 15 November.
UK Department of Industry (1975) *Business Monitor 4: Overseas Transactions 1973*. Business Statistics Office, London: HMSO.
UK Department of Industry (1974) *Census of Overseas Assets at End 1974, M4 Overseas Transactions 1972 – Part II*, London: HMSO.
UK Board of Trade (1968) 'Book Value of Overseas Investments', *Board of Trade Journal*, 26 January.
Reddaway, W. B., Potter, S. J. and Taylor, C. T. (1968) *Effects of UK Direct Investment Overseas. Final Report*. University of Cambridge, Department of Applied Economics, Occasional Papers: 15, London: Cambridge University Press.

Sweden

Swedenborg, B. (1979) *The Multinational Operation of Swedish Firms: An Analysis of Determinants and Effects*. Stockholm: Industrial Institute of Economic and Social Research.

Swedenborg, B. (1973) *Den svenska industrins investeringar i utlandet* (Swedish Direct Investment Abroad), Stockholm, Industriens Utredningsinstitut: Almqvist & Wiksell.

Federal Republic of Germany

Deutsche Bundesbank (1979) 'The level of direct investment at the end of 1976', *Monthly Report of the Deutsche Bundesbank*, vol. 31, no. 4, April.

Federal Ministry of Economics (1977) *Runderlass zur Aussenwirtschaft* (Circular on Foreign Trade and Payments), 11/77 vom. 4, April.

Federal Ministry of Economics (1976) *Runderlass zur Aussenwirtschaft*, 13/76 vom. 2, April.

Federal Ministry of Economics (1971) *Runderlass zur Aussenwirtschaft*, 10/71 vom. 1, April.

Federal Ministry of Economics (1966) *Runderlass zur Aussenwirtshaft*, 13/66 vom. 31, März.

Direct Foreign Production (Inward)

United States of America

US Department of Commerce (1976) *Foreign Direct Investment in the United States, Volume 2: Report of Secretary of Commerce: Benchmark Survey, 1974*, Bureau of Economic Analysis, Washington, DC: US Government Printing Office, April.

US Department of Commerce (1977) 'Foreign Direct Investments in the United States, 1976', *Survey of Current Business*, vol. 57, no. 10, October.

US Department of Commerce (1973) 'Foreign Direct Investment in the United States, 1962—71', *Survey of Current Business*, February.

Japan

Ministry of International Trade and Industry (1977) *Gaishi Kei Kigyo No Doko* (The Survey of Foreign Companies), Bureau of Industrial Policy, October.

Ministry of International Trade and Industry (1972) *Gaishi Kei Kigyo No Doko*. (The Fifth Survey of Foreign Companies), Enterprise Bureau, May.

Ministry of International Trade and Industry (1968) *Gaishi Kei Kigyo, sono Gittai to Eikyo*, (Foreign Companies – Reality and Impact), Bureau of Enterprises.

United Kingdom

UK Department of Industry (1979) *Report on the Censuses of Production 1974 and 75: Summary Tables: Enterprise Analysis*, Business Monitor PA1002, vol. 2, Business Statistics Office, London: HMSO.
UK Department of Industry (1973) 'Book values of overseas direct investments', *Trade and Industry*, 15 November.

Sweden

Statistiska Centralbyran (1978) *Utlandsaga Foretag 1975 och 1976*, Statistiska meddelanden Serie F 1978:8. More detailed breakdown from this source provided in private correspondence by Dr Lars Hakanson, Statens Industriverk, Stockholm, from the Register of foreign-owned enterprises.
Samuelsson, H. F., (1977) *Utlandska direkta investeringar i Sverige: en ekonometrisk analys av bestamnings factorerna* (Foreign Direct Investments in Sweden – an Econometric Analysis), Industriens Utredningsinstut, Stockholm: Almqvist & Wicksell. More detailed breakdown of data from the original source provided in private correspondence by Dr Lars Hakanson, Statens Industriverk, Stockholm, from the Register of foreign-owned enterprises.

Federal Republic of Germany

Deutsche Bundesbank (1979) 'The level of investment at the end of 1976', *Monthly Report of the Deutsche Bundesbank*, vol. 31, no. 4, April.
Federal Ministry of Economics (1977) *Runderlass zur Aussenwirtschaft*, 12/77 vom. 4, April.
Federal Ministry of Economics (1976) *Runderlass zur Aussenwirtschaft*, 12/76 vom. 2, April.
Federal Ministry of Economics (1966) *Runderlass zur Aussenwirtschaft*, 20/66 vom. 26, Mai.
Deutsche Bundesbank (1978) 'Reversal in the balance of direct investment', *Monthly Report of the Deutsche Bundesbank*, no. 10, October.

Deutsche Bundesbank (1974) 'Foreign interests in enterprises in the Federal Republic of Germany', *Monthly Report of the Deutsche Bundesbank*, November.

Deutsche Bundesbank (1972) 'Foreign interests in enterprises in the Federal Republic of Germany', *Monthly Report of the Deutsche Bundesbank*, November.

Deutsche Bundesbank (1972) 'Foreign interests in enterprises in the Federal Republic of Germany', *Monthly Report of the Deutsche Bundesbank*, January.

Deutsche Bundesbank (1969) 'Foreign interests in enterprises in the Federal Republic of Germany', *Monthly Report of the Deutsche Bundesbank*, May.

Deutsche Bundesbank (1965) 'Foreign ownership in German enterprises', *Monthly Report of the Deutsche Bundesbank*, May.

International Royalty Receipts and Payments (Unaffiliated)

OECD (1977 *Data Concerning the Balance of Technological Payments in Certain OECD Member Countries: Statistical Data and Methodological Analysis*, Directorate for Science, Technology and Industry, DSTI/SPR/77.2, 21 November.

United States

US Department of Commerce (1980) 'US International Transactions in Royalties and Fees, 1967–78', by M. L. Kroner, *Survey of Current Business*, January.

US Department of Commerce data supplied in private correspondence.

United Kingdom

UK Department of Industry (1978) *Overseas Transactions 1975*. Business Monitor 4, Business Statistics Office, London: HMSO.

UK Department of Industry (1975) *Overseas Transactions 1973*, Business Monitor 4, Business Statistics Office, London: HMSO.

UK Department of Trade and Industry (1972) 'Overseas Royalty Transactions', *Trade and Industry*, 30 March.

UK Board of Trade (1967) 'Overseas Transactions – Trade Credits and Royalties', *Board of Trade Journal*, 21 July.

Sweden

Statistiska Centralbyran (1977) *Forskningsstatistik 1975–1977* Statistiska meddelanden Serie U. 1977:23, Enheten for finansstatistik. Stockholm: Sveriges officiella statistik.
Statistiska Centralbyran (1971) *Forskningsstatistik for Industri 1969–1971*, Statistiska meddelanden nr 1971: 26, Enheten for finansstatistik, Stockholm: Sveriges officiella statistik.
Statistiska Centralbryan (1969) *Forskningsstatistik for Industri 1965–1967*, Statistiska meddelanden nr 1969:4, Enheten for finansstatistik, Stockholm: Sveriges officiella statistik.

Federal Republic of Germany

Deutsche Bundesbank (1976) 'Patent and Licence Transactions with Foreign Countries, *Monthly Report of the Deutsche Bundesbank*, April.
Deutsche Bundesbank (1972) 'Patent and Licence Transactions with Foreign Countries in 1970 and 1971', *Monthly Report of the Deutsche Bundesbank*, May.
Deutsche Bundesbank (1966) 'Patent and Licence Transactions with Foreign Countries in 1964 and 1965', *Monthly Report of the Deutsche Bundesbank*, April.

Research and Development Expenditure in the Business Enterprise Sector

OECD (1979) *International Statistical Year 1975: International Volume*, Directorate for Science, Technology and Industry, Paris, March.

United States

US National Science Foundation (1972) *Research and Development in Industry 1970*, NSF 72309, Washington, DC, April.

Japan

Bureau of Statistics (1976) *Japan Statistical Yearbook,* Office of the Prime Minister.
Bureau of Statistics (1971) *Japan Statistical Yearbook*, Office of the Prime Minister.

Bureau of Statistics (1966) *Japan Statistical Yearbook*, Office of the Prime Minister.

United Kingdom

UK Department of Industry (1977) 'Industrial Expenditure and Employment on Scientific Research and Development in 1975', *Trade and Industry*, 24 June.
UK Central Statistical Office (1973) *Research and Development Expenditure*, Studies in Official Statistics, no. 21.

Sweden

Statistiska Centralbyran (1977) *Forskningsstatistik 1975–1977*, Statistiska meddelanden serie U, 1977:23, Enheten for finansstatistik, Stockholm: Sveriges officiella statistik.
Statistiska Centralbyran (1971) *Forskningsstatistik for Industri 1969–1971*, Statistiska meddelanden nr U 1971:26, Enheten for finansstatistik, Stockholm: Sveriges officiella statistik.
Statistiska Centralbryan (1969) *Forskningsstatistik for Industri 1976–77*, Statistika meddelanden nr 1969:4, Enheten for finansstatistik, Stockholm: Sveriges officiella statistik.

Federal Republic of Germany

Statistisches Bundesamt (1978) *Statistisches Jahrbuch für die Bundesrepublik Deutschland,* Wiesbaden: Stifterverband für die Deutsche Wissenschaft (1974) *Forschung und Entwicklung in der Wirtschaft 1971*, Arbeitsschrift C, Essen.
Stifterverband für die Deutsche Wissenschaft (1969) *Wirtschaft und Wissenschaft* Nr 1/1969, Essen.

Research and Development Employment in the Business Enterprise Sector

As for Research and Development expenditure, except for:

United States

US National Science Foundation (1977) *Research and Development in Industry 1975*, NSF 77–324, Washington, DC.

United Kingdom

US Central Statistical Office (1976) *Research and Development, Expenditure and Employment*, Studies in Official Statistics, no. 27.

Employment

United States

US Department of Commerce (1978) *Annual Survey of Manufactures 1976, Industry Profiles,* Bureau of the Census, June, Washington, DC: US Government Printing Office.
US Department of Commerce (1973) *Annual Survey of Manufactures: 1970 and 1971,* Bureau of the Census, Washington, DC: US Government Printing Office.
US Department of Commerce (1968) *Annual Survey of Manufactures 1964–1965,* Bureau of the Census, May, Washington, DC: US Government Printing Office.

Japan

Bureau of Statistics (1978) *Japan Statistical Yearbook*, Office of the Prime Minister.
Bureau of Statistics (1972) *Japan Statistical Yearbook*, Office of the Prime Minister.

United Kingdom

UK Department of Industry (1979) *Report on the Censuses of Production 1974 and 75, Summary Tables; Enterprise Analysis*, Business Monitor PA1002, vol. 2, Business Statistics Office, London: HMSO.
UK Department of Industry (1976) *Report on the Census of Production 1970, Summary Tables*, Business Monitor C154, London: HMSO.

Sweden

Statistiska Centralbyran (1977 *Foretagan Hafte 1 and Hafte 2* Enheten for finansstatistik, 20/21 July, Stockholm: Sveriges officiella statistik.

Statistiska Centralbyran (1977) *Statistik Arsbok for Sveriges*, Stockholm: Sveriges officiella statistik. Statistiska Centralbyran (1972) *Foretagen 1970: Economisk redovisning*, Stockholm: Sveriges officiella statistik.
Statistiska Centralbyran (1972) *Statistik Arsbok for Sveriges*, Stockholm: Sveriges officiella statistik.

Federal Republic of Germany

Statistisches Bundesamt (1967, 1973 and 1978) *Statistisches Jahrbuch für die Bundesrepublik Deutschland,* Wiesbaden.

Domestic Production

United States

As for Employment.

Japan

As for Employment.

United Kingdom

As for Employment, except for:

UK Department of Trade and Industry (1971) 'Index of industrial production for November 1970' *Trade and Industry*, 20 January.

Sweden

As for Employment.

Federal Republic of Germany

As for Employment, except for:

Deutsche Bundesbank (1978) *Jahresabschlüsse der Unternehmen in der Bundesrepublik Deutschland 1965 bis 1976,* Sonderdrücke der Deutschen Bundesbank Nr 5, July, Frankfurt am Main.

Net Tangible Fixed Assets (Depreciable Assets)

United States

As for Employment, except for:

US Department of Commerce (1977) *Survey of Current Business*, Bureau of Economic Analysis, 57, no. 8, August.
US Department of Commerce (1976) *Survey of Current Business*, Bureau of Economic Analysis, 56, no. 4, April.
US Department of Commerce (1972) *Annual Survey of Manufactures: Special Geographic Supplement to 1962–1964*, Bureau of the Census, February, Washington, DC: US Government Printing Office.
US Department of Commerce (1976) *Survey of Current Business*, 56, no. 4, April.

Japan

Bureau of Statistics (1966, 1971 and 1977) *Japan Statistical Yearbook*, Office of the Prime Minister.

United Kingdom

UK Department of Industry (1978) *Company Finance*: Business Monitor 3, Business Statistics Office, 9th issue, March, London: HMSO.
UK Department of Trade and Industry (1973) *Company Finance*: Business Monitor 3, 4th issue, London: HMSO.
UK Ministry of Labour (1967) *Statistics on Incomes, Prices, Employment and Production*, no. 21, June, London: HMSO.

Sweden

As for Employment.

Federal Republic of Germany

As for Employment.

Wages and Salaries

United States

As for Employment.

Japan

Bureau of Statistics (1967, 1971 and 1977) *Japan Statistical Yearbook*, Office of the Prime Minister.

United Kingdom

As for Employment.

Sweden

As for Employment.

Federal Republic of Germany

As for Domestic Production.

General Sources

United Nations (1978) *Yearbook of Industrial Statistics, 1, Industrial Statistics*, 1976 Edition, New York: Department of Economic and Social Affairs, Statistical Office.
United Nations (1974) *The Growth of World Industry, 1, General Industrial Statistics, 1962–1971*, 1972 Edition, New York: Department of Economic and Social Affairs, Statistical Office.
United Nations (1969) *The Growth of World Industry, 1, General Industrial Statistics, 1953–1966*, 1967 Edition, New York: Department of Economic and Social Affairs, Statistical Office.

Appendix B
Sources of Additional Data

Appendix A details the sources of data used in the statistical analysis. While these sources also provide other information presented mainly in Chapter 3 and not used in the formal statistical work, this appendix records additional sources of information, mainly used in Chapter 3.

Outward Direct Foreign Investment

United States

US Department of Commerce (1982) Computer print of updated material from the 'Survey of Current Business', Bureau of Economic Analysis, Washington, DC, September.

US Department of Commerce (1981) *US Direct Investment Abroad, 1977*, Bureau of Economic Analysis, Washington, DC: US Government Printing Office, April.

US Department of Commerce, (1982) *Selected Data on US Direct Investment Abroad, 1950–76* Bureau of Economic Analysis, Washington, DC, February.

Japan

Ministry of International Trade and Industry, (1983) *The Fifteenth Survey of Foreign Capital Affiliated Companies for FY 1982*, News from MITI Summary, MIT. Information Office, 23rd May.

Ministry of Finance (1981), *Monthly Report on Financial Statistics*, no. 356, Special Report on Outward Investment Statistics, December.

Ozawa, T. (1981), *The Japanese Experience with the 'New' Forms of Investment: a Preliminary Exploration.* Paper presented at the Progress Evaluation Meeting for the Research Project on Changing

International Investment Strategies: the 'New' Forms of Investment in Developing Countries, Foreign Investment and International Banking Research Programme, Paris, OECD, 2–6 March.

United Kingdom

UK Department of Trade and Industry (1984) *Census of Overseas Assets 1981, Business Monitor MA4, 1981, Supplement*, Business Statistics Office, London: HMSO, May.

UK Department of Industry (1981) *Census of Overseas Assets 1978, Business Monitor MA4, 1978 Supplement*. Business Statistics Office, London: HMSO.

UK Bank of England (1982) 'An Inventory of UK External Assets and Liabilities: End-1981', *Bank of England Quarterly Bulletin*, 22, no. 2, June.

UK Bank of England (1978) 'An Inventory of UK External Assets and Liabilities: End-1977' *Bank of England Quarterly Bulletin*, 18, no. 2, June.

UK Bank of England (1975) 'An Inventory of UK External Assets and Liabilities: End-1974', *Bank of England Quarterly Bulletin*, 15, no. 2, June.

UK Bank of England (1971) 'An Inventory of UK External Assets and Liabilities: End-1970', *Bank of England Quarterly Bulletin*, 11, no. 2, June.

UK Bank of England (1970) 'An Inventory of UK External Assets and Liabilities: End-1969', *Bank of England Quarterly Bulletin*, 10, no. 3, September.

Inward Direct Foreign Investment

United States

US Department of Commerce (1983) *Foreign Direct Investment in the United States, 1980*, Bureau of Economic Analysis, Washington, DC, US Government Printing Office, October.

US Department of Commerce (1973) 'Foreign Direct Investments in the United States in 1972' *Survey of Current Business*, August.

Japan

Ministry of International Trade and Industry (1983) *The Fifteenth*

Survey of Foreign Capital Affiliated Companies for FY 1982. Summary, MITI Information Office, 23 May.

United Kingdom

As for Outward Direct Foreign Investment

Sweden

Statistiska Centralbyran (1976) *International Enterprises*, Press-Middelande Nr 1976:131, Stockholm: Sveriges oficiella statistik.
Samuelsson, H. F. (1973) *Foreign Direct Investment in Sweden 1965 to 1970*, unpublished paper.
Statistiska Centralbyran (1976) *Internationella Foretag, Kartlaggning per 31 December 1974*, Enheten for finanasstatistik, Stockholm.

Federal Republic of Germany

Deutsche Bundesbank (1981) 'International capital links between enterprises in 1978', *Monthly Report of the Deutsche Bundesbank*, vol. 33, no. 1, January.
Deutsche Bundesbank (1972) 'Foreign interests in enterprises in the Federal Republic of Germany' Monthly Report of the Deutsche Bundesbank, vol. 24, no. 1, January.

International Royalty Receipts and Payments

United States

US Department of Commerce (1973) 'US international transactions in royalties and fees: their relationship to the transfer of technology', *Survey of Current Business*, December.
US Department of Commerce data supplied in private correspondence by the Bureau of Economic Analysis.

Japan

Association for Economic Research (1976) *The 12th Survey of Capital Import by Companies*, (in Japanese).

Ministry of International Trade and Industry (1970) *Gijitsuyushutsu no Jittai nitsuito* (On the Actual State of Japan's Technology Exports), Tokyo.

United Kingdom

UK Department of Industry (1977) 'Overseas royalties and similar transactions in 1975', *Trade and Industry*, 28, July—September.

General Sources

International Monetary Fund (various years) *International Financial Statistics, Yearbook*, Washington, DC.
United Nations (1979) *Yearbook of National Account Statistics*, New York.
United Nations (1977) *Statistical Yearbook*, New York.
United Nations (1978) *Demographic Yearbook*, New York.

Appendix C
The Definition of a Direct Foreign Investment

The definition of direct foreign investment is an inherently practical set of guidelines, given that financial data are an imperfect proxy for the complex business linkages that can exist within the multinational firm. A set of practical proposals for improving this definition in line with the argument found in Chapter 1 are found in Billerbeck and Yasugi (1979).

The basic definition of DFI is provided by the IMF, being an investment conferring a 'lasting interest in an enterprise operating in an economy other than that of the investor, the investor's purpose being to have an effective voice in the management of the enterprise' (1977, p. 136). This covers the control of both incorporated and unincorporated foreign affiliates (branches), and all national definitions noted in Appendix D accord with this.

The central issue is the practical imputation of control. National practices vary (Appendix D) via the use of differing minimum qualifying thresholds for control to be deemed. Such thresholds are conventionally set at around 25 per cent or below, reflecting the observation that control can be effectively exercised with minority shareholdings as long as the source country/owners act in a unified manner, and particularly if ownership by the majority is disparate. Because a number of such variables are involved, arbitrary thresholds are employed for pragmatic reasons. However, in principle there is no reason why effective control cannot be exercised at very low shareholdings, given the manner in which the owners act is conducive to this. The lower thresholds used by the UK (20 per cent of equity) and the USA (10 per cent for outward, and inward after 1974) reflect precisely these considerations.

The nominal criteria adopted by the IMF employ similar reasoning.

Effective control is inferred from ownership of 50 per cent or more if the source country owner is a single entity or a group of owners acting in a unified manner. Furthermore, if specific groups from a particular source country are represented on the board of directors, then the equity ownership, however low a percentage, may count as a direct foreign investment. Under any of these circumstances the particular share of equity involved is used to apportion the source country stake in the book value of net assets of the foreign affiliate. This is then viewed as the financial value of the source country firm's interest in the affiliate. As noted in Appendix D some countries report the value of total assets or nominal capital instead. However, there is some general agreement over the imputation of effective control, which is the central issue whatever financial measure is employed. The empirical agreement between national conventions is made even stronger because of the tendency for direct investment shareholdings to be grouped away from the very lowest levels of ownership (as seen in Chapter 3).

The main drawback of this practice is that by allocating a share of the value of foreign involvement, the issue of whether total capital (however defined) is controlled remains unanswered. For this reason any such share is likely to undervalue the extent of true foreign commitment if there is effective control with substantially less than total ownership. However, in general, near-full ownership is preferred, reducing the absolute value of this discrepancy. For both Japanese outward and inward investment this is not tenable, although the measures taken in the estimation of sales abroad in this study were intended to minimise the problem. In formal terms this relates to the procedure of consolidation of accounts, which may be full (in the case of 100 per cent ownership) or partial. Normally the value of direct investment attributed to the parent enterprise by the affiliate is the figure used, given standard rules of consolidation.

According to the practice adopted by the IMF (1977), direct foreign investment consists of that investment abroad in subsidiaries, majority and minority-owned, and branches. The investing company's share in the net assets of overseas affiliates is calculated as:

i) the book value of fixed assets (net of depreciation) plus
ii) current assets (net of amounts owing by the investing company) less,
iii) current liabilities (net of amounts owing to the investing company) less,

iv) long-term liabilities (net of amounts owing to the investing
   company) less,

v) minority shareholders' interests in net assets.

(The above procedure is presented in the UK Census of Overseas
Assets Commentaries.)

For practical reasons the value of direct investment found in the
parent enterprise's accounts may be used for minority foreign investments.

All surveys must rely on the accuracy of the accounts kept by
enterprises. Although most countries have adopted the definition of
direct foreign investment given in the IMF Balance of Payments
Manual, there is still scope for relatively minor international differences in accounting practice to lead to divergences in estimation. For
example, the difference between US and UK accounting practice for
stocks and work-in-progress is noted in the UK Census of Overseas
Assets (1981) commentary.

The values for any financial variable are derived from the balance
sheets. In the case of direct foreign investment, this is based on net
assets, being fixed assets, less accumulated depreciation provisions,
plus current assets, less current liabilities. The book values of current
assets and liabilities are reasonably accurate with respect to true
current valuation, however this may not apply to fixed assets. Fixed
assets are frequently recorded at historical cost, unless there is a
recent revaluation, and thus may be appreciably lower than current
market or replacement values. This is recognised as a failing of the
measurement of direct foreign investment, although no improvement
can be made on it. Evidently this is not a problem of current-valued
statistics such as sales, and it is these which are used in statistical
analysis. From time to time data on direct foreign investment are
reported with a negative sign, although rather infrequently. This
could result from the net indebtedness of a parent enterprise to a
foreign subsidiary – a position which could have any number of
motives. This example is merely symptomatic of the more general
problem of using financial variables. It is evident that in certain
instances the direct foreign investment position can completely misre-
present the true nature of competition abroad in providing nonsense
figures.

Appendix D
A Note on National Sources of Data on Direct Foreign Investment

The sources of data used in the statistical work in this study are detailed in Appendix A. The quality of the basic data is briefly appraised here. Where some estimation has been necessary, this is noted in Appendix F.

UNITED STATES

Both inward and outward DFI statistics are official covering close to 100 per cent of the estimated universe by value. Data are collected by the Bureau of Economic Analysis, US Department of Commerce in periodic mandatory surveys. The minimum threshold for a DFI to be inferred is 10 per cent (25 per cent for inward DFI prior to 1974).

JAPAN

Outward data derived from the accumulated approved value of specific projects submitted to the Ministry of Finance under the Foreign Exchange Control Act (1949), beginning in 1951. Data cover all investments in which participation in management is intended. Inward data are from the Surveys of Foreign Companies conducted by the Bureau of Industrial Policy at the Ministry of International Trade and Industry, since 1967. The data covered 84 per cent of the estimated universe by capital value in 1975. The minimum ownership threshold for a DFI is generally 25 per cent.

UNITED KINGDOM

Both inward and outward DFI statistics are official and are estimates of the universe data, collected by the UK Department of Trade and Industry (formerly Board of Trade) since 1962 in periodic surveys. Since 1978 these have been mandatory. In this study, some additional data for 1965 were obtained from Reddaway *et al.* (1968), for outward investment. The effective minimum ownership threshold is 20 per cent.

SWEDEN

Data on Swedish outward DFI are available from surveys by the Industriens Utredningsinstitut (Industrial Institute for Economic and Social Research) and are published in Swedenborg (1973 and 1979). The coverage is 97 to 99 per cent of the estimated universe. The minimum ownership threshold is 10 per cent.

Inward DFI is derived from the Register of Foreign-Owned Enterprises, taken from the Official Register of Enterprises kept by the Swedish Statistiska Centralbyran (Central Bureau of Statistics), which covers all enterprises in Sweden. The minimum ownership threshold for DFI is 20 per cent.

FEDERAL REPUBLIC OF GERMANY

There are two separate series of annual data on inward and outward DFI, both produced by the Deutsche Bundesbank. The first series consists of cumulated balance of payments flows since 1952 for outward, and 1961 for inward DFI. The second consists of periodic surveys in 1976. The ownership threshold for all German data is 25 per cent.

The balance of payments statistics overestimated the survey data on outward DFI by 12 per cent in 1978 and underestimated inward DFI by 20 per cent.

Appendix E
A Note on National Sources of Data on International Non-Affiliate Licensing Transactions

This note records the differences in coverage between the national sources. However, all data on licensing are official. The general problem inherent in licensing data is that of undervaluation, although this is likely to be least in countries where data are collected under legal requirement.

UNITED STATES

Statistics are collected by the Current Account Services Branch, Balance of Payments Division, Bureau of Economic Analysis, of the US Department of Commerce. The coverage of the data is believed to be high as the reporting of statistics is required by law. The delineation between affiliated and non-affiliated transaction is based on a 25 per cent equity shareholding threshold.

JAPAN

Statistics on Japanese transactions are collected in surveys by the Ministry of International Trade and Industry. Since 1971 the reporting of such international transactions has been required by law, and the coverage of the estimated universe is about 90 per cent. There is no formal threshold for distinguishing transactions by ownership, but those which are related at all are in very low ownership classes, close to the IMF definition of 25 per cent. This applies mainly to receipts, as ownership in payments transaction is negligible.

UNITED KINGDOM

UK statistics are collected by the Department of Trade and Industry on a voluntary basis. These cover approximately 70 per cent of receipts and 80 per cent of payments. An estimate of the universe value of these transactions is provided in the data. The ownership threshold is 25 per cent.

FEDERAL REPUBLIC OF GERMANY

Statistics are collected by the Deutsche Bundesbank, from all firms resident in Germany who are required by law to report all such transactions over a minimum value. The description of the classes of ownership is somewhat different than for German DFI statistics. However, there is expected to be a good correspondence within the 25 per cent ownership threshold normally used.

Appendix F
A Note on Estimation Procedures

In certain instances, data have been estimated from related series. For example, data on direct foreign production may not be directly available, and in this case it will be estimated from direct foreign investment.

DIRECT FOREIGN PRODUCTION

Data on DFP were estimated from DFI for the following countries in respect of outward DFP: Japan, UK, Federal Republic of Germany, and for inward DFP: US, Japan, UK and Federal Republic of Germany. However, data were directly available for certain years even for these countries, providing a useful check on the estimation procedure.

The procedure adopted was to apply the output to capital ratio for domestic industry to the DFI position. This was conducted for each industry and each country, thus no assumptions were made about the homogeneity of the ratios across countries. The most appropriate definition of capital was chosen for each country.

LICENSED FOREIGN PRODUCTION

Some industrial details were in licensing transactions estimated for the US from partner country statistics, and data for 1965 were estimated from 1967 figures. For the Federal Republic of Germany data for 1965 was also estimated using 1967 data.

Notes

2 Theory and Evidence on International Production: A Critique and Development of Recent Work

1. There is now an ample body of reviews, notably Agarwal (1980), Swedenborg (1979), Parry (1975), Hufbauer (1975), Stevens (1974) and Dunning (1973). Calvet (1981) reviews the mainstream theories and Buckley and Casson (1976 and 1985) contain a critique of the different theoretical approaches to the MNE. A slightly extended version of this review appears in Clegg (1985, chapter 2).
2. See Appendix F.
3. Dunning (1979a) suggests that UK DFI abroad is high for both these reasons.

3 International Production by the Five Countries

1. For Japan the data are according to Japanese fiscal year, which begins on 1 April and runs until 31 March the following year. Thus, for example, FY 1975 refers to the period 1 April 1975 to 31 March 1976. This period corresponds closest to calendar year 1975, and this is the principal adopted here.
2. The International Standard Industrial Classification (ISIC) equivalents of the manufacturing industries referred to here are, within Section 3 of the ISIC code: Food, drink and tobacco – 311/2, 313, 314. Chemicals and allied products – 315, 352, 355, 356. Primary and fabricated metals – 371, 372, 381. Mechanical and instrument engineering – 382, 385. Electrical engineering – 383. Transportation equipment – 384. Textiles, leather, clothing and footwear – 321, 322 323, 324. Paper, printing and publishing – 341, 342. Other manufacturing industries – 331, 332, 361, 362, 369, 390. (See United Nations (1968) *International Standard Industrial Classification of All Economic Activities*, Statistical Papers, Series M, No. 4, Rev. 2, New York. The ISIC is used throughout the study.
3. Linder (1961) notes from Heckscher's (1919, 1949) history of Sweden that the initial exploitation of forest reserves in the second half of the nineteenth century industrial revolution was substantially carried out by foreign residents. At least in this instance the pattern of inward and outward involvement has come full circle, and this does provide some time series support for the concept of an international investment development

cycle (Dunning, 1981b) and the country-specific origins of ownership advantages (Dunning, 1979b).

4 The Determinants of International Competition

1. A more detailed analysis of multicollinearity in the context of the study is to be found in Clegg (1985, ch. 5).

6 Policy Implications

1. Caves (1982, chapter 10) provides a comprehensive review of policy options.

Bibliography

AGARWAL, J. P. (1980) 'Determinants of Foreign Direct Investment: A Survey', *Weltwirtschaftliches Archiv,* Band 116, Heft 4, pp. 739—73.

ALIBER, R. Z. (1970) 'A Theory of Direct Foreign Investment', chapter 1 in Kindleberger, C. P. (ed.), *The International Corporation. A Symposium,* Cambridge Mass.: MIT Press.

ALIBER, R. Z. (1971) 'The Multinational Enterprise in a Multiple Currency World', chapter 2 in Dunning, J. H. (ed.), *The Multinational Enterprise,* London: Allen & Unwin.

ARROW, K. J. (1969) 'The Organisation of Economic Activity: Issues Pertinent to the Choice of Market Versus Nonmarket Allocation', *United States Congress, Joint Economic Committee,* 1, pp. 47–64.

ARROW, K. J. (1974) *The Limits of Organisation,* New York: W. W. Norton & Company.

BALASSA, B. (1977) '"Revealed" Comparative Advantage Revisited: an Analysis of Relative Export Shares in the Industrial Countries, 1953–1971', *Manchester School of Economic and Social Studies,* no. 4, December, pp. 327–44.

BALDWIN, R. E. (1979) 'Determinants of Trade and Foreign Investment: Further Evidence', *Review of Economics and Statistics,* 61, no. 1, February, pp. 40–8.

BANDERA, V. N. and WHITE, J. T. (1968) 'US Direct Investments and Domestic Markets in Europe', *Economia Internazionale,* February, pp. 117–33.

BARANSON, J. (1970) 'Technology Transfer Through the International Firm', *American Economic Review,* 40, May, pp. 435–40.

BAUMANN, H. G., (1974) *The Determinants of the Pattern of Foreign Direct Investment: Some Hypotheses Reconsidered,* paper presented at the University of British Columbia, August 1.

BEHRMAN, J. N. (1969) 'Licensing Abroad under Patents, Trademarks, and Knowhow by US Companies', in Harris, L. J. (ed.), *Nurturing New Ideas: Legal Rights and Economic Rules,* Washington, DC: Bureau of National Affairs.

BILLERBECK, K. and YASUGI, Y. (1979) 'Private Direct Foreign Investment in Developing Countries', *World Bank Staff Working Paper,* Washington, DC, July.

BROWN, W. B. (1976) Islands of Conscious Power: MNCs in the Theory of the Firm', *MSU Business Topics,* Summer, pp. 37—45.

BUCKLEY, P. J. (1981a) 'A Critical Review of Theories of the Multinational Enterprise', *Aussenwirtschaft,* Heft 1, pp. 70–87.

194

BUCKLEY, P. J. (1981b) 'The Entry of Recent European Direct Investors in the USA', *Journal of Comparative Law and Securities Regulation*, 3, pp. 169–91.

BUCKLEY, P. J. (1983a) 'New Theories of International Business: Some Unresolved Issues', chapter 2 in Casson, M. C. (ed.), *The Growth of International Business*, London: Allen & Unwin.

BUCKLEY, P. J. (1983b) 'Macroeconomic Versus International Business Approach to Direct Foreign Investment: A Comment on Professor Kojima's Interpretation', *Hitotsubashi Journal of Economics*, 24, pp. 95–100.

BUCKLEY, P. J. and CASSON, M. C. (1976) *The Future of the Multinational Enterprise*, London: Macmillan.

BUCKLEY, P. J. and CASSON, M. C. (1981) 'The Optimal Timing of a Foreign Direct Investment', *Economic Journal*, 91, March, pp. 75–87, reprinted in Buckley, P. J. and Casson, M. C. (1985).

BUCKLEY, P. J. and CASSON, M. C. (1985) *The Economic Theory of the Multinational Enterprise*, London: Macmillan.

BUCKLEY, P. J. and DAVIES, H. (1981) 'Foreign Licensing in Overseas Operations: Theory and Evidence from the UK', in Hawkins, R. G. and Prasad, A. J. (eds), *Research in International Business and Finance*, vol. 2, pp. 75–89, Greenwich, Conn.: JAI Press.

BUCKLEY, P. J., DUNNING, J. H. and PEARCE, R. D. (1978) 'The Influence of Firm Size, Industry, Nationality, and Degree of Multinationality on the Growth and Profitability of the World's Largest Firms, 1962–72', *Weltwirtschaftliches Archiv*, Band 114, Heft 2, pp. 243–55.

BUCKLEY, P. J. and PEARCE, R. D. (1977) 'Overseas Production and Exporting by the World's Largest Enterprises – A Study in Sourcing Policy', *University of Reading Discussion Papers in International Investment and Business Studies*, no. 37, September.

BUCKLEY, P. J. and PEARCE, R. D. (1981) 'Market Servicing by Multinational Manufacturing Firms: Exporting versus Foreign Production', *Managerial and Decision Economics*, 2, no. 4, December, pp. 229–46.

CALVET, A. L. (1981) 'A Synthesis of Foreign Direct Investment Theories and Theories of the Multinational Firm', *Journal of International Business Studies*, Spring/Summer, pp. 43–59.

CARLSSON, B. and OHLSSON, L. (1976) 'Structural Determinants of Swedish Foreign Trade: A Test of Conventional Wisdom' *European Economic Review*, 7, February, pp. 165–74.

CASSON, M. C. (1979) *Alternatives to the Multinational Enterprise*, London: Macmillan.

CASSON, M. C. (ed.) (1983) *The Growth of International Business*, London, Allen & Unwin.

CASSON, M. C. (1984) 'General Theories of the Multinational Enterprise: A Critical Examination', *University of Reading Discussion Papers in International Investment and Business Studies*, no. 77, January.

CAVES, R. E. (1971) 'International Corporations: The Industrial Economics of Foreign Investment', *Economica*, 38, February, pp. 1–27.

CAVES, R. E. (1974) 'Multinational Firms, Competition and Host-Country Markets', *Economica*, 41, May, pp. 176–93.

CAVES, R. E. (1974) 'Causes of Direct Investment: Foreign Firms' Shares in Canadian and United Kingdom Manufacturing Industries', *Review of Economics and Statistics*, 56, August, pp. 279–93.

CAVES, R. E. (1982) *Multinational Enterprise and Economic Analysis*, Cambridge: Cambridge University Press.

CAVES, R. E., CROOKELL, H. and KILLING, J. P. (1983) 'The Imperfect Market for Technology Licenses', *Oxford Bulletin of Economics and Statistics*, 45, no. 3., August, pp. 249–67.

CLEGG, L. J. (1985) *The Determinants of International Production: A Comparative Study of Five Developed Countries*, PhD thesis, University of Reading.

COASE, R. H. (1937) 'The nature of the firm', *Economica*, 4, November, pp. 386–405.

COHEN, B. I. (1975) *Multinational Firms and Asian Exports*, New Haven: Yale University Press.

CONTRACTOR, F. J. (1980a) 'The "profitability" of Technology Licensing by US Multinationals: A Framework for Analysis and an Empirical Study', *Journal of International Business Studies*, Fall, pp. 40–63.

CONTRACTOR, F. J. (1980b) 'The Composition of Licensing Fees and Arrangements as a Function of Economic Development of Technology Recipient Nations', *Journal of International Business Studies*, Winter, pp. 47–62.

CORDEN, W. M. (1974) 'The Theory of International Trade', chapter 7 in Dunning, J. H. (ed.), *Economic Analysis and the Multinational Enterprise*, London: Allen & Unwin.

DAVIDSON, W. H. and McFETRIDGE, D. G. (1984) 'International Technology Transactions and the Theory of the Firm' *Journal of Industrial Economics*, 32, no. 3, March, pp. 253–64.

DAVIDSON, W. H. and McFETRIDGE, D. G. (1985) 'Key Characteristics in the Choice of International Technology Transfer Mode' *Journal of International Business Studies*, 16, no. 2, Summer, pp. 5–21.

DUNNING, J. H. (1971) Comment on Aliber, R. Z. 'The Multinational Enterprise in a Multiple Currency World', Chapter 2 in Dunning J. H. (ed.), *The Multinational Enterprise*, London: Allen & Unwin.

DUNNING, J. H. (1973) 'The Determinants of International Production', *Oxford Economic Papers*, 25, no. 3, November, pp. 289–336.

DUNNING, J. H. (1977) 'Trade, Location of Economic Activity and the MNE: a search for an eclectic approach', chapter 12 in Ohlin, B., Hesselborn, P.-O., and Wijkman, P. M. (eds), *The International Allocation of Economic Activity*, London: Macmillan.

DUNNING, J. H. (1979a) 'The UK's International Direct Investment Position in the mid-1970s', *Lloyds Bank Review*, no. 132, April, pp. 1–21.

DUNNING, J. H. (1979b) 'Explaining changing patterns of international production: in defence of the eclectic theory' *Oxford Bulletin of Economics and Statistics*, Special Issue: The Multi-National Corporation, 41, no. 4, November, pp. 255–67.

DUNNING, J. H. (1980) 'Toward an Eclectic Theory of International Production: Some Empirical Tests', *Journal of International Business Studies*, Spring/Summer, pp. 9–31.

DUNNING, J. H. (1981a) *International Production and the Multinational Enterprise,* London: Allen & Unwin.

DUNNING, J. H. (1981b) 'Explaining the International Direct Investment Position of Countries: Towards a Dynamic or Developmental Approach', *Weltwirtschaftliches Archiv,* Band 117, Heft 1, pp. 30–64.

DUNNING, J. H. (1981c) 'A Note on Intra-Industry Foreign Direct Investment', *Banca Nazionale del Lavoro Quarterly Review,* no. 139, December, pp. 427–37.

DUNNING, J. H. (1982) 'Non-equity Forms of Foreign Economic Involvement and the Theory of International Production', *University of Reading Discussion Papers in International Investment and Business Studies,* no. 59, February.

DUNNING, J. H. and BUCKLEY, P. J. (1977) 'International Production and Alternative Models of Trade', *Manchester School of Economic and Social Studies,* no. 4., December, pp. 392–403.

DUNNING, J. H. and CANTWELL, J. A. (1982) 'Joint Ventures and Non-Equity Foreign Involvement by British Firms with particular reference to Developing Countries: an Exploratory Study'. *University of Reading Discussion Papers in International Investment and Business Studies,* no. 68, November.

DUNNING, J. H. and NORMAN, G. (1983) 'Intra-Industry Production as a Form of International Economic Involvement: an Exploratory Study', *University of Reading Discussion Papers in International Investment and Business Studies,* no. 74, September.

DUNNING, J. H. and PEARCE, R. D. (1975) *Profitability and Performance of the World's Largest Industrial Companies,* Economists Advisory Group Business Research Study, London: Financial Times Ltd.

DUNNING, J. H. and PEARCE, R. D. (1981) *The World's Largest Industrial Companies,* London: Gower Press.

DUNNING, J. H. and RUGMAN, A. M. (1985) 'The Influence of Hymer's Dissertation on the Theory of Foreign Direct Investment', *American Economic Review,* 75, no. 2, May, pp. 228–32.

GOLDBERGER, A. S. (1964) *Econometric Theory,* New York: Wiley.

GRAY, H. P. (1982) 'Macroeconomic theories of foreign direct investment: an assessment', chapter 8 in Rugman, A. M. (ed.), *New Theories of the Multinational Enterprise,* London and Canberra: Croom Helm.

GRUBER, W. H., MEHTA, D. and VERNON, R. (1967) 'The R and D Factor in International Trade and International Investment in United States Industries', *Journal of Political Economy,* 75. February, pp. 2–37.

GRUBER, W. H. and VERNON, R. (1970) 'The Technology Factor in a World Trade Matrix', in Vernon R. (ed.), *The Technology Factor in International Trade,* New York: National Bureau of Economic Research, Columbia University Press.

HECKSCHER, E. F. (1919) 'The Effect of Foreign Trade on the Distribution of Income', *Ekonomisk Tidskrift,* 21, pp. 497–512, reprinted (in English) in Ellis, H. S. and Metzler, L. A. (eds), *Readings in the Theory of International Trade,* Blakiston, 1949, pp. 272–300.

HELLEINER, G. K. (1978) 'Transnational Corporations and Trade Structure: The Role of Intra-Firm Trade', in Giersch, H. (ed.) *On the Economics of Intra-Industry Trade: Symposium*, Tübingen: JCB Mohr (Paul Siebeck).

HELLEINER, G. K. and LAVERGNE, R. (1979) 'Intra-Firm Trade and Industrial Exports to the United States', *Oxford Bulletin of Economics and Statistics*, Special Issue: The Multi-National Corporation, 41, no. 4, November pp. 297–311.

HIRSCH, S. (1976) 'An International Trade and Investment Theory of the Firm', *Oxford Economic Papers*, 28, July, pp. 258–70.

HOOD, N. and YOUNG, S. (1979) *The Economics of Multinational Enterprise*, London: Longman.

HOOD, N. and YOUNG, S. (1981) 'Recent Strategic Expansions by British Corporations in the United States', *University of Strathclyde Working Paper* no. 8109, November.

HORST, T. (1972a) 'The Industrial Composition of US Exports and Subsidiary Sales to the Canadian Market', *American Economic Review*, 62, March, pp. 37–45.

HORST, T. (1972b) 'Firm and Industry Determinants of the Decision to Invest Abroad: An Empirical Study', *Review of Economics and Statistics*, 54, August, pp. 258–66.

HUFBAUER, G. C. (1970) 'The Impact of National Characteristics and Technology on the Commodity Composition of Trade in Manufactured Goods', in Vernon, R. (ed.), *The Technology Factor in International Trade*, National Bureau of Economic Research, New York: Columbia University Press.

HUFBAUER, G. C. (1975) 'The Multinational Corporation and Direct Investment', in Kenen, P. B. (ed.) *International Trade and Finance: Frontiers for Research*, London: Cambridge University Press.

HYMER, S. H. (1960) *The International Operations of National Firms: a Study of Direct Foreign Investment*, PhD, MIT, 1960, Cambridge, Mass.: MIT Press, 1976.

IMF (1977) *Balance of Payments Manual*, 4th edn, Washington, DC.

JOHNSON, H. G. (1968) *Comparative Cost and Commercial Policy: Theory for a Developing World Economy*, Wicksell Lectures, Stockholm: Almqvist & Wiksell.

JOHNSON, H. G. (1977) 'Technology, Technical Progress and the International Allocation of Economic Activity', chapter 9 in Ohlin, B., Hesselborn, P-O. and Wijkman, P. M. (eds) *The International Allocation of Economic Activity*, London: Macmillan.

KEESING, D. B. (1965) 'Labour Skills and International Trade: Evaluating Many Trade Flows with a Single Measuring Device', *Review of Economics and Statistics*, 47, pp. 287–94.

KEESING, D. B. (1967) 'The Impact of Research and Development on United States Trade', *Journal of Political Economy*, 75, pp. 38–45.

KEESING, D. B. (1968) 'Labour Skills and the Structure of Trade in Manufactures', in Kenen, P. B., and Lawrence, R. (eds) *The Open Economy: Essays on International Trade and Finance*, New York: Columbia University Press.

KINDLEBERGER, C. P. (1969) *American Business Abroad: Six Lectures on Direct Investment*, New Haven: Yale University Press.

KNICKERBOCKER, F. T. (1973) *Oligopolistic Reaction and Multinational Enterprise*, Boston: Harvard University Press.

KOJIMA, K. (1973) 'A Macroeconomic Approach to Foreign Direct Investment', *Hitotsubashi Journal of Economics*, 14, June, pp. 1–21.

KOJIMA, K. (1978) *Direct Foreign Investment: A Japanese Model of Multinational Business Operations*, London: Croom Helm.

KOJIMA, K. (1982) 'Macroeconomic Versus International Business Approach to Direct Foreign Investment', *Hitotsubashi Journal of Economics*, 23, no. 1, June, pp. 1–19.

KOMIYA, R. (1972) 'Direct Foreign Investment in Postwar Japan', chapter 6 in Drysdale, P. (ed.), *Direct Foreign Investment in Asia and the Pacific*, Canberra: Australian National University Press.

KOUTSOYIANNIS, A. (1977) *Theory of Econometrics*, London: Macmillan.

LALL, S. (1973) 'Transfer Pricing by Multinational Manufacturing Firms', *Oxford Bulletin of Economics and Statistics*, 35, no. 3, August, pp. 173–95.

LALL, S. (1979) 'The International Allocation of Research Activity by US Multinationals', *Oxford Bulletin of Economics and Statistics*, Special Issue: The Multi-National Corporation, 41, no. 4, November pp. 313–31.

LALL, S. (1980) 'Monopolistic Advantages and Foreign Involvement by US Manufacturing Industry', *Oxford Economic Papers*, 32, no. 1, pp. 105–22, reprinted in Lall, S. (1980) *The Multinational Corporation*, London: Macmillan.

LALL, S. and SIDDARTHAN, N. S. (1982) 'The Monopolistic Advantages of Multinationals: Lessons from Foreign Investment in the US', *Economic Journal*, 92, September, pp. 668–83, reprinted in Lall, S. (1983) *Multinationals, Technology and Exports*, London: Macmillan.

LEFTWICH, R. B. (1973) 'Foreign Direct Investment in the United States 1962–71', *Survey of Current Business* United States Department of Commerce, Bureau of Economic Analysis, February, pp. 35–40.

LINDER, S. B. (1961) *An Essay on Trade and Transformation*, New York: Wiley.

LIPSEY, R. E. and WEISS, M. Y. (1981) 'Foreign Production and Exports in Manufacturing Industries', *Review of Economics and Statistics*, 58, no. 4, November, pp. 488–94.

LUNDGREN, N. (1975) *International koncerner i industrilander (International Enterprises in Industrial Countries)*, summary in English, Stockholm: National Central Bureau of Statistics, SOU 1975: 50.

MAGEE, S. P. (1977a) 'Information and the Multinational Corporation: an Appropriability Theory of Direct Foreign Investment', chapter 13 in Bhagwati, J. N. (ed.), *The New International Economic Order: the North South Debate*, Cambridge, Mass.: MIT Press.

MAGEE, S. P. (1977b) 'Multinational Corporations, the industry technology cycle and development', *Journal of World Trade Law*, II, no. 4, July–August, pp. 297–321.

McMANUS, J. (1972) 'The Theory of the International Firm', in Paquet, G. (ed.), *The Multinational Firm and the Nation State*, Ontario, Canada: Collier-Macmillan.

MUNDELL, R. A. (1957) 'International Trade and Factor Mobility', *American Economic Review*, 47, no. 3, June, pp. 321–35.

ORR, D. (1973) *Foreign Control and Foreign Penetration in the Canadian Manufacturing Industries*, unpublished paper, Vancouver, Canada: University of British Columbia, July

ORR, D. (1975) 'The Industrial Composition of US Exports and Subsidiary Sales to the Canadian Market: Comment', *American Economic Review*, 65, March, pp. 230–34.

OSHIMA, K. (1973) 'Research and Development and Economic Growth in Japan', in Williams B. R. (ed.), *Science and Technology in Economic Growth*, New York: Wiley.

OWEN, R. F. (1982) 'Inter-Industry Determinants of Foreign Direct Investments: A Canadian Perspective', chapter 11 in Rugman, A. M. (ed.), *New Theories of the Multinational Enterprise*, London and Canberra: Croom Helm.

OZAWA, T. (1978) 'Japan's Multinational Enterprise: The Political Economy of Outward Dependency', *World Politics*, 30, no. 4, July, pp. 517–37.

OZAWA, T. (1979) *Technology Transfer and Control Systems: the Japanese Experience*, paper presented at a conference on technology transfer control systems, Seattle, 6–7 April.

OZAWA, T. (1981) *The Japanese Experience with the 'New' Forms of Investment: a Preliminary Exploration*, paper presented at an OECD meeting on 'Changing International Investment Strategies: the "New Forms" of Investment in Developing Countries', Paris, 2–6 March.

PANIĆ, M. and JOYCE, P. L. (1980) 'UK Manufacturing Industry: International Integration and Trade Performance', *Bank of England Quarterly Bulletin*, March, pp. 42—55.

PARKER, J. E. S. (1978) *The Economics of Innovation*, London: Longman.

PARRY, T. G. (1975) *The International Location of Production: Studies in the Trade and Non-Trade Servicing of International Markets by Multinational Manufacturing Enterprise*, PhD Thesis, the School of Economics, University of London, July.

PARRY, T. G. (1976) 'Methods of servicing overseas markets: the UK-owned pharmaceutical industry', *University of Reading Discussion Papers in International Investment and Business Studies*, no. 27, May.

PEARCE, R. D. (1977) 'British Investment in Less Developed Countries – a General Survey', *University of Reading Discussion Papers in International Investment and Business Studies*, no. 31, January.

POSNER, M. V. (1961) 'International Trade and Technical Change', *Oxford Economic Papers*, 13, October, pp. 323–41.

ROEMER, J. E. (1975) *US – Japanese Competition in International Markets. A Study of the Trade-Investment Cycle in Modern Capitalism*, monograph, Institute of International Studies, Berkeley, University of California.

ROEMER, J. E. (1976) 'Japanese Direct Foreign Investment in Manufactures: Some Comparisons with the US Pattern', *Quarterly Review of Economics and Business*, 16, no. 2, Summer, pp. 91–111.

RUGMAN, A. M. (1978) Review of Hymer, S. H. *The International Operations of National Firms: a Study of Direct Foreign Investment*, 1976, in *Journal of International Business Studies*, Fall, pp. 103–4.

RUGMAN, A. M. (1979) *International Diversification and the Multinational Enterprise*, Lexington Books: Lexington, Mass., D. C. Heath.

RUGMAN, A. M. (1980) 'Internalisation as a general theory of foreign direct investment: a re-appraisal of the literature', *Weltwirtschaftliches Archiv,* Band 116, Heft 2, pp. 365–79.

SAMUELSSON, H. F. (1977) *Utlandska directa investeringar i sverige. En ekonometrisk analys av bestamningsfaktorerna (Foreign Direct Investments in Sweden – an Econometric Analysis)*, Stockholm: Industriens Utredningsinstitut.

SCAPERLANDA, A. E. (1967) 'The EEC and US Foreign Investment: Some Empirical Evidence', *Economic Journal,* March, pp. 22–6.

SCAPERLANDA, A. E. (1968) 'The EEC and United States Foreign Investment: Some Empirical Evidence – a reply', *Economic Journal,* September, pp. 720–3.

SCAPERLANDA, A. E. and MAUER, L. J. (1969) 'The determinants of US direct foreign investment in the EEC', *American Economic Review,* 59, September, pp. 558–68.

SCAPERLANDA, A. E. and MAUER, L. J., (1972) 'The Determinants of US Direct Investment in the EEC: Reply', *American Economic Review,* September, pp. 700–4.

SEKIGUCHI, S. and KRAUSE, L. B. (1980) 'Direct foreign investment in ASEAN, by Japan and the United States', chapter 4 in Garnaut, R. (ed.), *ASEAN in a Changing Pacific and World Economy*, Canberra: Australian National University Press.

SIMON, H. A. (1978) 'Rationality as Process and as Product of Thought', *American Economic Review,* 68, no. 2, May, pp. 1–16.

STEVENS, G. V. G. (1974) 'The determinants of investment', chapter 3 in Dunning, J. H. (ed.), *Economic Analysis and the Multinational Enterprise*, London: Allen & Unwin.

STOBAUGH, R. B. (1968) *The Product Life Cycle, US Exports and International Investment*, DBA Thesis, Harvard University Graduate School of Business Administration.

STOPFORD, J. M. (1976) 'Changing Perspectives on Investment by British Manufacturing Multinationals', *Journal of International Business Studies,* 7, Fall/Winter.

SWEDENBORG, B. (1979) *The Multinational Operations of Swedish Firms. Analysis of Determinants and Effects,* Stockholm: Industrial Institute of Economic and Social Research.

TEECE, D. J. (1981) 'The Multinational Enterprise: Market Failure and Market Power Considerations', *Sloane Management Review,* 22, Spring, pp. 3–17.

TELESIO, P. (1979) *Technology Licensing and the Multinationals*, New York: Praeger.

TUGENDHAT, C. (1971) *The Multinationals,* London: Eyre & Spottiswoode.

VERNON, R. (1966) 'International Investment and International Trade in the Product cycle', *Quarterly Journal of Economics,* 80, June, pp. 190–207.

VERNON, R. (1971) *Sovereignty at Bay: the Multinational Spread of US Enterprises*, New York: Penguin Books.

VERNON, R. (1974) 'The Location of Economic Activity', chapter 4 in

Dunning J. H. (ed.), *Economic Analysis and the Multinational Enterprise*, London: Allen & Unwin.

VERNON, R. (1979) 'The Product Cycle Hypothesis in a New International Environment', *Oxford Bulletin of Economics and Statistics*, Special Issue: The Multi-National Corporation, 41, no. 4, November, pp. 255–67.

WALLIS, K. F. (1968) 'The EEC and United States Foreign Investment: Some Empirical Evidence Re-examined', *Economic Journal*, September, pp. 717–9.

WILLIAMSON, O. E. (1971) 'The Vertical Integration of Production: Market Failure Considerations', *American Economic Review*, 61, part 2, May, pp. 112–27.

WILLIAMSON, O. E. (1975) *Markets and Hierarchies: Analysis and Anti-Trust Implications: a Study in the Economics of Internal Organisation*, New York: Free Press.

WILLIAMSON, O. E. (1979) 'Transaction-Cost Economics: The Governance of Contractual Relations', *Journal of Law and Economics*, 22 (2), October, pp. 233–61.

WILLIAMSON, O. E. (1981) 'The Modern Corporation: Origins, Evolution, Attributes', *Journal of Economic Literature*, 19, December, pp. 1537–68.

WOLF, B. M. (1977) 'Industrial Diversification and Internalisation: Some Empirical Evidence', *Journal of Industrial Economics*, 26, no. 2, December, pp. 177–91.

YOUNG, S. and HOOD, N. (1980) 'Recent Patterns of Foreign Direct Investment by British Multinational Enterprises in the United States', *National Westminster Bank Quarterly Review*, May, pp. 20–32.

ZELLNER, A. (1962) 'An Efficient Method of Estimating Seemingly Unrelated Regressions and Tests for Aggregation Bias', *Journal of the American Statistical Association*, 57, no. 298, June, pp. 348–68.

Index